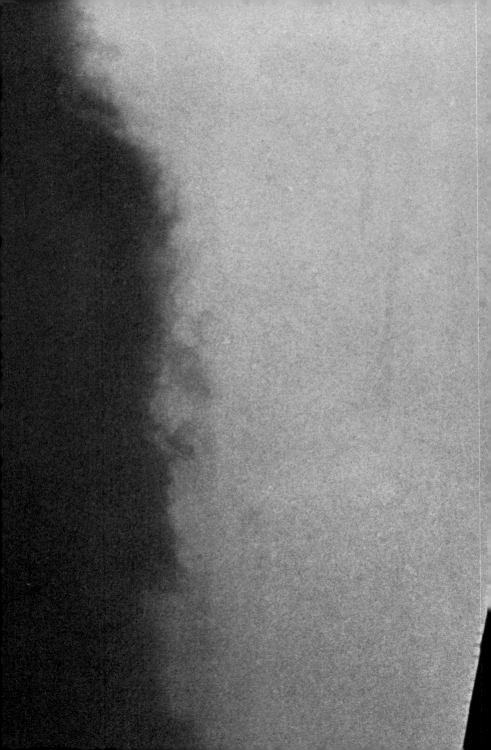

IN
SEARCH
OF
CANADA

IN SEARCH OF CANADA

The Reader's Digest Association (Canada) Ltd., Montreal

SBN: 0-88850-026-2

Printed in Canada

First Edition

Contents

Foreword

This book is a rich assembly of Reader's Digest stories
about Canada and Canadians. It tells of people and places,
institutions and resources; it sings sad songs and joyful paeans.
Complementing this fascinating story of a fascinating country
is a superb collection of illustrations—many published
here for the first time.

The Editors

My Own Dear Land

A portrait of Canada
by a great Canadian writer
who shows us our country
through the eyes of a poet

By Robert Choquette
of the French-Canadian Academy

My country, *mon pays*. My Canada.
I want to speak of you the way
a man speaks of the woman he loves—
for the one wonderful reason
that you are *you*.
I know full well your shortcomings,
but no other can take your place
in my heart.

Yet where do I find the words
to paint your lovely portrait,
to sing my hymn to your beauty?
You have such an abundance
of scenery; your soul blends
such a rich diversity of elements.
It would be so much easier
to whisper the simple words:
"My own dear land, I love you so!"

At the mere thought of you,
my imagination takes wing.
Does the stranger realize
that within your immense territory,
caressed by Pacific swell
and Atlantic wave,
the province of Quebec alone
could contain all of Spain, France
and Italy? Or that when noon
reaches Halifax it is only 8 a.m.
in Vancouver? . . .
Oh, dear land of mine, so great,
so new—where one feels
on the threshold of things,
where hope *matters*—
you are the stuff of epic poetry.
Homer would have glorified
your waves, Virgil your prairies,
Dante your Rockies.

What do I think of when I think of you?

I think of your forests. Forests of valley and hilltop, of plain and mountain;
forests winding around lakes and rivers and towns and villages, overhanging gorges
and ravines . . . trees dying as other trees are born, leaves withering
where new leaves will bud . . . forests forever renewing themselves, endless.

I think of national parks that your greatness makes possible,
huge sanctuaries where wild creatures wander uncaged,
great green museums sheltering works of art shaped by Nature's own all-powerful hands.

I think of your rivers and streams, and your lakes—
one-seventh of all the world's fresh water.
I think of the Yukon River, the Columbia,
the Saskatchewan, the Churchill, the Nelson,
the never-ending Mackenzie, the untamed Fraser,
the St. Lawrence escorting ocean-going vessels
deep into the heart of America.
I think of the Richelieu, the St. Maurice, the Yamaska,
the Saguenay.... I stand enthralled by your inland seas
and your gigantic waterfalls: Niagara, Montmorency,
Alexandra, Twin Falls in Yoho Park, Takakkaw Falls.

I thrill to your mountains. In the east
the harmonious Laurentians, begowned in color, alive
with the melody and the flutter of birds. In the west,
thrusting savagely to the sky, your snowclad, ice-topped
Rockies, so often peaking far beyond the clouds,
in the lofty realm of imagination . . . and in the Yukon,
Mount Logan, which would overshadow mighty
Mont Blanc. Sheep and mountain goats clamber
where eagles soar, valleys flower high in the skies—
and Lake Louise, Lake Cameron, Lake Eva,
Moraine Lake . . . all glisten like precious stones.

I salute the prairies, where oily black gold bubbles in fields of golden wheat,
where the gigantic arch of sky is thronged by white clouds
and one almost hears the ringing of the Angelus at the end of day.
Blessed are the prairie nights, too, when man is alone with his God
and can reach out to pluck a handful of stars.

I watch the dancing mirage of Aurora Borealis. I see icebergs
drifting toward Newfoundland, where teeming cod clog the sea.

I sweep over your immeasurable north, where daylight sleeps
despite the dawn; your north of ice and snow,
where the polar bear hides in his coat of camouflage white;
your north of the tundra, where fox skulks and rabbit crouches.
And I salute its people: the 40,000 natives and whites of this
enormous land once known only to whalers and missionaries,
now destined to become a vital part of Canada.

I think of your highways, so many that they would encircle
the entire earth three times over. I think of the network
of air routes, the maze of railroads, the wave upon wave
of human voices in daily communication. . . .
I think of all these umbilici which bind your provinces together
so that, in defiance of reason, you are one and the same country.

VANCOUVER

CALGARY

EDMONTON

REGINA

I think
of your cities.

Vancouver with its back to the mountains and its gaze to the sea,
hard by the great island where Victoria slumbers. Vancouver and its rain
and parks and gardens, its harbor mingling waters from far-off seas,
the loftiest trees in the world, sockeye salmon, totem poles, Chinese music.

Edmonton, jumping-off place for the rush to the Klondike,
now a university city amid the seas of wheat.

Calgary, city of big hats and the smiling handshake of friendship, city of the Stampede
with wild horses bucking, twisting, kicking—throwing their daring cowboy riders.

Regina, oasis in a seeming desert, the endless terrain
that is one of the world's great granaries.

Winnipeg, where Red and Assiniboine meet, crossroads and communications hub,
a commercial city nevertheless open to things of the spirit.
And St. Boniface, the good neighbor whose closest kin are a thousand miles to the east,
whose heart beats *à la française*.

WINNIPEG

OTTAWA

TORONTO

Toronto, the cosmopolitan Queen City,
not long ago stiffly corseted in respectability,
today so liberated by Old World immigrants
that her rainbow clotheslines sing of washday
in Naples. Toronto, mistress of high finance
and big business, lover of the arts,
trailblazer in education and research—
and ever more curious about good wines
and the rules of French grammar. . . .

Ottawa, born Bytown, where woodsmen
with rough-hewn tongues and hearts of gold
took off for the Gatineau;
where, high above the water and the trees,
the Peace Tower carillon rings out its message
of goodwill. Ottawa, capital city,
daily more beautiful—as it should be.

QUEBEC

MONTREAL

I think of Montreal, epitome of energy, dynamism. . . .
Where once slums huddled, now skyscrapers reflect the lights
and the dreams of a metropolis throbbing with ambition—
and impatience. Its dim little streets? Broad boulevards now.
What was is no more—or is somewhere else, or soon will be.
Montreal, leaven of Canada. Montreal, a city for man and his world.

Quebec City. So much has been said so many times (and so well)
about Lower Town, Upper Town, the Plains of Abraham, the Citadel,
the Basilica, the Château, the *calèches*, Laval, the Winter Carnival. . . .
It does indeed seem that everything has now been told
about these twisting streets in which one can read
the opening chapters of your history, *mon pays*—these hilly streets
where a "French Frenchman" might fancy himself in Angoulême
or Poitiers. But while men have been saying all this, over and over,
Quebec has become young again, has faced the present for what it is,
and has renewed its very soul, all the while remaining true to itself.

FREDERICTON

Fredericton, city of well-tended streets and trim houses and, close by on its hill,
the university. Not far away the colossal tides of the Bay of Fundy,
world-famous focal point of New Brunswick, that checkerboard of forest and fields
sprinkled with snow that is really the powder-white flower of the potato,
a province where Acadian tenacity compels History to retrace its steps.

Halifax. The ever-present sea, the lap-lapping of the water, the gloomy rhythm
of the foghorn, the constant comings and goings. And the whole, long scalloped coast
of Nova Scotia, each little harbor with its halo of gulls,
where men built mighty wooden sailing ships. (And one was *Bluenose*.)
Grand Pré and the little church of Evangeline, among the apple blossoms
of the Annapolis Valley; Cape Breton, the Fortress of Louisbourg, the black mines
where men with flickering lamps search for coal that is their daily bread.

Charlottetown, where hope became Confederation,
the promise of a land that men everywhere would respect and envy.

St. John's, capital of Atlantic-tossed Newfoundland, a province wet with fog
and fragrant with the perfume of wildflowers; a weathered land where habit dies hard
and old men still say: "One of my boys lives up in Canada."

HALIFAX

CHARLOTTETOWN

ST. JOHN'S

Canada. I hear your name and my heart overflows with sights and sounds and scents in such bountiful profusion that they go to my head. And the more I drink, the thirstier I get.

Autumn, and the splendorous miracle of a living tapestry of trees where one's glance leaps from copper to gold, from scarlet to vibrant yellow to rose to purple. Up on the wind the great fraternal din of wild geese winging toward skies where summer still lives. . . .

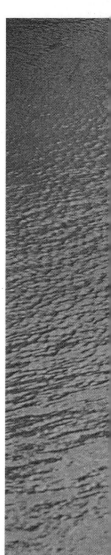

Autumn is cold and wind and rain and broad hints of winter to come, of houses quilted in snow under skies blue and gold, of ski slopes where mortal man has the feet of Mercury, of the joyous crunch of new-fallen snow underfoot. And Christmas. And a New Year. . . .

Now spring! The clink of falling icicles, the fir tree's
soft surrender of its armful of snow, and everywhere
the gurgle of water, the happy sound of the annual melting.
The sap of maple slaps the countless pails, drop by drop
by note by note, and the sugarbush becomes a gigantic
seasonal xylophone. Suddenly (oh, the *surprise* each new time
it happens!) naked branches bud again. . . .

Now summer settles in, and the smell of new paint
and new-mown grass, and the sharp, clean smell of wood
as the great saws whine, ripping the blue silence of the countryside.
Summer travel, summer fishing—each to his own sport,
in a land of space and freedom and beauty. . . .

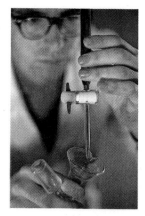

Dear land of mine, I hear the song your
sons and daughters sing. Their song of
labor, the hum of all your human effort:
machines throbbing in steel mills
and smelters, the sounds of airports
and shipyards, factories, offices,
laboratories, universities and hospitals,
stadiums and theaters. . . . It is everywhere:
the noise of pistons and piledrivers, levers
and winches, saws, hammers, electric
motors, computers, the roar of presses
and the clanking of reapers and threshers,
the grinding derricks and screaming drills
and whirring turbines . . .
and church bells pealing out
from steeples of every denomination.

MAHONE BAY, N.S.

It excites me when I think of millions of men and women—
different from me and different one from another in origin,
language, culture, history and tradition—who, too, think of you
as their country. And I love the thought that everyone,
or almost everyone, has always wanted you to be greater still,
more beautiful, more confident of yourself and your destiny.
Those who discovered you felt that way. So did those who came later
and toiled to develop the broad expanse waiting for plow and people.
So did those who followed them. So do those who continue to arrive
on your shores—because they have faith in you, because for them
and for their children you represent security and freedom
and are the best answer to their hopes.

Because, my own dear land,
you are as young as tomorrow,
as young as hope itself.

The Treasure
and
The Challenge

Sympathy with nature
is a part
of the good man's religion

FREDERICK HENRY HEDGE

Our Wonderland of Mountain Parks

By Paul Friggens

Sunlight breaking through thick cloud bathes the familiar profile of Mount Rundle (above), near the southern end of the magnificent Banff-to-Jasper highway, which runs 178 miles through the heart of glacier country. Mount Rundle was named in honor of Robert Terrill Rundle, the first Protestant missionary in Alberta, who served from 1840 to 1848.

High amid the snow-clad peaks, and the mammoth glaciers and crystal lakes of Canada's Selkirk and Rocky mountains, is the world's largest, most spectacular chain of national parks. Strung along the mountain tops, this lofty wonderland of awesome alpine grandeur covers an area of 8,638 square miles (larger than Lake Ontario).

These breathtaking parks—seven in all—aren't yet a hundred years old, but nature started molding the site and sculpting it 750,000,000 years ago when the oceans over the aeons of time began depositing sediment on the earth's crust. The Rockies are a living textbook in geology, recording the upthrust of rock 70,000,000 years in our

past, the Great Ice Age, and the relentless grinding of glaciers through hundreds of thousands of years.

Located on the East-West traffic routes, the mountain parks are easily accessible by air (to Calgary, 80 miles away), by the Trans-Canada Highway and by exciting vista-dome trains and tour buses. At night you have your choice of campgrounds, motels, "bungalow" cabins, lodges, chalets and hikers' hostels. Or, after roughing it in the wilderness, you can enjoy continental cuisine and a concert.

For our first sighting excursion into the parks, my wife and I took the 187-mile Banff-to-Jasper highway, often called the finest scenic

A tiny lake mirrors mighty Mount Robson, at 12,972 feet the highest peak in the Canadian Rockies. Just outside Jasper National Park, it lies over the Continental Divide in British Columbia and gives its name to Mount Robson Provincial Park. High in Jasper Park's peaceful Tonquin Valley, where masses of wildflowers bloom in summer—and where World War II commandos were taught to ski—a log cabin nestles warmly in the winter snows.

road in North America, and one of the great "highroads" of the world. Leaving the lovely little town of Banff, Alta., with its prideful shops and old-world charm (it's named after the town of Banff in Scotland), we followed the new highway 36 miles up the glacier-scoured Bow Valley, through fragrant evergreen forests, past meadows riotous with yellow arnica, blue lupine and flaming Red Indian paintbrush.

Climbing to nearly 6,000 feet, we dropped down on breathtaking Lake Louise—a mile and a half long, three-quarters of a mile wide and 275 feet deep—lying in a hanging valley, carved probably 10,000 years ago at the close of the Ice Age.

World-famous Banff Springs Hotel, a huge building with accommodation for more than 1,000 persons, is dwarfed by the towering peaks that surround the broad Bow River valley. At evening, more than 150 miles to the north, two fishermen wait patiently on a calm lake whose majestic backdrop is 11,033-foot Mount Edith Cavell, named for a British nurse whom the Germans accused of espionage and shot in 1915.

Set amidst green forest and jagged peaks, with gleaming Victoria Glacier as a backdrop, Lake Louise is probably the most photographed and painted scene in the Rockies—and understandably so! The waters are a turquoise blue, which in the early morning light reflect the glacier in fleeting, iridescent beauty. Up at dawn, I shot two rolls of film trying to capture the ever-changing scene. Named in honor of Princess Louise, daughter of Queen Victoria and wife of the Marquis of Lorne (Canada's governor-general from 1878 to 1883), Lake Louise is a memorable gateway to more superb sight-seeing. It's a thrilling day's round trip to adjacent Yoho (Indian for "how wonderful") National Park to view spectacular Takakkaw Falls, plunging a sheer 1,250 feet over the rim of Yoho Valley. Another day took us across the Continental Divide into Kootenay National Park, where, after motoring through red-walled canyons and evergreen valleys, we relaxed in the invigorating waters of Radium Hot Springs.

Hot springs were discovered in the Rockies in 1883. Surveyors of the Canadian Pacific Railway, intent on driving a track across the rugged terrain to link the West with the rest of Canada, spotted wispy steam rising from the top of a mountain near what is now Banff. Investigating, they found a bubbling, emerald-hued hot spring in a limestone cavern. The subsequent clamor to "claim" the springs led the Privy Council of Queen Victoria in 1885 to set aside a ten-square-mile reserve for its "sanitary advantage to the public." This was the beginning of Banff National Park and a system that now covers more than 30,000 square miles in 24 parks from coast to coast. The hot springs of Banff, Radium and Miette in Jasper are among the major attractions for visitors to the parks. Radium Hot Springs has a flow of nearly half a million gallons of the healthful waters a day!

Basing at Lake Louise, we traveled into back country, seeing the wilderness splendor of the Valley of the Ten Peaks, boating on Emerald Lake and hiking around beautiful Lake O'Hara in Yoho.

Hiking back-country trails is the best way to "feel" the mountains, to see nature at its most minute and to savor the vistas carved by the mighty forces of time. At our feet were the lichens, the most primitive of plants, growing on barren rocks, gradually building a layer of soil that will one day support more complex plant life. On either side of the trails, the alpine firs and tenacious plants like the moss campion wage an endless struggle for existence, recycling the waste products of nature so that nothing goes begging at these rarefied altitudes.

Wildlife species range from beaver to buffalo, mink to moose, mountain goat to the fast-vanishing grizzly bear. Also fighting for survival are the majestic Bighorn sheep which, along with mountain goats, populate the high Rockies. Once common throughout the mountains of western North America, and even on the prairies, the Bighorn sheep have been decimated by hunters and disease. Park official Ron Langevin at Banff made a study of this extraordinary animal: "His eyesight is probably about equal to an eight-power telescope. The Bighorn's feet are developed for rough terrain. The hoof has a hard rim for strength and endurance, while inside is a remarkable rubberlike base or suction cup designed for steep climbing. With his cleft toes and dewclaws, the Bighorn can brake downhill."

Wildflowers abound in the mountain parks, sprinkling and splashing their color along nature trails, through the valleys and far up into the high alplands—even edging the permanent snow. Flowers may not be picked. Like birds, animals, trees and rocks, they are protected. "Take only pictures," state the park regulations, "leave only footprints." Hiking in the high country (opposite) and along back-country trails gives visitors an intimate sense of the staggering size and stunning beauty of the mountain parks. Trails are safe and well marked.

At Lake Louise, we left the Trans-Canada Highway to travel northward over a spectacular route completed in 1940. Finally we crossed the broad, sweeping North Saskatchewan River, climbed Sunwapta Summit, and entered Jasper, Canada's largest mountain park, embracing 4,200 square miles. Ahead, "on the roof of the Rockies," there's the great Columbia Icefield, a remnant of the Ice Age and the largest mass of ice south of the Arctic. To get the full benefit of the scenery, we flew over the 150 square miles of glacial ice and snow astride the Continental Divide, and had a vivid view of how much of North America must have looked when covered with the continental

Big animals are no threat to mountain park visitors if kept at a distance. But most are dangerous if approached. Binoculars are a tourist's best bet in the high country (left) where glimpses of fauna—like the two lambs silhouetted on the ridge—are not uncommon. Among the most fascinating animals in the parks are the sharp-eyed Rocky Mountain Bighorn sheep (above, left). The clumsy-looking Rocky Mountain goat (above), about the size of a domestic sheep, moves swiftly and surely on two-toed blunt hooves.

Athabasca Glacier, one of nine glaciers in the 150-square-mile Columbia Icefield, comes to within a mile of the Banff-to-Jasper highway. Sightseers stop at the Columbia Icefield Chalet (foreground, at the side of the highway), then go by snowmobile to the edge of the ice and, by an access road (left), up alongside the glacier. Eleven of the Canadian Rockies' 24 highest peaks border the icefield. It is the biggest body of permanent ice and snow between the Arctic and Antarctic, reaching a depth of 2,000 to 3,000 feet. The Athabasca Glacier recedes approximately 90 feet a year.

ice cap. Today, melting waters of the Columbia Icefield pour into great rivers flowing in three directions: the Athabasca, a tributary of the Mackenzie, to the Arctic; the North Saskatchewan, to Hudson Bay and the Atlantic; and the Columbia, to the Pacific. Columbia Icefield is thus the hydrographic center of North America. Air-conditioned by the great ice mass, summer weather here is invariably chilly.

Returning to Lake Louise, we drove over the Continental Divide, dropping down into the Rocky Mountain Trench, a great 1,000-mile-long gash or geologic "fault" in the earth, extending from the U.S. border northwestward up into Yukon Territory. Through the flat-bottomed, steep-sided Trench, flow portions of the Columbia, Fraser, Kootenay and other great rivers of the North. There we climbed to Glacier and Mount Revelstoke national parks, set amidst the spiky peaks and ragged ridges of the Selkirk Mountains. Millions of years older than the Rockies and weathered down to solid rock, the Selkirks are rugged and wild. Over 100 glaciers have sculpted the final touches; nurtured by record snowfalls—728 inches during the winter of 1966-67 and 370 inches *average*—they should be here to stay for a while.

A curious attraction at the Athabasca Glacier is this arch of permanent ice.

Our final stop was entrancing Waterton Lakes National Park, lying on the Canadian-American border, adjacent to Glacier National Park in Montana. The two parks are virtually one. At a goodwill gathering in 1931, the Rotarians of Alberta and Montana joined hands across the border, and the following year legislation was approved by the United States and Canada, creating the first international peace park in the world.

You cruise seven miles of international waters from Waterton, Alta., to the end of the lake at Goathaunt, Mont., and return, without so much as a driver's license for identification, and back at the Swiss-styled Prince of Wales Hotel you toast the two-fisted Irish trader and frontiersman, John George (Kootenai) Brown, who dreamed that some day the lovely lakes would become a national park. He campaigned for his dream, and when it came true, he became its first "game guardian" and forest ranger just after the turn of the century. Passing his grave, near the lakes he loved, we saluted his memory—and all those who gave to Canada the world's most spectacular complex of mountain parks.

Where
Tomorrow Is Now

A rare breed of men, Eskimos are caught between two cultures, the old and the new, the primitive and the sophisticated, the comfortable and the sometimes frightening. Those employed by Panarctic Oils Ltd., searching for oil on Melville Island (above and opposite), may own snowmobiles—but, as Eskimos, are given special leaves which enable them to stock family larders by hunting, as Eskimos have for thousands of years.

"There are only a few Eskimos but millions of whites, just like mosquitoes. It is something special to be an Eskimo. They are like snow geese. If an Eskimo forgets his language and his ways, he will be nothing but just another mosquito."

Eskimos—snow geese in that eloquent imagery of one Eskimo elder—call themselves simply People. They are a rare and primitive breed of men who have lived for 4,000 years as nomadic hunters in an unforgiving terrain. There are fewer than 60,000 of them across the roof of the world, and in the Northwest Territories they number no more than 12,300, strung out across a harshly daunting land as vast as all of Canada east of Manitoba. For the Eskimo of yesteryear, it was triumph enough at the end of each day just to have lived through it. But in these times an Eskimo's survival is rarely in doubt. *Kabloona* (the white man) has introduced him to the succor of the welfare state—just as *kabloona* is wreaking huge changes on the entire fabric of the Arctic's indigenous culture. In Canada's new North, the era of the snow geese is swiftly coming to a close. Modern machines—from helicopters to hovercraft—crisscross the land in a great search for the treasure trove of oil and minerals locked under the windswept ice.

Going north, as sometime Arctic traveler Pierre Trudeau has observed, "is stepping into Canada's future." In the Northwest Territories' capital of Yellowknife, it is no longer fashionable to speak of the Great Tomorrow Country. By northern lights, tomorrow is here. On the north slope of the Beaufort Sea, extending in an arc from Alaska's catalytic Prudhoe Bay oil discovery north into the Arctic Archipelago, 500 miles from the North Pole, oilmen confidently talk of finding a new Arabia in the Arctic.

Every major oil company is in on the play, and so is the Canadian government, with a 45-percent stake in Panarctic Oils Ltd., which is drilling test wells on Melville Island, 1,700 miles north of Calgary. By the mid-'70s, the oil industry may spend as much as $1,000,000,000 on exploratory drilling and development in the far North. Seismic soundings on the north slope and the Arctic islands lead normally cautious geologists to guess that possibly as many as 300,000,000,000 barrels of oil may lie beneath the ice—a pool that would indeed be of Middle East proportions.

If the hunt for oil in the North is exciting, the search for hard minerals is only slightly less so. Mary River on Baffin Island is estimated to contain 100,000,000 tons of ore of up to 70 percent iron. At Hope and Dismal lakes, some 100 companies have staked out 2,000,000 acres in their search for copper. Mineral production is beginning to zoom.

Nowhere in the Northwest Territories is the impact of the new North more strikingly evident than in the capital city of Yellowknife. Pacific Western Airlines jets fly in daily with businessmen, oil roughnecks and prospectors; in the terminal, the PA system straight-facedly announces that "transportation is now leaving for downtown Yellowknife." Downtown is 50th Street and 50th Avenue; when the muddy crossroads of the "new" town were laid out in 1946, the town fathers decided to start off with the nice round sound of high numbers.

Since the seat of the territorial government was moved from Ottawa to Yellowknife in 1967, the gold-mining town has taken on a cosmopolitan air that draws native northerners by droves "just to see the city." The population of Yellowknife has grown rapidly to 7,000 with the arrival of civil servants and the development of a territorial administration to take over the functions of government which formerly fell to Ottawa. At 52nd Street and 53rd Avenue is the North's first skyscraper, a 14-story apartment tower which boasts a swimming pool. A few blocks away, grizzled prospectors sit next to gray-suited civil servants in a cocktail lounge called the Hoist Room, which is dominated by a huge stone fireplace containing ore from nine mines,

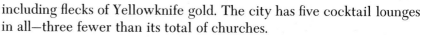

Larger communities in the North have most of the amenities and services of southern towns: hotels, restaurants, stores, theaters, churches, hospitals. Yellowknife even boasts paved streets, tennis courts and a golf course—that's *sand*, that "green"! In the heart of downtown Yellowknife are the Northwest Territories government building (left) and the Yellowknife Inn, here reflected in the roof of a car.

including flecks of Yellowknife gold. The city has five cocktail lounges in all—three fewer than its total of churches.

Of the 61 settlements in the North, two others have joined Yellowknife as major centers.

Frobisher Bay is the administrative center of the eastern Arctic and has the largest Eskimo settlement in the North—a few more than 1,200 in a population of 2,100. Now only three hours from Montreal by Nordair jet, Frobisher Bay has attracted the Territories' largest private enterprise development, a $13,000,000 modular precast town center financed by an Edmonton consortium. The complex has 26,000 square feet of offices, a 49-room hotel, a theater that holds 300 persons, a swimming pool, 158 apartments and 76 townhouses. Other private enterprise also flourishes. One example is Arctic Ventures, the hippest shop in the Arctic. Run by English-born Bryan Pearson—one of the ten elected members of the Northwest Territories Council—the store sells Pakistani wedding vests and $150 mod suits.

Eighteen hundred air miles west of Frobisher Bay and 665 miles north of Yellowknife is Inuvik, with a population of more than 3,000. This $30,000,000 government town is the distribution center for the

burgeoning Mackenzie Delta. Completed in the late '50s as the first model town in the Arctic, Inuvik is built on stilts to stop the heat of the houses from thawing the permafrost underneath. Water, sewers and heating pipes are carried to each house in a metal-clad, surface "utilidor" system. Once a Chinese Wall that separated whites from natives, the utilidor has now been extended into Indian and Eskimo parts of town where prefab frame houses painted in pastels present a panorama that is a northern version of suburbia.

Where the Eskimo fits into this great tomorrow country is uncertain. Only the past seems clear. The Canadian government acquired the 2,500,000 square miles of Rupert's Land and the North-Western Territory from the Hudson's Bay Co. for £300,000 in 1870. But apart from sending the Mounties north, Ottawa largely forgot about the empty Arctic until the cold war brought on the DEW line's radar trip wire against Soviet attack from over the pole. It was not until 1953 that Canada set up a Northern Affairs Department. In that year, Prime Minister Louis St. Laurent admitted that "apparently we have administered these vast territories in an almost continuing state of absence of mind."

Since the early '50s, Ottawa's spending on social development of the North has increased more than twentyfold. It has transformed the old nomadic life of the Eskimo by creating a network of 60-odd settlements with hospitals, nursing stations and, in most cases, schools. Everywhere across the North, the snowhouse and skin tent has been replaced by a government-subsidized frame home. The dogteam has given way to the snowmobile, the kayak to the canoe.

On Ellesmere Island, framed by a hole in the ice of a glacier, a snowmobile races a snowdrift whose shape is remarkably like —a snowmobile. On Baffin Island, at a time of neither snow nor ice, Eskimos heft into place a plastic house shaped remarkably like—an igloo.

But the program does not satisfy everyone. What good, critics ask, is it to take the Eskimo away from his hunter's livelihood but fail to provide him with an alternate occupation? Said former Territorial Councillor Duncan McLean Pryde: "Where are the Eskimo managers of Hudson's Bay posts? Where are the Eskimo police, the radio operators, the nurses? I'll tell you where they are. They are down at the welfare office drawing relief."

Like the Canadian West at the turn of the century, the North of the future will be as competitive as it is tough, an aggressive society of adventurers and boom-timers. In a population that could well grow to 100,000, the Eskimo will find himself even more in a minority. Already it is too late for him to turn back to the isolation of the traplines. Where and how, then, will the native population fit in?

The 1,200 miles of the Mackenzie River from Great Slave Lake to the Arctic Ocean can be navigated by cabin cruisers. At the Mackenzie Delta (below) are the historic settlements of Aklavik and Tuktoyaktuk and the newer Inuvik. East from here the Arctic tundra stretches almost 1,500 miles to Hudson Bay. Beyond Hudson Bay, at Baffin Island's Frobisher Bay—which has the biggest Eskimo settlement in the North—a little girl practices her printing. "Five yellow ducks come to take a drink," she writes, "Six floating lily pads . . ."

Duncan Pryde wholeheartedly endorses Prime Minister Trudeau's approach—that the government's goal should be "not to assimilate these people, but permit them to participate in the determination of their future as equal citizens of our society." Pryde argues that even major oil finds will not give a great many native people immediate or lasting jobs unless Canadian attitudes change. Many companies have shied away from Eskimos and Indians, claiming they have little notion of living by the clock and that they are apt to disappear once the hunting season starts. Says Pryde: "It may be true that the older ones find it hard to adapt to the clock, but the children are learning this in school."

And perhaps attitudes are changing. Panarctic Oils employs some Eskimos and President C. R. Hetherington acknowledges that Eskimo employes must take advantage of some seasonal hunting to provide for their families during the dark months in the Arctic. Accordingly, Panarctic feels it must give Eskimo employes special leaves for prolonged periods.

A better long-term source of employment could well be mining. The Territories' biggest mining operation, the Cominco lead-zinc pit work at Pine Point, is a major employer of native labor. A government employment liaison officer works with Cominco staff to recruit northern residents and train them on the job. The 350-man work force at Pine Point includes 150 northerners. A handful of Eskimos have proved successful as operators, welders and engineers on the fully-automated Pine Point Railroad.

The heart of the problem seems to be that Ottawa has not had a completely coordinated policy on education and employment of native people—or, if it has, the policy hasn't proved suitable to the rapidly shifting northern employment scene. Civil servants, like private concerns, have tended to judge the natives' prospects by their formal education. A government advertisement asking for welding trainees in Inuvik with a minimum of grade eight would have ruled out three members of the Territorial Council at that time: Loucheux Chief John Tetlichi, Eskimo Simonie Michael and Gordon Gibson, a self-made Vancouver millionaire. Victor Allen, an Eskimo heavy-equipment operator at the Canadian Forces Station at Inuvik, whose schooling stopped at first grade, said: "When education came into the North, it was for our children only. There should be some way the knowledge we have picked up on the job could be exchanged for grades."

Even with most native children in school, there is still doubt that northern schools are on the right track. While the same can be said of most provincial school systems, perhaps the unique situation in the North adds urgency to the search for solutions to the native education-employment dilemma. It is not enough to copy a curriculum because it works well in another jurisdiction. It may have little relevance either to the North or, more damagingly, to native culture.

All told, the economic promise of its natural resources gives the new North a chance to redress the balance, to build a Just Society north of the 60th parallel. But if it is to be done, the North needs, perhaps above all else, to catch the sympathetic imagination of southern Canada.

Kabloona the white man is a Mountie, a Hudson's Bay Company storekeeper, an oil man from Alberta . . . and a group from Liverpool whose music is one more influence in the shaping of the new North.

The Changing, Changeless Lakes

By Noel Mostert

Inland they lie and their waters are fresh, but the Great Lakes are seas nonetheless, brimming with raw power, vast and often violent. This Lake Ontario "seascape" is at Toronto's Cherry Beach lighthouse.

The Great Lakes are the immemorial surprise of middle North America. They are the greatest natural wonder of our whole continent, and yet, I am convinced, the most undervalued and unsung.

My own first introduction to them came from the spectacular stretch of Canadian Pacific track that runs along the north shore of Superior. The train comes drumming down from the bushland plateau, doubling and turning in the cuttings, and suddenly the emerald water heaves below, spreading from the white empty sands to a horizon as vast and open as the sea. That far horizon has always struck me as being the truest measure of North America's breadth: it is hard to grasp that a land should contain several freshwater seas so big that a ship can steam out of sight of the shore for a day or more, or even founder in giant waves, as happens from time to time.

Yet there they are, these changing, changeless lakes, flung upon the map, almost dead center, spilling eastward and southward across the Middle West. Ontario, the only province that fringes them, sprawls along their northern coasts, and eight American states—New York, Pennsylvania, Ohio, Michigan, Indiana, Illinois, Wisconsin, Minnesota—crowd their lower shores. More than 40 percent of the total dollar income from farming, mining and manufacturing in the United States is earned around their basins; 80 percent of Canada's industry is settled there—so that in a most literal sense it is the breathing, pulsing, coursing heart of the continent.

This is the largest group of lakes in the world and the biggest body of fresh water, covering 96,000 square miles in surface, draining a 300,000-square-mile area, and flowing to the sea at the rate of 240,000 cubic feet a second—more than the Seine, Thames and Danube combined.

The lakes were the single greatest asset this land endowed to its pioneer man. Their spacious waters were a natural highway for the exploring French and, two centuries later, for the main westward rush of settlement. And when ore was discovered on Superior's shores, in the nineteenth century, the cheap transportation provided by the lakes became the lever of continental prosperity and boom.

Let us approach the lakes the best way: along the course of history, up from Montreal along the St. Lawrence and its Seaway. We book on a big Swedish freighter that is on its way into the lakes to pick up grain and general cargo for Australia.

Under way, we slide out of Montreal harbor and nose through the deepening twilight into the first lock of the Seaway, at St. Lambert.

Gulls promenade at the edge of Lake Huron as breakers crash onto the beach of Nottawasaga Bay. Across the bay is the Niagara Escarpment, backbone of the Bruce Peninsula. Tobermory, at the end of the peninsula, is linked by ferry (below) with Manitoulin Island, the largest freshwater island in the world. Almost 100 miles long, it lies in the northern part of Lake Huron and is an extension of the escarpment.

Suddenly a siren wails, bells ring, booms descend, the lock gates start swinging shut, lights flash red, and a drawbridge behind us descends while another in front rises, the heavy road and rail traffic shifting imperturbably and without pause from one to the other. There is a roar of water, the ship rises, and in minutes we have been lifted high enough to sail on.

The Seaway is 110 miles long and has seven locks. Through our first night and the following day, these lift us steadily higher, into Lake Ontario. Ontario is the smallest of the Great Lakes, but it is deep, with a maximum sounding of 778 feet. It is 193 miles long, east to west. While the other lakes have distinct personalities, Ontario's is more elusive. The Niagara Escarpment with its sheer thunderous drop has been an effective barrier between this and the other lakes, and the St. Lawrence sluicing out its eastern end draws Ontario's attention seaward. Its commerce has always been in that direction—or south, to New York. Its mood is sedate. Here no vulgar echoes of the westward push, the immigrant scramble; that essential pioneer familiarity of the upper lakes is missing.

On the bridge, the pilot tells us that the lake sailor speaks a different nautical language. The lakeman came originally from the farm, and he brought with him a homey terminology. He goes steam-boating, as he describes his calling; he calls the rail his fence, the bow the front end. When a propeller loses a blade he says the boat has "thrown her bucket." After the Seaway brought in the ocean ships, pilotage was introduced and enforced, and the lakeman has grudgingly come to recognize that the Great Lakes are no longer his private preserve.

In the morning we enter the Welland Canal, whose 27 miles and eight locks will lift us over the Niagara Falls escarpment to Lake Erie. We drift down the canal, past orchards and towns. We sail between backyards. Then past the back porch of a small farmhouse.

The cataract made Niagara Falls "the honeymoon capital of the world"—and the Welland Canal a necessity. The Horseshoe Falls, wholly in Canada, are 176 feet high and 2,200 feet wide, and the water below the falls is 180 feet deep. The 27.6-mile canal, also in Canada, bypasses the Niagara River. Its eight locks raise ships 326 feet from Lake Ontario's level to Lake Erie's.

Next morning we break out past the last lock into Lake Erie. The ship suddenly begins to sway. Doors bang and the air pours cold and strong through the porthole. We are at sea.

Though Superior is the worst storm lake, with waves reported as high as 35 feet, Erie is the one that is talked about: a killer of small craft. It has a reputation for treacherous flash storms. The shallowest of the lakes, it can be pale as glass, and as smooth—then a few hours later be insensately churning under a fugitive sky. Its shores are low-lying, its beaches often narrow, and except for the gritty imprints pawed by industry in that dense line of cities between Buffalo and Toledo on the south shore, it is succulently pastoral.

All day we push southwest. By evening the air is much colder, and a rainstorm washes away Cleveland's profile as we pass in through the breakwater and tie up there. A group of officials wait on the sodden dock, all solemnly patient in their wet clothes, motionless as pavement pigeons in a downpour. This is our first port in the United States, and they are here to clear the ship. One man goes down into the holds to look for beetles; no vigilance is too small to protect the mid-continent farmland against some unknown blight.

A German freighter bound for Toronto harbor passes sailboats off the west end of the city near the Canadian National Exhibition grounds.

51

Heavy-laden downbound ships at the south end of Lake Huron wait their turn to enter the St. Clair River at Sarnia, Ont.

We never really see Cleveland; in the morning it remains hidden in dark mist, and the foghorn on the breakwater sounds steadily. The cargo winches are busy, and the ship lists to starboard as the cranes work the port side, probing and nodding over the hatches like weird skeletal giraffes at feed; crates of beer and canned fish swing upward.

At dusk we pass the Detroit River lighthouse, situated at the junction of river and lake. Detroit lies beside us now, an immense suffusion of light on the mist, with glowing red patches from the torches of the plants at River Rouge. The night rattles and growls with the sleepless discontent of industry on the nearby shore. A strange melody as one lies in one's bunk, listening.

The unity between metropolis and water at Detroit forms an extraordinary junction. The other great cities stand back from the water, seem to bend their gaze inland toward the plains. I feel this in Chicago, even in Milwaukee. But not in Detroit and its Ontario neighbor, Windsor. Nowhere else does human traffic converge so spectacularly, with such pace and purpose and pride.

In the next day and night we run the 206-mile south-north length of Lake Huron, the second largest of the lakes. Its deepest sounding is 750 feet, and its shores are sparsely populated. Except for Bay City, Mich., Owen Sound, Ont., and the twin cities of Port Huron, Mich., and Sarnia, Ont., it is still wild country. You can smell the north here; the wind has the resinous taste of pine and stings from having blown a long way across cold water.

52

A dark spirit is in the air; on the bridge one of the Swedes is sorting the charts, and the names marked on them run like an incantation to the presence that suddenly seems manifest about us—Manitowoc, Manitowaning, Manitou North, Manitoulin—and we take our sense of awe below with us, where we slowly and thoughtfully eat the rich meal and listen as the pilot, a Canadian, talks solemnly about ghosts and storm and wreck.

We enter the St. Mary's River at the upper end of Huron at twilight. The river is wide and still. On either side of it the forest comes down to the water, a stony shore; the country behind rises to low, hunched mountains. The overwhelming impression is of absolute silence. Not even Huron itself seemed so wide, so empty, soundless, as these woods pressing thickly to the very edge of the water. A gull, solitary as fear, the only movement in this primeval desolation, rises beside the rail and then wheels and soars high and catches that final light on its wing, floats for a moment, then vanishes.

Our destination now is Thunder Bay, Ont., at the top of Lake Superior. Superior is 360 miles long, the largest freshwater lake in the world. It is also the deepest of the Great Lakes—with the deepest sounding at 1,302 feet, its bottom lies several hundred feet below sea level—and it holds almost half the water of the entire system.

There is an antique stillness on Superior, a feeling of immense brooding age. Round-humped mountains around the shores look like burial mounds of the gods, their surfaces rubbed to a hard polish by glaciers through aeons of cold sleep.

Out through these ancestral mists move the long lake barges bearing prairie grain and Minnesota ore. If there is a distinctive sound that man has brought to this region, then surely it is the harsh clanging of shunting freight cars, which re-echoes night and day in the ports —Marquette, Duluth, Superior, Thunder Bay—where the trains crawl in with their mile-long loads of golden seed or tinted nuggets.

We slowly steam up to Thunder Bay. It wears the look of any city: sidewalks, paved streets and urban architecture. Yet the gleaming tracks and lines of cars, fringing the wilderness, strike me as being among the most remarkable things we have experienced so far; one feels that one has indeed come to some junction of the continent, between past and present, between frontier and factory.

Forty-eight hours later, having recrossed Lake Superior to the St. Mary's River and Lake Huron, we pass through the Straits of Mackinac and enter Lake Michigan. Michigan, the only one of the lakes entirely within the United States, is the lake that built Chicago. It is the main route of the ocean-going ships. Its shores are green and tangled in the north, and white with dunes to the east.

Now the whole lake has gone glassy, and the sky black. There are distant rumbles, and suddenly the wind comes. In no time the ship begins to lift and roll. The bulkheads creak; the curtains swing; lightning illuminates the whole ship. From that windless dusk to this black rage. A steward comes in to secure the porthole.

"Tomorrow Chicago," he says, as if to convince himself as well as me. It still doesn't seem true. He should have said Cherbourg or Southampton. Chicago? I lie and listen to the water.

Grain elevators at Thunder Bay, Ont. —monuments to an industry that has thrived because of cheap transportation on the Great Lakes.

Colossus
at Churchill Falls

By Paul Friggens

"Up here we have a saying that the good Lord made the earth in six days, and on the seventh he threw rocks at Labrador!"

So said my young helicopter pilot as we flew across the desolate Labrador wilderness 700 miles northeast of Montreal. This glacier-gouged, rock-strewn land of lonely lakes, scrub spruce and muskeg is the scene of the biggest and boldest hydroelectric power project in the free world. It underwrites a new era of growth and development for eastern Canada, with important implications in engineering and power development for countries everywhere.

Though colossal in size, the fabulous Churchill Falls power project is surprisingly simple in concept. Here, in Labrador, 6,000 years ago, the retreating Ice Age left a vast saucerlike depression or bowl, with frequent dents or gaps in the rim. Enterprising Canadian engineers are plugging 40 miles of these gaps with glacial debris and granitic dikes so that the Churchill and smaller rivers now draining the area will no longer escape. The backed-up waters will create a huge natural reservoir of 2,567 square miles, about one-third the size of Lake Ontario; then, instead of cascading down from the Labrador plateau in a thundering waterfall as it does today, the Churchill River will be diverted to drop a thousand feet into the world's greatest underground powerhouse.

Located in one of the last great hydro sites left on the North American continent, the Churchill Falls project will guarantee Canada 5,225,000 kilowatts—7,000,000 cheap horsepower—for industrial and domestic use. In what Paul Dozois, then Quebec's finance minister, hailed as the "biggest power contract ever signed in the world," Hydro-Québec contracted to buy $5,000,000,000 in power over a 65-year period. The utility will sell some electricity to Ontario and New Brunswick on a short-term basis; but, as the new territory develops, it will need more and more of the Churchill Falls power for its own use.

The great power project was the dream of Newfoundland's aggressive premier, Joseph (Joey) Smallwood, who envisioned the growing need for industry and power development in this remote region. On a journey to London in August 1952, Smallwood interested Winston Churchill in his idea.

Churchill opened doors to the Rothschilds and other British financiers who, the following year, incorporated Brinco (British Newfoundland Corporation) to explore the Labrador potential. Through subsidiaries, Brinco built a small power site, Twin Falls, on a tributary

In the spectacular Labrador wilderness, where the mighty Churchill River roars, men with bulldozers and giant earthmovers —and shovels—begin the task of building the western world's largest hydroelectric power plant.

of the Churchill River. The $60,000,000 Twin Falls plant supplies vital power for the development of new iron mines in western Labrador and energy to construct the Churchill Falls power project. Inaugurated on July 17, 1967, the vast hydroelectric project is expected to remain fully competitive with thermonuclear power sources.

The Churchill Falls area was explored by John McLean, a Hudson's Bay Company trader, as far back as 1839. Until a few years ago it remained a remote wilderness frequented only by trappers and Indians. But when I visited the site during the peak of the underground excavation work, I found a sprawling trailer town winterized for Arc-

tic-like weather and complete with phone service, television, movie theater, recreation center, elementary school, hospital, 300 miles of road and daily aircraft service. The work force, which reached 6,000 in the summer of 1970, enjoys most of the amenities of home, though the wilderness is always close at hand. Wolves prowl just outside the main camp, and a black bear once snatched a lunchbox from a construction worker, taking a chunk of his pants in the process.

Construction of the mammoth project is under the supervision of ACB (Acres Canadian Bechtel), a joint venture of two companies. At the company offices and nerve center in Montreal, and at the busy field offices in Churchill Falls, a staff of engineers monitors more than 100 separate, precisely timed and dovetailing contracts, ranging from a few million to $50,000,000 apiece. Computers in Montreal keep a constant check on progress and enable project manager Harold L. Snyder to run a tight ship. Daily transportation reports, for example, permit instant inventory of supplies and equipment needs, and allow the staff in Churchill Falls and Montreal to spot potential delays and make necessary corrections.

Result—the project, despite its huge size, keeps on time and within estimates.

It is a monumental achievement. Take the primary task of building dikes to plug the gaps in the saucer's rim. While we watched a fleet of yellow bulldozers and giant earthmovers churn over the bleak Labrador plateau, one of the engineers told me, "Altogether we'll move more than 31,000,000 cubic yards of glacial till, rock and gravel, and build 90 dikes." The carefully compacted dikes range from a few hundred feet to nearly four miles long and up to 90 feet above natural terrain. Each dike must be constructed at exactly the same level in relation to the others. "We'll be draining about one-quarter of Labrador," the engineer explained, "and we can't risk overflow through a dike that is too low."

Logistics and climate are perpetual obstacles. Contractors moved at least $50,000,000 in heavy equipment to the job, working at times at 50° below zero in winter snows and whiteouts. All vehicles, equipment and supplies had to be shipped 500 miles by boat from Montreal down the Gulf of St. Lawrence to the port of Sept-Iles, thence transshipped 286 miles by rail and 113 miles by truck—altogether more than 900 miles. Amazingly, the huge project has never been shut down on account of weather.

The crowning achievement at Churchill Falls is the world's greatest underground powerhouse: located nearly 1,000 feet beneath the surface in granitic gneiss, it's nearly 1,000 feet long, 81 feet wide and up to 154 feet high.

Before deciding on the site for the powerhouse the Churchill Falls engineers first had to determine that the rock was stable or "competent." Drilling holes 1,000 feet and more, geologists used "borehole" photography to check the rock. Lowering mini-cameras, which take circular pictures, into the bores, they looked for open fractures, slippage or fault zones. When they detected "bad rock" in a major fault zone, engineers selected a new location 1,000 feet east of the site originally chosen. As the excavation progressed, engineers watched

Five million tons of rock was removed in creating the huge underground complex at Churchill Falls —and it took 5,000,000 pounds of explosives to dislodge it. At its deepest, in the turbine pits, the powerhouse (below, lower photo) is 984 feet beneath the surface. Also underground are an immense surge chamber and transformer gallery, 11 penstocks which lead the water to the turbines (immediately below, a penstock under construction) and two tailrace tunnels (one is shown opposite).

with an array of highly sensitive instruments for any signs of instability.

The whole underground complex is so big you enter by bus! You travel through a mile-long access tunnel, 33 feet wide and 28 feet high, easily able to accommodate two-lane traffic and to truck in components for the giant generators and turbines. During the excavation work you slogged through a maze of tunnels and cavernous chambers thundering with the roar of huge drills and acrid with powder smoke from recent blastings. Flashing their warning lights and sounding sirens, 35-ton behemoths barreled through with their towering loads of rock—up to 15,000 tons a day—and you flattened yourself against the tunnel walls for safety. WHOOM! WHOOM!—the blasting resumed.

Excavating the mammoth powerhouse and its miles of shafts and access tunnels was a remarkable engineering feat. About the time that workmen began tunneling the mile-long bus route to the powerhouse in October 1967, another crew commenced sinking a 958-foot *vertical* shaft for speedy access to the completed structure. The two crews were scheduled to meet at the powerhouse. Drilling horizontally and vertically at the same time, from positions more than a mile apart, the two crews hooked up a year later—and were only four inches off the original survey.

The whole powerhouse complex consists of three enormous structures, which alone cost nearly $50,000,000 to excavate. The largest is the powerhouse proper, where 11 giant turbines and 11 generators will produce the 7,000,000 horsepower. Upstream from the powerhouse in the transformer gallery, the generators' output will be boosted from 15,000 to 230,000 volts of alternating current, and power will travel to the surface for a second transformation to 735,000 volts. Downstream is the surge chamber, where surges or fluctuations in the water flow from the turbines will be smoothed out before the water exits through the tailrace tunnels and into the Churchill River—otherwise, violent surges could cause pressures and strains that might wrench installations apart.

Transmitting 7,000,000 horsepower is in itself a new feat and technological milestone. Until recently, it was uneconomical to transmit such great blocks of power over long distance. But there have been recent breakthroughs in transmission technology, and engineers have been using higher and higher voltages to push these blocks of power over increasing distances. In 1962, after scouring the United States and Europe for the most sophisticated hardware and switchyard equipment, Hydro-Québec built what was the first 735-kilowatt line in the world.

In 1976 the entire project should be in operation. Then Churchill Falls will settle down to a permanent community of about 1,000 souls. Already permanent staff have moved their families into comfortable, all-electric homes. The Churchill Falls (Labrador) Corporation has constructed houses and four three-story, 12-unit apartment houses (rentals, $60 to $100 a month, with free utilities). It built a $3,000,000 town center complex, with 21-room hotel, supermarket, department store, bank, theater, gymnasium, curling rink, community library and fine modern school. "I figure this new town is a safe place to raise my kids. And with fishing and boating, hunting and skiing right at

The swank Town Center and well-equipped school belie Churchill Falls' reputation as a wilderness settlement. *This frontier town has a hospital, churches, two TV channels, several bridge clubs, a cocktail lounge, bowling alley and laundry. There are judo classes, dental service and daily air connections with Montreal and St. John's. Most construction workers live in trailers but long-term staff and their families live in the permanent community (opposite).*

my door, you'll never get me back to the cities," vows one engineer.

Which is the way it was planned. The late Donald McParland, when president of the Churchill Falls (Labrador) Corporation, once said: "Canada's destiny depends on opening and developing the resources of the Northland, and we think this permanent town is a demonstration that with careful and imaginative planning, people can live comfortably in our remoter areas."

Indeed, the whole bold, billion-dollar Churchill Falls project, from engineering to human planning, is an object lesson for Canada and the world.

A Walk in the Wilds

By Fred Bodsworth

I stood on jutting Skinner Bluff, 300 feet above the blue waters of Georgian Bay, soaking in the panorama of forest, shore and distant islands. Tulips were pushing up in the Toronto area, which I'd left a few hours before, but here the snow was still so deep that we'd had to tramp in on snowshoes.

My awe for the grandeur of the view suddenly heightened when I turned and gazed back at the chain of white-paint tree blazes marking the way we had come. I felt a heartening thrill at the knowledge that this modest footpath went on and on, ahead and behind, a primitive yet strangely dramatic challenge to hikers.

For this was the Bruce Trail, which stretches 450 miles from the Niagara River to the tip of Ontario's Bruce Peninsula. It was planned as part of a vast network: New York State hiking clubs are well advanced with a 500-mile path to link the Bruce with the famed Appalachian Trail. Then there'll be a continuous hiking route through rural and wilderness lands from Georgian Bay to Georgia, beckoning to a continent that's showing eager signs of wanting to get back on its feet.

In this age of "no trespassing" signs and superhighways, the Bruce Trail symbolizes a new attitude toward the outdoors. The North American urge to subjugate the continent, to fence it in and cover it with concrete, has here made an about-face. In one of Canada's most populous and industrialized regions, the man who wants freedom to walk in lonely places is having his innings again.

In building the Bruce, trail-blazers met with a surprising degree of cooperation from the 1,500-odd landowners whose permission was needed for routing the trail across their property.

It's anybody's guess how many people use the Bruce Trail. "They come onto it from hundreds of access points," says Ray Lowes, secretary of the trail association, "and they walk anywhere from one mile to the whole 450. All we can say for sure is that the ground is well packed down!"

"I knocked at a farmhouse once," recalled Phil Gosling, an ardent naturalist from Guelph, Ont., "and the farmer asked me in. I told him we'd like to put a Bruce Trail path somewhere on his land. 'Yes siree, read all about you in the papers,' he said. Then he pointed to a door off the kitchen. 'You can put your trail anywhere you like on my place, except through there,' he told me. 'That's my wife's bedroom.'"

Indeed, although Canada has no great hiking tradition, the Bruce Trail was built largely across privately owned lands—by an eager army of volunteers—and without one cent of government money.

It began as a dream of one man, a soft-spoken metallurgist from Hamilton. Ray Lowes learned to hike in Saskatchewan, where he had to walk eight miles to school. When he moved east, he soon fell in love with the rugged, wooded ribbon of the Niagara Escarpment, which loops around Hamilton and winds on far to the north. At the same time, Lowes acquired a pet aversion: "I got tired of walking into 'keep off' signs whenever I tried to hike in the country."

Behind his idea for a Niagara escarpment trail lay two purposes. He hoped it would get people back to nature, in a place where they could hike freely, and also encourage preservation of a great scenic resource. As Lowes told the Federation of Ontario Naturalists in 1960, the escarpment was ideal for hiking—wild woodlands with rocky glens, waterfalls and breathtaking views from towering limestone bluffs. Moreover, it was reasonably close to Ontario's main centers of population. But the naturalists needed little persuading. The FON promptly set up a Bruce Trail committee, with Lowes as secretary.

Suddenly, donations and well-wishing letters poured in from across Canada. When Lowes outlined the plan on a radio program, many shut-ins who would never see the trail wrote that they were thrilled just to know it would be there. A Calgary woman offered to donate a bench or trail-side shelter. After *The New York Times* suggested a link with the Appalachian Trail, a flood of mail came from the eastern United States.

The FON submitted a brief to the Atkinson Charitable Foundation of Toronto and received $12,000 to cover initial expenses and to pay a full-time trail director for one year. So Phil Gosling put his Guelph real-estate business on ice for a year and went to work for the newly incorporated Bruce Trail Association.

In no time he'd organized nine Bruce Trail Clubs—grass-roots

Trees along the trail are blazed with white paint. The sign at a stile warns: "This is private land. Please refrain from damaging trees, fences & other property. No camping, no fires except at authorized areas." Some hikers walk the Bruce alone; group hikers include youth organizations, geology students and natural history classes.

Color is everywhere on the trail, from the deep, cool green of fern . . . and the delicate mauve of woodland flowers . . . to the gentle gold of sunlight on rolling hills and a weathered barn.

support—in communities between Niagara and Tobermory. Members pored over topographical maps and aerial photos, then explored the ground itself, selecting routes that would be scenic but not too rugged for hiking. Next came the big job of getting landowner permissions. And finally, the trail building itself—clearing and blazing, erecting signs, building hundreds of footbridges and fence stiles.

In the rare cases where landowners denied permission, the trail was routed along unused, overgrown road allowances to bypass their property. Refusals came mainly from city residents with rural retreats.

"Can you blame them?" Gosling asked. "They buy country land to get away from people, and then we come along and ask if we can put a public hiking trail past their door."

But most landowners agreed. "I want to say no," growled a Toronto architect with property on Bruce Peninsula, "but this trail thing is bigger than I am. Go ahead."

Almost all farmers welcomed the trail, offering their wells for drinking water and haymows for sleeping places. Ronald Gatis of Colpoy's Bay gave three miles of his shore line and became so enthusiastic about it that he wound up helping the Lower Bruce Club to blaze a 20-mile section.

Since owners' permission can be withdrawn if hikers become a nuisance, the trail association hammers hard on the respect-for-property theme. When one of the first completed sections was opened, in the Dundas Valley near Hamilton, several hundred people jammed the trail; but when it was later checked for litter and damage, all that was found was one discarded facial tissue and the remains of a lunch stuffed in a hollow tree.

All types have been attracted to the project. The first association president was Prof. Norman Pearson of Waterloo University, a noted town planner. Trail-clearing teams included lawyers, printers, machinists and housewives, and many firms donated cash, lumber, nails, tools and paint.

By the time Phil Gosling's year as coordinator ended, in mid-1963, more than 1,000 persons had worked on the trail. Their methods varied. Some clubs pushed their sections through with crash programs, using hundreds of volunteers; other sections grew more slowly. In the Collingwood area, where no club was organized, lab technician Walter Blacklock and his wife contacted 50 landowners, built 37 stiles, blazed and cleared 35 miles of trail almost by themselves.

The trail begins at Queenston Heights, near where General Sir Isaac Brock died repelling the American invasion of 1812. It wends westward through the Niagara fruitlands toward Hamilton, following escarpments that on clear days provide sweeping views across Lake Ontario to the skyscrapers of Toronto, 40 miles away.

As the trail loops around Hamilton, hikers can look down on the city's checkerboard street patterns as though from an aircraft. To keep to a woodsy setting here, the footpath had to be routed up and down the escarpment and ravine banks, requiring more than 500 steps and 25 footbridges. After a midwinter building bee, one volunteer looked ruefully at his chapped, cold hands and christened a new span "Blue Knuckle Bridge"—a name that has stuck. Despite its proximity to the city, this section of the trail is beautiful, winding past picturesque waterfalls and under cliffs of fossil-filled shale. Jan Kamermans, the Hamilton trail boss, said proudly, "We hardly cut a living tree."

Much further north, at the base of Bruce Peninsula, Owen Sound citizens adopted the trail as a community project. They went at it so enthusiastically that a 60-mile stretch was cleared, blazed and bridged in just six months. Here is a magnificent region of deep gorges, trout streams and hidden caves with bucolic legends about old recluses who are said to inhabit them.

The northernmost segment, which twists for almost 150 miles up the Bruce Peninsula, is the wildest, ruggedest and probably most beautiful part of the whole trail. For here the escarpment forms a sheer and towering shore line; in many places, Georgian Bay's white surf beats the rocks a dizzying 300 feet directly below. It is a region of rare ferns, orchids—and occasional bears.

Though the complete trail was originally conceived as 250 miles, the loops and bends around towns and impassable terrain have almost doubled its length. Most people hike in small sections. But some—probably many—do it all in one trip. For hardened hoofers it's a three-week hike, for strollers five or six weeks.

The day after my hike to Skinner Bluff, I drove on to the Cape Croker Indian Reserve, where John Nadjiwon and his Chippawa band blazed many miles of the Bruce Trail across their land. Nadjiwon showed me parts of his trail and the campground on Sydney Bay that his people have created. "I take no credit," he said modestly, "but I take pride."

I saw a shine in John Nadjiwon's brown eyes, mirroring an ancestral memory of a time long gone. And I knew, as I had known on Skinner Bluff, why Nadjiwon and hundreds of others rallied behind Ray Lowes' simple idea. For the Bruce Trail has tapped a yearning that thousands feel in this mechanized time—a yearning for primitive places where a man can walk on and on and still be alone.

Legend lends a touch of mystery to the northern part of the trail. In some caves, people say, live strange and scary old hermits. You believe or not, as you wish.

Escape
to Canoe Country

By Fred Bodsworth

"... we distributed small loads between the two children, and set out in Indian file. We camped that night on Happy Isle."

If you look at a highway map of eastern Canada, you will see the tentacles of roads reaching northward here and there into the hinterland. Many of them end at chains of lakes and rivers linked by portage trails first trod by Indian hunters long before the white man came. This is canoe country, and beyond it are yet more waterways waiting, beckoning, rarely traveled—as primeval still as the retreating ice left them ten thousand years ago.

The canoe that makes it all accessible is a unique and versatile craft that evolved to fit the travel requirements of this lake-laced wilderness. It is the only water craft sturdy enough to carry two or three people and a two- or three-week outfit, yet light enough to be portaged overland by one man. It can be loaded and unloaded quickly and easily. It can take you away from cars, cottages, motorboats—and people—as no other mode of travel can. It is the only way to enjoy and see wilderness as the voyageurs and explorers saw it. A canoe can turn back the clock and make *you* feel like an explorer, too.

The year that we decided, with tenderfoot trepidation, to try our first wilderness canoe-camping trip is fading now into family history. Today we are veterans of many trips, and the toddler we carried across his first portage is now a strapping adolescent. Our canoe is rock-scarred, our sleeping bags are patched, our wilderness maps are tattered and faded, and our memories are filled with vivid recollections of a kind of fun and adventure that no other vacation can give.

Our first canoe trip began one August evening at the public campsite on Opeongo Lake in Ontario's Algonquin Park, 194 miles north of Toronto. We had bucked highway traffic all day to reach it, only to find ourselves squeezed in among other campers. Half a dozen radios blared within earshot, half a dozen outboards cut silver figure eights on the lake.

I gazed northward up Opeongo Lake, vaguely picturing what lay beyond in the almost 2,000,000-acre wilderness and lakeland of Algonquin Park. About ten miles up there, I knew, Opeongo ended, and there should be a portage into Happy Isle Lake, another to Merchant, to Big Trout . . . my memory of the map stopped, but a teasing reverie had begun. One could start paddling and portaging here and go on and on for a thousand miles to the Arctic Ocean. It struck me then that the Opeongo campsite was not an end, but a beginning.

As the radios squawked around us we made our decision. Next morning we bought a detailed map of the park, rented life jackets, packsacks and a canoe. We loaded our camping gear, left the car in a parking lot, and paddled a greenhorn's zigzag course up Opeongo.

In a couple of hours we were getting the knack of it and the zigzags were straightening out. That afternoon we reached the head of the lake, studied our map and found the footworn burrow through the trees that was the portage to Happy Isle Lake, a mile and a half away.

I recalled my camp-lore reading and tied two paddles athwart the canoe so that the blades would form a carrying yoke for my shoulders. I rolled a sweater for shoulder padding and with my wife's help struggled under the canoe—and immediately made my first startling canoe-trip discovery. To the uninitiated, a 16-foot canoe on a man's back looks like a weight-lifter's burden. I was amazed to find that it isn't. Most people go through life carrying only with their arms, never discovering that what is a burdensome armload is no real burden at all when it is balanced squarely on one's shoulders so that the legs and not the arms are supporting it.

My wife wrestled into the shoulder straps of a food pack, we distributed small loads between the two children, and set out Indian file. We camped that night on Happy Isle. I caught a lake trout and while the golden fillets fried, a beaver and five loons swam back and forth in curious sentry patrols off our campsite.

Darkness came and we scanned the lakeshore for the orange flicker of another campfire. There was none. It was another canoe-tripping discovery. We had seen many boating parties coming up Opeongo that day, but one portage had been enough to put the outboard crowd behind us. Happy Isle that night belonged to us, the loons and beaver, and we crawled into our sleeping bags with the proud and weary knowledge that we had earned its solitude. We've been canoe-trip devotees ever since.

We've had thrills that a lifetime of highway camping could never provide. We've been serenaded by a wolf pack and we've slipped up so close to a moose feeding in the shallows that we could almost slap its rump with a paddle. One memorable night on Burnt Island Lake we disputed a campsite with three bears that refused to be frightened away. We finally settled for an uneasy truce, with the tent flaps tied tight and the bears in possession outside until dawn.

Once, in Quebec in 1954, we camped on Lac Ogascanane, near the Ontario border about 250 miles north of Toronto. Ogascanane can hardly be called remote; like thousands of other Canadian lakes, it is just far enough off the beaten track to demand a modest tribute of sweat and toil from those who would paddle or fish its waters. (We had reached it with three days of leisurely paddling and portaging.) We camped on an island with a beach of vivid green sand. The mineral coloring baffled me, and intrigued the children so much they didn't want to leave. Next morning before pushing on, we left the tent poles we had cut propped up in a spruce tree so that they would resist decay and serve other campers who might follow. And we left some firewood neatly piled beside the stone fireplace we had made.

That single night's camp was to become a symbol I treasure. We have never been back, but a companion on that trip, Dr. Carl Atwood, a forest entomology professor, went back ten years later.

"Don't worry about children: they take naturally to canoe-tripping."

"Remember the island with the green beach in the Ogascanane narrows?" Carl asked me on his return. "Remember the tent poles and the firewood? They haven't been touched. There doesn't seem to have been another soul on it since we were there ten years ago!"

That's wilderness, unsullied and unspoiled.

Canoe-camping will throw you on your own resources. There will be no groceterias for replenishing the sugar or milk powder that you haven't rationed properly to the trip's end. But those simple things—your watertight tin of matches, or the final egg painstakingly packed in the flour or oatmeal to be intact for the last day's breakfast pancakes—will assume critical value. And wherever you go, you will have the zestful satisfaction of knowing that you got there on your own power. It's hard work—make no mistake—and if you are a city softie, as I am, for the first couple of days of each trip you will be persecuted with blisters, torn fingernails and pains in a myriad of muscles you never knew you had. But with the physical pain and toil will come a psychic rest and peace, and you will feel your body toughening, adapting to the new physical demands.

For the shop- or desk-bound man this is a healthy, ego-boosting experience. For example, there is a canoe route into Algonquin Park that calls for a portage going in and coming out—an arduous, up-and-down mile-and-a-halfer between Blackbear and Ink lakes. Hitting that portage the first day out is a grueling test. I have taken as long as two hours to make the trip across, and at the end my canoe is so heavy that I can barely move. But outbound two weeks later, toughened by paddling and portaging, I can cross that same portage in 40 minutes.

On every canoe trip I relive that adolescent experience of feeling myself once more become a man. My canoe weighs 85 pounds (heavier than normal: the average is 70), and I weigh 145, so canoe-tripping is not just for brawny athletes—it is for anyone who can swim and is reasonably active.

Want to try it? Okay, where do you go, and how do you get started?

The best canoe country is where Ice Age glaciers gouged out rock basins and left a labyrinth of lakes behind. I prefer the lake regions instead of following a single river because, in lake country, you have a choice of routes always beckoning, and the challenge of finding your way by map and compass. There is good wilderness lake country in Maine, the Adirondacks of New York and northern Minnesota, but the canoer's paradise is the vast hinterland reaching northward from the

fringes of settlement in Quebec, Ontario, Manitoba and Saskatchewan. Canada's lake and river chains provide thousands of routes that can keep you paddling a lifetime without ever covering the same mile twice.

Two good schooling grounds for novices are Algonquin Park and Quetico Park on the Ontario-Minnesota border. Here the lakes are small, the portages reasonably short and well used so that they are easy to find and follow. Select a route with short portages—even half-milers will be grim if it's your first portaging experience.

For a first-year shakedown run, you don't need your own outfit. In the popular canoeing regions there will be outfitters who will rent you canoes and camping gear, and provide light, dehydrated canoe-trip foods. They will plan your route, mark it on a map and, if you need it, give you some instructions on how to handle a canoe. The rates for full outfit will be comparatively inexpensive.

Don't worry about children: they take naturally to canoe-tripping. Lecture them in advance on the need for sitting still in a canoe, and let them work off their energy on the portages. Make sure they have, and wear, approved life jackets while on the water, and impress upon them that they must stay on the portage trails, because to leave a trail invites getting lost in the forest.

Avoid rapids until you are experienced and know the ways of canoes and rapids well. Avoid big lake stretches in stormy weather. When you have to cross a big lake, check the skyline for approaching thunderstorms. If you do get caught in a sudden squall, head against the wind for the closest land.

Don't overload. Maximum load for the average 16-foot pleasure canoe is 550 pounds. Remember, probably several times each day you will have to carry the canoe and its contents on your backs.

There are books full of camping and canoeing lore, but you will learn best by trial and error. You won't learn from a book how to put that final golden-brown crust on a reflector-oven's biscuits, and by the time you have carried your tent across half a dozen portages you'll know—from the crick in your back—whether you want a lighter one.

If you have done some automobile camping and acquired a feel for outdoor living, you will have a basis of experience on which to build. The switch to living out of packsacks is a considerable one, but if you are the kind of person who wants to, you can paddle your own canoe into a thrilling new world of family fun.

"One could . . . go on and on for a thousand miles . . . the Opeongo campsite was not an end, but a beginning."

67

The Fabulous Yukon

By Ben Lucien Burman

He's retired now and his "yellow fever" has subsided a bit. In a Dawson hotel, remembering all his brave young dreams of gold, an old prospector lives on bittersweet memories of a lifelong search for eldorado.

The last glow of the Yukon sun disappeared over the distant mountains. Sitting opposite me, a black-bearded prospector called Hot Stove Johnny chewed his cud of tobacco thoughtfully. "The one bad thing you got to watch here is you don't catch yellow fever," he drawled.

"I knew the mosquitoes were bad," I said, in surprise. "But I thought that only the tropical kind could give you the fever."

The grizzled miner beside him, who went by the name of Deep Hole, chuckled. "This ain't the kind of yellow fever you get with bugs," he said. "It's the kind you get with a pick and shovel. Hunting gold."

We were sitting in a log cabin in the Klondike. Outside, a foaming stream rushed over the tailings of gravel left by grimy miners and whining dredges since the days of the great Gold Rush of 1898. In all, more than $250,000,000 worth of the glittering metal has been taken from the frozen ground of the Yukon Territory.

"It's going to happen again. You'll see," said Hot Stove. "The Mother Lode ain't been even touched."

Deep Hole nodded in agreement. "If they ain't on the trail of the Mother Lode, why has somebody in the last month been buying up all the land in Dawson City?"

I drove to Dawson with my two friends. The town—population less than 1,000—is a faint shadow of its former self, when 25,000 people crowded its muddy streets. Here and there the traveler still sees a building whose very name conjures up the old-time glory: the Flora Dora Hotel, the Palace Grand Theater (reconstructed in magnificent detail in 1961), the shop where Madame Tremblay sold the latest Paris gowns to the wives and mistresses of suddenly rich miners.

"Was the biggest town west of Winnipeg," said Deep Hole. "More saloons than you could count, and plenty of dance-hall girls, too."

"Some of 'em were beautiful," added Hot Stove. "Most times nobody knew their right names, just nicknames like everybody else up here. There was Bubbling Lil, and Giggling Gertie and Nellie the Pig and the Oregon Mare that whinnied like a horse."

We went into the beer parlor of the Westminster Hotel. Long-haired Indians, bearded prospectors and burly construction workers sat about, discussing the mysterious figure who was buying up all the property in Dawson. The bartender prepared their drinks solemnly.

"Ain't like the bartenders used to be," declared a red-shirted individual. "Them days the miners didn't have money. Just carried a poke of gold dust. The bartender'd put a wet towel under the scales for weighing the dust and flick the scales with his fingers so a little

Southeast of Whitehorse, the Alaska Highway skirts the eastern shore of Teslin Lake (left), whose superb wild setting is typical of the Yukon landscape. Dawson (below), a bustling city of 25,000 at the peak of the Klondike Gold Rush of the 1890s, dozes peacefully in the late-afternoon sun.

Some Dawson streets and many saloons, bars and other buildings have changed little since the heyday of the "City of Gold." The excitement and the color of old Dawson are revived each summer in such buildings as the Palace Grand Theatre, where the girls of The Gaslight Follies make it all seem like only yesterday. . . .

dust'd fall off. Later he'd pan the towel and get maybe $30 or $40."

I left my two companions and went to my room in the Whitehouse cabins, built of lumber from the boats in which the early prospectors, after crossing the forbidding coastal mountains, had floated down the turbulent Yukon River. In the late August moonlight outside, I could see its waters racing swiftly toward the Bering Sea, 1,500 miles away. Off in the distance I could hear the dogs of the Indian quarter howling dismally.

In the morning I climbed into a little seaplane that rose quickly from the choppy water. Soon the towering Ogilvie Mountains were beneath us; at times jagged blades of stone thrust into the air like the teeth of a saw. We flew into a cloud that quickly became a snowstorm. The plane floundered like a ship in a heavy sea, yet the pilot flew on as calmly as if he were riding a commuter train. We emerged from the storm and rapidly went into another.

The mountains grew lower. The snowstorms ended. Caribou wound their way across a green valley; here and there a moose drank at the edge of an emerald lake. This is one of the emptiest regions in the world; in the more than 200,000 square miles of the Yukon there are under 20,000 people.

We came down on a narrow lake and taxied up to a camp along the shore. Ragged strips of canvas lay scattered on the ground nearby.

"It's all that's left of my new tent," declared the pilot. "Had a little visit from a grizzly. That's normal for Mr. Grizzly. Now I'll show you something that isn't." He picked up an empty can punctured by three enormous holes. "This was a can of motor oil. I'd just brought out 24 quarts. The grizzly bit each one open and poured out every drop."

We flew back to Dawson. I collected Hot Stove and Deep Hole and drove out to see a prospector friend of theirs up a neighboring creek. We chatted with the snowy-haired old man about the unpredictable ways of gold. How, during the Gold Rush, a dog digging for a rabbit had uncovered a find that brought his hungry master a fortune. How two newly arrived tenderfeet asked some bearded old-timers where to dig. The old-timers, as a joke, told them to dig high up on a hill, knowing that gold had been found only in the low valleys. The tenderfeet dug, and found one of the richest mines in all the Klondike.

As we talked, two large dogs came through the door, dark, shaggy animals with great, sad eyes. "They're malamutes," said our host. "Part wolf. Finest dog there is."

"That's sure right," said Hot Stove. "Friend of mine over near Carcross was out with his team once when he got caught in a blizzard. He was walking in snowshoes ahead of the dogs, breaking a trail, and his lead dog, a young female malamute, kept putting her paws on his snowshoes so he'd fall head over heels. He scolded the dog, but she kept on doing it. Finally he figured there must be a reason, and he found out that instead of coming to his cabin he was going away from it. If it hadn't been for that dog, he wouldn't be alive today."

We drove to several other isolated cabins, seeing more men whose lined faces bore the marks of the years they had spent with picks and

In 1900, right after the Klondike rush, Yukon gold production was $22,275,000. Five years later, when men had worked all the richest and easiest ground, came the switch from hand-mining to dredging—and markedly less output. But the search has never ended. Huge dredges still dig deep into the gold-bearing earth, still bring up enough of the yellow metal for profitable refining. Great heaps of tailings force Bonanza Creek—originally known as Rabbit Creek—into unnatural pools and channels. The creek, a commonplace little stream, is where it all started in 1896—and where many an old-timer believes the Mother Lode is yet to be discovered.

In wild, wide-open Dawson, the Red Feather Saloon—and scores of others—ran 24 hours a day . . . butter was $3 a pound, eggs $1 each, champagne $60 a bottle, doughnuts and coffee $1.25. . . . Here for a while lived more than 20,000 souls, among them rhymester Robert W. Service, novelists Rex Beach and Jack London, promoter Tex Rickard . . . Suddenly, after only a few years, the boom turned to bust, population dropped to 2,000 . . . and Dawson City took its colorful place in Canadian history.

shovels. "You got to be tough to prospect in the Yukon," said Hot Stove. "Be all by yourself for a whole year maybe. It's all right till something happens. Like the man broke his hip over in Hart River country. He couldn't move more than a few feet, but he lived for seven months till they found him, just crawling around, living on rabbits he killed by throwing sticks at 'em."

I left Dawson a few days later and flew to Whitehorse, the booming little capital of the Yukon. Its two fashionable restaurants were crowded with government men and their smartly dressed wives. But the shops and bars, like those of Dawson, were full of shaggy Indians and unshaven prospectors. The frontier began again where the few sidewalks ended, a quarter of a mile away.

I sat in a café with some long-time residents of the area.

"We've had some wonderful characters here in the Yukon," said a twinkling-eyed, sandy-moustached individual called Charley. "I guess you have to be a character or you wouldn't stay.

"Take that fellow just come through the door." Charley called the newcomer over. "This is the champion gut fighter of the Yukon," he declared.

"That's right," said the dark, burly man. "That's me."

I asked him to explain.

His round face lighted. "It's a stomach fight, a game we have in the Yukon. I stand up at one end of the beer parlor and a second fellow stands up at the other. The bartender drops a handkerchief. And we each put out our stomachs and charge." He affectionately patted a massive expanse of stomach. "That stomach's the champion," he boasted. "It ain't been beat yet."

Charley and I left the café and drove out to an Indian fishing camp. Here several Indian families were out after the huge salmon swimming to their spawning grounds from the far-off ocean. A wrinkled old Indian called Gus was the head of the camp. As he hung new strips of fresh-cut salmon over the fire to smoke, we talked of the changes time had brought to his people.

"Young Indians not same old ones," he said, tossing a bit of raw fish to one of many skinny dogs. "Can't hunt, can't do nothing right. Chief come here all way Yellowknife looking for caribou feed his dogs. Hunters all young. Can't find nothing. Chief has to send telegram white boss Yellowknife: CAN'T FIND NO CARIBOU FOR DOGS. PLEASE SEND PLENTY CANS PET FOOD."

Charley chuckled. "He's dead right. The other day I met two young Indians out hunting. As I passed, they called out, 'Mister, you know where there's some caribou?'"

We left the camp, soon after.

"They're great people, the old-timers like Gus," said Charley. "Once I heard about an old Indian out in the wilderness who'd had some kind of accident and was lying in his cabin freezing to death. I went out and brought him to the hospital in town. Curious thing, he'd spent all his life in the remote mountains, but he never said a word about the things he was seeing for the first time—electric light, radio, even an automobile. Then we took him to an airport to transfer him to another hospital. He studied the concrete runway a long time, then reached down and felt it carefully. At last he spoke. 'This plenty good trail,' he said."

Back in Whitehorse again, I boarded a little plane with Charley and flew to the mountain-fringed camp of one of those numerous organizers of hunting and fishing expeditions.

The men sitting around the spacious log-cabin headquarters began to talk of the coming winter.

"I've seen it officially 81 below zero at Snag," commented the camp proprietor, weather-beaten until his skin was the color of the moosehead on the wall. "At 50 below, it sizzles when you breathe; at 70 it sounds like breaking glass."

"It's square-tire country," added Charley with a grin. "When it's that cold, your tires freeze in any shape you've left 'em; so, when you first start out, instead of being round, the tires are square as a box. The trick is to keep the four square sides running together."

They grew serious, and I heard again how it is the intense cold that gives the Yukon its unique character. How even today, in the wilderness, there is never a lock on a cabin door. For this is the sacred, unwritten law of the North: when a traveler is in trouble, he can walk into any cabin he encounters; he can use the firewood and eat the canned goods. His only obligation is to replace the wood and write a note telling what food he took and saying that he will leave a credit at the nearest trading post.

When, at last, I decided to leave the Yukon, I dropped in for a final drink at the noisy bar of the Whitehorse Inn. To my delight, I saw Deep Hole and Hot Stove, just up from Dawson. They joined me.

"Things in Dawson are getting hotter by the minute," said Deep Hole. "Even on the hills around town, you can't buy an inch of land. I don't know whether it's the Mother Lode, or copper or oil like they're finding along the Arctic Ocean, but somebody sure knows something."

"Pretty soon a new stampede'll be starting all over," added Hot Stove. "And it could happen in Whitehorse, too. All them scientific fellows that come here say there's every kind of mineral in the Yukon ain't been even touched. Right here in this hotel we might be sitting over a million dollars."

The fantastic way that things have happened in the Yukon, he may be right.

Despite its name and location, Whitehorse is no rugged wilderness community. The many fine stores carry a range of goods astonishing to persons who have pictured the Yukon's capital city as a primitive frontier town. Tourist attractions include an excellent museum, various frontier-day relics, a log cathedral and several two- and three-story log "skyscrapers," built soon after World War II.

Incredible
British Columbia

By Bruce Hutchison

Nothing in North America, writes Bruce
Hutchison, can compare with Vancouver's
glorious setting . . . nor is there much to
match the wild beauty of a misty morning
at Long Beach, 125 miles up the Pacific
shore of Vancouver Island from the capital
city of Victoria.

More than 7,000,000 tourists a year romp through that vast region of natural wealth and wild beauty known as British Columbia, spending some $400,000,000 for the sheer fun of it. Why?

The reason is simply that B.C.—as residents like to call it—rekindles the old North American folk-dream of the wilderness, still unspoiled, yet open to man's easy access. Here are snowcapped mountains, valleys, rivers, lakes, deserts, impenetrable forests and shimmering seashore, a continent in microcosm that shames all the travel literature. No photographer, painter or poet has been able to catch more than a fragment of its immensity.

Vancouver, Canada's third biggest city, sparkles with exciting contrasts. It has the second largest Chinese community in North America, next only to San Francisco's. And it has ultramodern Simon Fraser University, named after the North-West Company's great fur-trader and explorer. Situated atop Mount Burnaby, the university was inspired—said one of the architects—by "the Acropolis at Athens, the hill towns of Italy and the Inca ruins of Machu Picchu in Peru."

Industrial smoke rising against a mountain background near Squamish is reflected in the still waters of Howe Sound.

This westernmost province of 366,255 square miles, larger than California, Oregon and Washington combined, is too big and diverse to explore in a single lifetime. But more than 23,000 miles of roads have exposed part of this complex anatomy and opened some of its secrets to the stranger who expects comfort in his travels. The hunter, fisherman, horseman, skier and mountain climber, seeking adventure in primitive solitude, will find it a few miles from any highway.

Though most of B.C. is a maze of mountain ranges behind a twisted 5,560-mile shoreline, it can be easily approached by land or air from the Canadian prairies or from Washington, Idaho and Montana. Four railways and four highways have been blasted east and west through the Rockies, while many U.S. roads cross the southern border.

Once the traveler arrives, his only problem is to choose between an embarrassment of riches. In any case, he will probably start or end at Vancouver.

Nothing in North America can compare with Vancouver's stage set: the blue-and-white backdrop of mountains, the green gash of the harbor and, to the south, the Fraser River's gleaming estuary. In this third largest Canadian city, with a population near the 1,000,000 mark, new skyscrapers abut directly on sandy beaches and the virgin forest of Stanley Park. Its harbor swarms with ships of the seven seas and a navy of pleasure craft moving under lofty bridges. Residential areas ablaze with flowers and crawling halfway up the mountains, a seaside university campus where Harvard or Oxford could be accommodated in one corner, the miles of boulevard and grass carpeting are all man's work.

But Vancouver's peculiar life is mainly the product of climate. Thanks to the genial Japan Current, weather around Vancouver is seldom unpleasantly cold in winter, never too hot in summer. True, the cargo of moisture rolling in from the Pacific in winter temporarily depresses even Vancouver's buoyant mood and supplies a standing joke for the cartoonists of other Canadian cities. Nevertheless, it is British Columbia's primary asset.

Rain nourishes the rank evergreen coastal forest, which springs up as fast as loggers remove it and feeds one of the world's largest industries of lumber, plywood, pulp and paper. The recurring crop is harvested with massive machines, processed in gigantic mills and shipped all over the globe.

Except for the mill towns, the logging camps, a few fishing villages, a mine here and there, the aluminum industry of Kitimat and the port of Prince Rupert, a serrated coast as long as North America is wide remains largely uninhabited. In recent years, however, pleasure yachts have been sailing the old sea route of B.C.'s Spanish discoverers—past the cliffs, fiords and glaciers that stretch all the way to Alaska. Many summer homes, on a cluster of adjoining islands, are the outposts of a profitable invasion from Vancouver.

Older than the metropolis and more British Columbian, the capital city of Victoria stands on the southern tip of Vancouver Island, 15 minutes from Vancouver by air, two hours by car ferry and much further in temperament. Victoria and its surroundings are the nearest

Victoria is a city of gardens, one unbroken flower bed from the sea to the gentle hills of Vancouver Island. Victoria's very English residents, says Bruce Hutchison, "hang flowers on the downtown lampposts [and] entertain ... with crumpets in the rich dowagers' haunt of the Empress Hotel." North of Victoria the mountains stretch for almost the whole 300-mile length of Vancouver Island.

British Columbia is a sportsman's paradise, and mountain climbing is a major sport in both the Rockies and, nearer the sea, the Coast Mountains. One of the toughest bicycle races anywhere is held annually on Mount Seymour, near Vancouver.

approximation of England in North America. The genuine Victorians, who profess to look down on their brawling mainland neighbor, have made their town one of the most captivating on the west coast. Its unbroken flower bed from the sea to the gentle island hills and its quiet, antique air have appropriated a big share of British Columbia's tourist revenue. The natives hang flower baskets on the downtown lampposts, entertain their guests in horse-drawn tallyhos and ply them with crumpets in the rich dowagers' haunt of the Empress Hotel. They devise replicas of Ann Hathaway's cottage and Madame Tussaud's waxworks. They fill their over-quaint secondhand stores with imported English furniture and silver.

Even nature has cooperated to make Victoria distinctive from the mainland. Thanks to a freak of vegetation, only around the city is the evergreen forest broken briefly by open meadows, outcroppings of mossy rock and glades of crooked oaks. Since his first landfall here in 1843, man has regarded his life as separate and privileged in a natural haven and has tried to keep it so.

Vancouver Island north of the capital is a heavily timbered mountain range almost 300 miles long with a narrow shelf on its eastern side. Protected from the Pacific gales and fully tamed by man, the eastern shelf is a playground of beaches, summer camps, safe anchor-

ages for small craft and salmon fishing resorts, all crammed with holi-daymakers from spring to fall.

The coast and the offshore archipelago are merely the outer rim of B.C. Its bulk lies behind the Coast Range, a barrier which has so far been pierced by only three channels.

From Vancouver the Trans-Canada Highway winds beside the lazy brown swell of the lower Fraser River and across a flat delta of green farmland ringed by white pinnacles. A hundred miles east of Vancouver the traveler approaches the river's canyon and enters the dark defile that led Indians and white men to the sea. Here Simon Fraser ran the rapids by canoe in 1808. Gold miners of 1862 built the first road by hand, hanging it from the cliffs by crazy scaffolds and crutches of wood.

From the highway's several summits, far above the two railways, the Fraser is no more than a thin brown thread. At the water's edge it is a whirling vortex, misted with spray. The drainage of half of B.C. writhes through the constricted gut of Hell's Gate, its clamor drowning all other sound, its current yearning for the sea.

As suddenly as it began the canyon ends. Following the tributary Thompson, the motorist emerges from rain forest and mountain jumble upon a rolling desert. He has crossed the first divide into the interior

In "floating classrooms" on English Bay, junior sailors of the Royal Vancouver Yacht Club are taught water safety, boat han-dling and racing rules. Surfing is great at Long Beach, on the west coast of Van-couver Island.

A church stands white and welcoming in sunny upcountry rangeland.

Dry Belt where Pacific winds, their moisture already spent on the coast, parch a land of clay gullies, tinted buttes, sagebrush, cactus and spicy air.

This is the southern fringe of the Cariboo plateau, perhaps better known to outsiders than to Canadians. At every dude ranch or fishing camp, automobiles carry license plates from far parts of the continent. They have been driven here mainly because the Fraser and its tributaries breed an unequaled multitude of trout. Anyone can catch them.

A long day's drive from Vancouver takes the motorist to Prince George, geographic center of B.C. North lies half the province, a black spruce forest with few traces of human life.

Now he can turn west toward the canyon of the Skeena, which will carry him to the coast at Prince Rupert. Or he can drive northeast across the Rockies into the Arctic watershed and the prairies by a low pass to join the Alaska Highway.

Unless he turns aside for a day or two he will overlook Canada's most ambitious engineering project in the North. Not far from the oil and gas fields around Fort St. John the B.C. government has dammed the mighty Peace River to impound its current in a gigantic man-made lake and build one of the world's greatest hydroelectric plants. In 1970, five generating units were placed in service. The plant's ultimate capacity, with ten units operating, is 2,300,000 kilowatts.

The central Cariboo route appeals especially to fishermen, hunters and horsemen, but most cars emerging from the Fraser canyon turn eastward to the Rockies. For the man who has time to spare that is a blunder. He should swing north at Kamloops and investigate the surprising valley of the North Thompson which is covered by rain forest and countless mile-high trout lakes. East of Kamloops, at Revelstoke, the traveler can drive up the reconstructed and fully paved Big Bend Highway. Along the way he'll enjoy panoramic views of the Columbia, an international river which has been dammed at three points to create a second vast supply of hydro power.

Now, straight ahead loom the Rockies' bared fangs. They should be approached slowly, for the Rockies are better than their photographs. Canada carried its first railway over two distinct ranges in 1885. In a stupendous feat of engineering, the continental spine was

80

breached again by the Trans-Canada Highway at Rogers Pass in 1962, and the whole travel pattern of the West was changed.

Until then the motorist from Vancouver usually drove to the prairies through Washington, Idaho and Montana, a detour of two or three days. Now he can reach Calgary in a single day of some 700 miles, if he is foolish enough to ignore the scenery.

Fortunately, few drivers are. From the luxury hotels of Banff and Lake Louise to motels and camps along meandering side roads, tourist traffic is leisurely. It takes a while to study even the accessible pockets of the Rockies, their friendly animals and new enchantments around every corner.

In some ways, British Columbia's southern compartment is the most interesting of all. Starting from Vancouver, you must leave the

Mount Assiniboine Provincial Park is a magnificence of mighty peaks and serene lakes. The park gets its name from 11,870-foot Mount Assiniboine (right), known as the Canadian Matterhorn because of its similarity to the peak of that name in the Pennine Alps on the Swiss-Italian border. The lakes in this photograph are Elisabeth (foreground), Cerulean, Sunburst and Magog, nestling under Mount Magog (center, top). The 92-mile Rogers Pass section of the Trans-Canada Highway (above) takes travelers through excitingly wild valleys and past the magnificent peaks of Revelstoke and Glacier national parks. It has been called "the world's most spectacularly beautiful main-highway drive." It is also one of the safest. Steel and concrete snowsheds (background) help keep the Rogers Pass route open for winter traffic.

Looking like the subject of an early Group of Seven painting, a lone tree stands sentinel at the edge of Kootenay Lake in the southeast corner of British Columbia.

Fraser near the western entrance of its canyon, turn eastward on the Hope-Princeton Highway and, crossing a high summit, drop steeply down into the improbable Okanagan Valley.

Here a dozen immaculate towns stand on the shores of a 100-mile-long lake system. All around stretch green orchards in froth of spring blossom or the autumn red of apples. Irrigation has transformed semi-desert into a luxuriant garden.

Eastward the highway climbs Anarchist Mountain, descends into another farm area beside the U.S. boundary and crosses two more summits into the far-flung drainage system of the Columbia. The Kootenays, as British Columbians call this country, include an accurate reproduction of Switzerland—the same frosty peaks, blue mountain

lakes, scented forests, lost villages and a web of casual roads leading nowhere in particular.

This pleasure land, long neglected by Canadians, has been accidentally discovered by Americans as they drive north from Washington to the Rockies. But only the wiser sort steer for the prairies by the Crow's Nest Pass, the most southern Canadian route, which has the virtues of stark solitude. Nearby, if he had a week to spare, a horse and a durable pair of legs, I could take the stranger to certain remote heights of sheep and goat and painted glens of wildflowers. Then at last he would glimpse the ultimate spectacle—the Rockies and the plains side by side. Only from such a dizzy perch can any man grasp British Columbia's size, diversity and rumpled splendor.

Botanical Columbus

By Robert O'Brien

Among nature's noblest creations is the mighty Douglas fir. It lifts its lovely, blue-green crown to heights of 200 feet and more. Its massive trunk, armored by dark, furrowed bark up to a foot thick, may measure 50 feet in circumference. It grows prodigiously in the most productive forest on earth—25,000,000 acres of green glory extending from British Columbia, south to California's Mount Shasta.

The Douglas fir takes its name from David Douglas, an intrepid Scots botanist who came across the tree during his exploration of the Pacific Northwest more than 140 years ago. Other European travelers had seen and described the fir before him—Captain James Cook used it to build shipmasts while exploring Vancouver Island in 1778—but Douglas was the first to collect its seeds and cones, the first to ship them back to England.

As a result of ten years of collecting, during which he walked, canoed, snowshoed or rode on horseback across 10,000 miles of unmapped forest, Douglas introduced into Britain more plants than any other scientist: Californian poppies, several species of phlox and lupin, Mariposa lilies, yellow globe tulips, the red flowering currant, the evergreen Madrona, Western dogwood, the beautiful Sitka spruce, the great sugar pine, Monterey pine and some 200 other trees and flowers.

One horticulturist wrote, a century after Douglas' death: "There is scarcely a spot deserving the name of a garden in which some of the discoveries of David Douglas do not form the chief attraction. To no single individual is modern horticulture more indebted."

Born in Scone, Scotland, Douglas was an inquisitive and high-spirited child. He found his life-long and only love—botany—at the age of 11, when his father apprenticed him to the head gardener of a nearby estate.

When 23, he won a coveted post as field collector for London's Horticultural Society, and at 25 he sailed to Fort Vancouver (now Vancouver, Wash.), a Hudson's Bay Company outpost on the Columbia River. For the next two years he blazed trails across a vast region never before explored by a white man. Often he traveled alone. Sometimes he hired Indian guides, or accompanied Hudson's Bay Company fur brigades.

Douglas' first shipment home included hundreds of specimens, all carefully preserved and meticulously described in his notes. One was the great evergreen that today bears his name.

"The wood," he wrote, "may be found very useful for a variety of

domestic uses ..." He was absolutely right. The wood of the fir—pound for pound stronger than concrete—has been used for a host of building purposes and became the core of British Columbia's giant forest products industry. And thin sheets of fir are bonded together to form the tough B.C. plywood that now is exported to every part of the world.

On the slope of Mauna Kea, on the island of Hawaii, a stone cairn marks where Douglas died in 1834. Behind it rises a grove of young Douglas firs, planted in 1934 to commemorate the hundredth anniversary of the scientist's death. But Douglas' proudest memorial ranges from the Cascades to the Pacific and towers over the lonely ridges and swift rivers that he loved. It is made of giant firs reaching for the wide Northwest sky.

The Best
of All Places

*. . . even in those times,
the farm was
the best of all places
for a boy to grow up*

ROBERT COLLINS

My Saskatchewan Boyhood

By Robert Collins

There was always a ragbag around our farmhouse when I was little. It was a plain five-pound flour sack bleached white, but inside—ah! All the treasures of an Oriental bazaar: fragments of silks, satins, denims, ginghams, polka dots, stripes, floral reds, buttercup yellows and noble purples, all washed clean and tumbled together waiting further duty. Ultimately the rags would patch torn overalls, line a jacket, or show up in a hooked or braided rug. But until then, they were cloaks for small Hamlets in rainy-day dramas, ribbons for kittens, bedclothes for teddy bears.

That ragbag was a symbol of our life-style. Every day was a ragbag brimming with possibilities. Even work tested our strength and our wits, and brought with it the prospect of something tangible at the end: a field of yellow wheat, a flock of Plymouth Rocks, a stout fence. And often the chore could be coupled with pleasures: husking corn while the organlike tones of Orson Welles resonated from the radio; poring over *For Whom the Bell Tolls* while herding cows; mending a bridle while someone read aloud the latest Paul Gallico story in *The Saturday Evening Post*. Somehow this made the work easier and each day richer. And in all of this was something of value that we have almost lost today.

Our farm was near the village of Shamrock, Sask. The Depression was on and, even in those times, the farm was the best of all places for a boy to grow up.

It was no calendar-cover kind of farm. No shiny silos, shady elms or white board fences. Just a barn and granaries weathered silver-gray; miles of barbed-wire fence enclosing 320 acres of grass, clay loam and stone; a gnarled caragana hedge, stubborn as the country itself; and a one-story frame house that had once been white and green.

It stood on a little hill under an ocean of sky. My father built it for my mother after he came home from the Great War. On dewy mornings when the mists played tricks on the eyes, the grain elevators of Gravelbourg miraged on the horizon 20 miles away. Gravelbourg was the center of our universe. On rare occasions we drove there in the '29 Chev for a treat: a Nelson Eddy-Jeanette MacDonald movie and dinner in the Chinese restaurant. At night, lonely pinpoints of light on other distant hills were a roll call of our neighbors—Scots, Germans, Irish, Swedes, English, Russian, French, pioneers all, tilling one land. But wasn't that what the world was all about? I thought so then.

Our house faced the sun and hunched its back against a wind

that sometimes sighed, sometimes howled, but *always* blew. In summer it carried the scent of grassy slough bottoms, sharp and sweet as peppermint, and the creaking rusty-hinge call of redwing blackbirds, the faint perfume of ripening wheat.

In autumn it plucked up dry gray Russian thistles and tumbled them, like marching armies, into the fencerows. Then, as winter came, it grew sharper, and in the white-clad stubbled fields our shaggy horses turned their rumps against the 20-below-zero nights, burrowed into strawstacks and looked out in the mornings with white whiskers and false eyelashes of hoarfrost.

Finally, with the gurgle of spring thaw, the gossipy quack of ducks V-ing in from the south and the first triumphant gopher squeak, the wind said, "Now let us begin again."

So here I grew and learned to cope with living. I discovered that loneliness bites deeper than blisters, but that it, too, heals. I learned to wake at sunrise, drive six horses abreast, build wheat stacks that would shed the rain, and, at milking time, squirt the white stream into a grateful cat's mouth at ten paces. I found out how to mend anything with a length of haywire or a few nails and cedar shingles.

We respected the other inhabitants of our little world. A few predators had to be killed for our own survival, but most days were spent in coaxing forth new life, helping chicks struggle damp and scrawny from hatching eggs, watching calves emerge wobbly-kneed from the womb, and carrying baby meadowlarks to safety from under the mower blade.

We even tolerated the sparrows that nested under the eaves of the house. Their gravelly voices at 5 a.m. sent my city-bred Uncle George into virtuoso flights of cursing, and their droppings ruined our porch, but we let them stay. They belonged; it was their world, as well as ours.

There were cruel days, too. Days when my father fell on the couch, too exhausted to wipe the black dust-mask from his face after 12 hours of prying a living from dry soil. Days when clouds of grasshoppers dimmed the sun, then settled to strip every green stalk. Days when a white fury of hail wiped out a year's hopes in ten minutes. A day when a sandstorm turned a morning into night, and the school closed at noon. Yet even on that awful day, walking home through a gray fog of topsoil, my brother and I blithely picked crocuses.

It was always that way. Nothing seemed to defeat us for long. We ad-libbed our pleasures. A handful of empty spools from the sewing machine became wheels for a truck, a carved shingle a six-gun. When a blizzard marooned us for a week, the coal-oil lamps ran dry so we threw open the Quebec heater and sang and told stories by firelight.

We built skating rinks by hauling pails of water until our drenched trousers turned to armor, but that homemade ice was surely better than Maple Leaf Gardens. We had a two-acre backyard and, when that became confining, hundreds of acres beyond. Sometimes I ran for miles with my close friend, Pedro Gonzales the gunfighter, a totally mythical Mexican with a slovenly brother named Pancho. (Unfortunate are the children who never have to make-believe.)

I saw the house intact for the last time the day they drove me to the train to join the air force. Years later when I went back, the place had been sold to a modern farmer, one of those who live in town and drive out to till the land with modern machinery in great half-mile swoops.

The house was a derelict, huddled on its hill, doors flapping raggedly in the wind, pigeons roosting on the kitchen counter. The ash, poplar and maple we had nursed through the droughts were choked with weeds. Barns, fences, windmill, all were gone. I cried. It was like the death of an old friend.

Seven Crows a Secret

By Ernest Buckler

I awaken. It is early summer, and the sun is just coming up. Light, finding things, draws their shadows from them slantwise on the ground. Dandelions dazzle themselves with yellow. Swallows shimmer, hills kindle. A hush of freshness walks on the air like Christ.

My blood springs with the hallelujah of downstairs and outdoors. I race downstairs.

My mother is scalding the wooden churn. The steam from it glistens in the sunlight from the open door. She cools the scalded butter tray with water pumped from the deep well in the cellar. As I eat, I watch the mesmeric motion of the dash in her hands and listen for the "breaking" sound that means the kernels of butter have begun to separate.

Lit velvetly with food, I don't know whether to stay with her or go out with Father. It is a morning for being with everybody. I watch Mother press the shining butter into the mold that has the pattern of acorns carved on it by my father.

Father comes into the kitchen and pumps himself a drink. "Aaaaaah!" he says, as he takes the dipper from his lips.

I go out with him. I take the brush off the long flower beds that run from the house to the road.

In a little while Mother comes out with us. I can see that this is a day when Father and Mother too like to keep the perimeter of their presences touching.

I pick up a marigold head. Its seeds are like little commas. They radiate from the center to form a perfect circle.

"Do you want to save this?" I ask Mother.

"No," she says. "I never have to worry about planting marigolds. They seed themselves."

"I'm glad" Father says. "I like yellow flowers."

It is not like Father to say anything like that. He never says anything like that. He puts his hand on my shoulder for a moment and draws me against his leg. He never does that. I am almost trembling with self-consciousness, but I've never felt so alive and happy in all my life.

And then, suddenly I have to see the brook. As if to stamp its voice, the voice of the very morning, on me, like the acorn on the butter.

I walk down the road to the bridge and sit and watch the brook. It is never for an instant the same, yet more than anything it stays itself, close and chatting. I shred pieces of bark off the bridge rail

92

and drop them into the chuckling current. I drop pebbles, one by one, into the water.

I see a small trout suspended between the surface of the water and its shadow on the pebbled bottom beneath, more electric with motion than if it were moving. Once or twice it flicks itself an inch ahead, like an impulse to certainty that sees itself as soon mistaken. And then, hitting the answer fair, it flashes straight into a dark cavern beneath the bank.

I open my shirt and let the sun touch my chest. I listen to the brook, and my own flesh and I are such snug and laughing brothers that I know we are forever mingled with the sun's pulse (or the wind's or the rain's) and forever unconquerable.

I walk back up the hill. I hear a strange voice in the kitchen. The way Father and Mother are talking sounds strange, too. I have a funny, still feeling, as when you hear a clock stop. I go in.

A neighbor is there. All three are standing, or moving purposelessly about. The neighbor's eyes are out of breath. His face looks as if he were carrying it rather than wearing it, like a garment snatched up. He is still white with the news he has brought: Jim Stedman just fell off the staging on his barn roof and broke his neck.

I look at Father. He looks as if his breath had toppled. And then he looks at Mother as if otherwise his look would have no place to go. Her look locks hands with his in the same way.

There seems to be some sudden terrible question in the air. In this great stroke of silence from the dead, it shrieks to be answered.

I am stunned. I go outside.

I look at things. And look at them. But they don't tell me anything. They've retreated inside themselves, inside that ring of deafness where they talk only to each other. In silences. The wild roses seem bowed with their own helpless color. I pick up a stone. I stare at it. It doesn't tell me anything. I drop it.

That night, we go to the dead man's house. Its windows do not speak.

Mother has cautioned herself not to "break down." Father opens the kitchen door as Mother slips her rubbers off, to leave them on the porch. Jim's wife, Annie, is sitting by the stove, pleating her handkerchief, her stricken face almost a childlike pink from tears parched dry.

"No, Mary," she says to Mother, with a faint smile of greeting even now, "don't leave your rubbers out there."

There's something about this being so much their ordinary exchange that Mother breaks down. She controls herself, but later when she says to Annie, "If you want that black hat of mine . . . ," she breaks down again.

The men sit in the kitchen, cumbersome with solemnity, looking like children who don't know their lessons. They spring up too quickly to offer their seats to a newcomer. They do not look at their wives, in a way that is suddenly like the way they hadn't looked at them in a crowded room when they were first courting. The family of the dead are awesome to me in their grief.

Visitors are shown into the parlor, where the coffin is. They move as if walking is a precarious thing they've just learned. Their eyes are kept in sober check, as if to take notice of anything in the room but the dead man would be shameful.

I stare at the dead man.

His face is whiter than water could ever wash it. The lamp is turned down to the color of his fingernails. I stare at his hands. They don't tell me anything.

The afternoon of the funeral, I sit on our veranda steps. I hear Mother and Father talking inside the house. My father is to be one of the carriers.

"Mary," he calls to her from the bedroom. "Where's my fine shirt?"

"It's in the second drawer there," she calls from the kitchen, "under the . . . just wait a minute. I'm coming up to change now, myself."

"These the right studs?" he says to her in the bedroom.

"Yes, I'll put them in for you." It is strange, this feeling they have today for each other's clothing. They never help each other dress.

"Which dress are you wearing?" my father says. He never says anything like that. "The blue one or the brown one?"

"I think the blue one'd look better today. It's old, but . . ."

"I always liked that dress on you."

"Did you like that old dress? You never said."

"Yes. It always looked good on you. What's my boots look like? Are they shined all right?"

"Yes. They look like new. That sock don't hurt where I darned the heel, does it?"

"No. Not a bit."

"Poor Annie!" Mother says. "She's takin' it so hard. Some said she drove her pigs to a poor market when she married Jim, but . . ."

"I never saw nothin' wrong with Jim," Father says. "Do you mind that morning it darkened up so when I had all the clover down and Jim never said a word, he just come over and started rakin' with his own horse?"

"Yes, I remember. And those children certainly thought there was no one like him," Mother says. "You never saw Jim anywheres without young Jim at his heels."

"I know. Do you want your beads?"

"Yes, I think so. They don't look gaudy at a time like this, do they?"

"No, they look nice. Here, I'll fasten that catch for you." Father never does anything like this. "Do us carriers set all the time, like the mourners," he says, "or do we stand up for the singin'?"

"No," Mother says, "you set all the time. Oh, Joe . . . when I think . . . if it was you . . ."

Father doesn't say anything for a minute, or so—and when he does speak his voice sounds different. "Well," he says, "I better get my coat on and walk along. I'm supposed to be there a little early. Maybe if you and Mark go out in a bit and stand by the gate you'll get a ride with someone."

"No," Mother says, "I want to go with you. We'll walk along with you. And wait."

"Maybe you'll get a chance back."

"No. We'll walk back with you. Unless *you* could get a chance. You've been working up there in the graveyard ever since daylight. You must be tired."

"No," Father says. "I'll walk along back with you."

The fields are still. Even the nostrils of the coal-black hearse horses are still. The mourners, in the front pew, are still.

And then when the first notes of the organ sound, the mourners themselves seem to break a little at the neck. It seems as if the clouds I can see through the church window are black-capitaled with the word NEVER.

The singing begins. "Shall we gather at the river/Where bright angel feet have trod . . ."

I close my eyes and try to see, really see, the river "flowing by the throne of God." They sing "In the sweet ('In the sweet,' the two splendid basses echo) by and by ('by and by')/We shall meet on that beautiful shore . . ."

I cry.

At the grave, a poplar leaf blows onto the coffin and dances the length of it. The carriers pay out the straps that let the coffin sink. I see my father's hands tremble. I notice a wrinkle in my mother's face that the sunshine seems to engrave there.

I feel like running.

We walk home together. Father and Mother look the way they do when they are working in the fields together, sowing seeds. When something comes out of them that is neither one of them but more than both. I take both their hands. I have never done this before.

"I remember when Jim and I was kids," Father says. "We used

to put green apples on the end of a withe and flick 'em at a bottle we'd set up on the stone wall. And every time there was a fresh snow we'd go back and try to track a fox to its den. . . . And hot afternoons I remember we'd strip our clothes off and wade into the lake for the white water lilies."

I look back at the churchyard. A flock of crows is circling overhead. I count them. One crow sorrow, two crows joy; three crows a wedding, four crows a boy; five crows silver, six crows gold; seven crows a secret never to be told.

A Son's Discovery

By Ernest Buckler

Call the man Joseph. Call his son Mark. Two scars had bracketed Mark's left eye since he was 12. But they were periods, not brackets, in the punctuation of his life. The reason had to do with his father.

Joseph had none of the stiffness that goes with rock strength. He was one of those men who cast the broadest shadow, without there being any darkness in them at all. Yet there was always a curious awkwardness between him and his son. In a neighbor's house of a Sunday afternoon, Mark might stand nearer to him than to anyone else; but he never got onto his lap the way the other kids got onto *their* fathers' laps. Joseph never teased him. He never made him any of those small-scale replicas of farm gear that the other farmers made their sons: tiny oxcarts or trail sleds.

96

In any case, that kind of fussy workmanship was not his province. His instrument was the plow.

One day he came across Mark poking seeds between the potato plants. "What's them?" he asked.

Mark could dodge anyone else's questions; he could never answer his father with less than the whole truth. "They're orange seeds," he said.

He'd saved them from the Christmas before. Oranges were such a seldom thing in Nova Scotia that it was as if he were planting a mystery.

"They won't grow here," Joseph said.

Mark felt suddenly ridiculous, as he so often did when his father came upon anything fanciful he was doing: as if he had to shift himself to the sober footing of common sense. He dug the seeds out and planted them, secretly, behind the barn.

The night of the accident was one of those cold, drizzly evenings in early summer when animals in the pasture huddle like forlorn statues. The sort of night when the cows never come.

School had ended that day. Mark was very excited. All the time his mother washed the supper dishes, he kept prattling on about the kings and queens of England he'd have in his studies next term. He felt two feet taller than the "kid" he'd been yesterday.

His father was waiting to milk. "Ain't it about time you got after the cows?" he said at last. He never ordered Mark.

Cows! Mark winced. Right when he could almost *see* the boy Plantagenet robed in ermine and wearing the jeweled crown!

"They'll come, won't they?" he said. (He knew better.) "They come last night."

He never used good speech when his father was around. He'd have felt like a girl.

"They won't come a night like this," Joseph said. "They're likely holed up in a spruce thicket somewheres, outa the rain."

Mark went then, but, as Joseph couldn't help seeing, grudgingly.

At the pasture gate, Mark called, "*Co*-boss, *co*-boss . . ." But there wasn't the tinkle of a bell. He picked his steps down the pasture lane to the first clearing. The cows were nowhere to be seen. But Pedro, the horse, was there—hunched up and gloomy-looking in the drizzle. Mark couldn't bear to see him so downcast and not try to soothe him.

He went close and patted Pedro's rump. The horse moved just far enough away to shake off the touch. It was the kind of night when the touch of anything sends a shivery feeling all through you.

Mark should have known that Pedro wanted to be left alone. But he kept at it. He'd touch him, the horse would move ahead; he'd follow behind and touch him again. The horse laid back his ears.

And then, in a flash, Mark saw the big black haunch rear up and the hoof, like a sudden devouring jaw, right in front of his left eye. The horse wasn't shod, or Mark would have been killed.

He was stunned. But in a minute he got to his feet again. He put his hand to his face. It came away all blood. He began to scream and run for home.

Joseph could hear him crying before he came in sight. He started to meet him. When Mark came through the alder thicket below the barn, and Joseph saw he was holding his hand up to his face, Joseph broke into a run. Before he got to the pasture gate he could see the blood.

He didn't stop to let down a single bar. He leaped them. Mark had never seen him move like that in his life. Joseph grabbed the boy and raced back to the house.

Within minutes, the place was a hubbub of neighbors. Mark gloried in the breathless attention that everyone bent on him. He asked Joseph to hold him up to the mirror over the sink. "No, no, Joseph, don't," his mother pleaded, but Joseph obeyed him. Mark's face was a mass of cuts and bruises. He felt like a Plantagenet borne off the field with royal wounds.

Afterward, he didn't remember his father doing or saying anything unusual. But Joseph was the one who quietly put the extra leaves in the dining-room table so they could lay Mark on it when the doctor came, at last, to take the stitches. And when the doctor put Mark to sleep, it was Joseph's hand that held the chloroform cone without a tremor.

The doctor said that Mark must stay in bed for two weeks. Joseph came in to see him once during each day and again just before bedtime. Mark's eye was now swollen shut and the color of thunder sunsets. Maybe he'd have the mirror in his hand, admiring his eye, when he heard his father coming. He'd thrust the mirror under the bedclothes. They exchanged the same awkward sentences each time. Joseph was the sort of man who looks helplessly out of place in a bedroom. He never sat down.

The first morning Mark was allowed outdoors again, he had planned to walk. But Joseph picked him up without a word and carried him.

Mark didn't protest. This time, however, there was no tumult of excitement, as just after the accident, to leave him mindless of his father's arms about him. Now the unaccustomed feel of them seemed to make him aware of every ounce of his own weight. Yet, though this was merely an ordinary fine summer morning, it struck him as the freshest, greenest, sunniest he had ever seen.

The moment they left the house, it became plain to Mark that this was not just an aimless jaunt. His father was taking him somewhere. Joseph carried him straight across the house field and down the slope beyond—to where he'd stuck the orange seeds in the ground.

Mark saw what they were headed for before they got there. But he couldn't speak. If he had tried to, he'd have cried.

Joseph set him down beside a miniature garden. Miniature, but with the rows as perfectly in line as washboard ribs. This had been no rough job for the plow. It had been the painstaking work of fork and spade and then the careful molding by hands. Joseph must have started it right after the accident, because the seeds were already through the ground. And he hadn't mentioned it to a soul.

"This can be yours," he said to Mark.

"Oh, Father," Mark began, "it's . . ." But how could he tell his father what it was? He bent down to examine the sprouts. "What's them?" he said, touching the strange plants in the outside row.

"Melons," Joseph said, pointing. "And red peppers and citron."

Things almost as fanciful as orange seeds!

"You never know," Joseph said. "They might grow here."

Mark could not speak. But his face must have shown the bright amazement that raced behind it, or else what Joseph said next would never have broken out.

"You don't think I'da made you go for them cows if I'da knowed you was gonna get hurt, do you?" he said. Almost savagely. "I wouldn'ta cared if they'da never give another drop o' milk as long as they lived!"

Mark gave him a crazy answer, but it didn't seem crazy to either of them then, because of a sudden something that seemed to bridge all the gaps of speech. "You jumped right over the bars when you saw I was hurt, didn't you?" he said. "You never even took the top one down. You just jumped right clear over 'em!"

His father turned his face away, and it looked as if his shoulders were taking a long deep breath.

When they went back into the kitchen, Mark's sister said, "Where did you go?"

For no reason he could explain, Mark felt another sudden compact with his father, that this should be a secret. "Just out," he said.

"Just around," Joseph echoed.

And Mark knew that never again would he have to shift himself at the sound of his father's footsteps. Not ever.

The Rooster
Who Served The Lord

By H. Gordon Green

Like most men whose faith is really profound, Father lived quietly with his religion. And as I look back now, I cannot help but marvel that he achieved so sure a belief in a Creator who was all good and always concerned, when his life had so much of struggle and heartbreak in it.

The soil of our farm in Ontario was heavy and sour, and there were but 40 acres of it to sustain eight children. Father, one of a pioneer family of 11, had had only three years of schooling, and it had taken him 20 years of hard labor and frugal saving to accumulate the down payment for the farm. Now the Great Depression was stalking the land.

Yet through all that grim time I can never remember him voicing the slightest doubt of the essential goodness of the Master Plan. To him, the proofs of the Lord's goodness were everywhere. Not least of these was our friend Prunejuice, the Dark Brown Leghorn.

It all started at the camp meeting held annually in a nearby woods by a nonsectarian group known simply as "The Saints." Our family attended every summer. One morning it was announced that the treasury was dangerously low, and the evangelist that year—a colorful old glory-thumper from Kentucky—treated us to a special sermon on stewardship.

"Now see here, brethren!" he shouted. "It's a downright disgrace for us to be so hard up for money! The Lord is a good provider, isn't He? Then why are we scraping the bottom of the barrel? I'll tell you why! Because, brethren, we're afraid to put our faith to work for us, that's why! Well, this morning we're going to change all that!"

Gradually he made his plan clear to us. Instead of taking up a collection, the ushers would pass among us with new dollar bills which he had induced the board to withdraw from the meeting's bank account.

"This time," cried the evangelist with a dramatic shake of his jowls, "these here ushers are asking you to *take* money! There's $700 in those collection baskets right now—$700 of the Lord's money. And we're asking you to take out what you figure would be a right share and invest it for the Lord. I'm not going to advise you how to invest it, because the Lord will tell you that when you get around to asking Him. All I'm asking is that, whatever you do, you do it with faith that the Lord will attend to His own. Then, when next camp-meeting time rolls around, and we pass these here baskets out to you again, we'll ask you to just give the Lord back His own money."

100

I can still recall the look of bewilderment on the faces of the congregation. Here was a preacher full of the spirit and all that, but after all he *was* an American. And these Americans were sometimes more spectacular than sensible.

Father had reservations, too. "Seems as though we're supposed to put God on trial," he whispered to Mother. But he took five one-dollar bills, the same as most of the others did.

"It's too late to do any planting with it," he said on the way home. "Looks to me as if it will have to buy some sort of livestock."

After some discussion, he and Mother decided that the five dollars should buy a setting of chicken eggs. The only trouble was that Mother had chickens of her own—a lovely flock of White Wyandottes. "We'll have to buy some kind that's different," she said. "Else we won't be able to keep track of them handy."

Father had several reasons for choosing Dark Brown Leghorns. One was that in those impractical days a farmer would often choose a particular breed for its beauty of feathering as much as for its earning power—and of all the fowl which ever strutted in the sun the Dark Brown Leghorn is surely one of the most gorgeous. Another reason was that Dark Brown Leghorns cost $5 per setting of 15 eggs; the other kinds were much cheaper. The Lord was getting the very best.

One of Mother's hens, carefully selected, was given the divine mission of hatching out the Lord's eggs. She was faithful to the end. But, for all her trouble, only three chicks broke out of their shells on the 21st day. This was bad luck; still worse was to come. Two of the chicks gave up the ghost that first day. The one remaining had now become so precious that Father took it away from the hen and gave it a box behind the kitchen stove.

"Isn't it pretty?" one of my little sisters cried, hugging the chick to her cheek. "Just the color of prune juice!"

"Well, Prunejuice," Father said, "you're sure going to have to lay one awful lot of eggs between now and next camp-meeting time if you're going to pay the Lord back His five dollars!"

A few weeks later, however, when fluff gave way to feathers and a little scarlet comb began to bud, it became quite evident that this chicken would never lay *any* eggs. Prunejuice was going to become a rooster.

The affection that soon developed between this special young bird and the family was, of course, inevitable. Father kept him in a little box near the head of the bed with the lamp burning in it all night to keep him warm. It was the maintenance of that lamp which caused the first entry in Prunejuice's expense account: "Extra coal oil—10 cents," Father wrote on the back of the calendar.

When Prunejuice no longer needed mothering, we tried leaving him in the henhouse with the other fowl. But he would have nothing to do with such ordinary creatures, and every time the screen door was left open he would come into the kitchen. If someone tried to catch him, he would go upstairs. When he was two or three months old, he began to follow Father to his work in the fields. "Never saw a bird like him," Father would say to the neighbors. "Sometimes you'd swear he was part human."

But there came a day when Father wasn't quite so affectionate. Prunejuice was strutting around the back porch when one of the girls gave a saucer of milk to the cat. Immediately Prunejuice laid claim to it. There was a battle, in the middle of which the rooster suddenly rose in the air like a helicopter and descended into a half can of cream cooling in the water tank by the well.

"I ought to drown you in it!" Father said as he pulled out the sputtering bird. He threw the cream to the pigs and chalked up the second entry in Prunejuice's account.

Two days later the cat and the rooster had another argument, and before it was over two panes of glass in our hotbed cover had been broken. Then, late in August, Prunejuice got a leg under a wheel of our Model T when Father was backing it out of the garage. The veterinarian had a good laugh when Father came in. "I've prescribed for goldfish and canaries," he said. "But, so help me Hannah, this is the first time I've ever been asked to splice a drumstick!"

Now Prunejuice was shut up in the duckpen back of the woodshed to recover. "I really don't know why we're keeping him," Father said to Mother one night. "He'll never amount to anything more than he does right now." We kept him nonetheless.

Then one blustery night there was a great commotion at the window of our parents' bedroom. Prunejuice, who had been carefully locked in the duckpen, was outside, squawking as if a banshee were

at his tail. Father slid into his trousers, grabbed his shotgun and went outside. He was none too soon. The two boys who had unlatched the duckpen door were just leaving with two of our ducks in a bag.

"We were hungry, mister!" the older of the pair begged.

Father emptied the sack of its terrified booty and studied the shivering lads closely. He recognized them both. "You're not working now?" he asked the older youth. "All right, I need a hired man to help in the bush. You report here tomorrow morning and cut wood with me, and we'll say no more about this. And you," he said to the younger one, "you're supposed to be in school these days, aren't you? Well, you just mind that I don't hear of you playing hooky if you don't want me to turn you in. Understand?"

The boys, sobbing with relief, disappeared into the night. And, bright and early next morning, our new man timidly declared himself ready for work. He stayed with us until the very last load of firewood came out of the woods that winter. "Come seeding time, I'd like to get that lad back," Father said when the boy finally left us. "Yes, sir, Prunejuice did us a mighty good turn that time! It's worth something to find a good hired man these days."

But how much was it worth? Now Prunejuice's account ran something like this:

EXPENSES		TO THE GOOD	
Camp-meeting money	$5.00	Two ducks saved	$3.50
Coal oil	.10	One hired man found	? ? ?
Half can cream all shot	3.25		
2 panes glass busted	1.20		
Veterinarian—leg busted	1.00		
Feed (approx.)	.32		
	$10.87		

"Of course, there's still the worth of his carcass to be figured in," Father said. "But, at a quarter a pound, say, for a five-pound bird, we're still on the minus side."

It wasn't time yet to strike the final balance, however. One bright morning in May a big Packard drove into our lane. "You've got Dark Brown Leghorns here, I believe," the man behind the wheel said. "Henry Becker tells me he sent you a setting last year."

"We didn't have very good luck," Father said. "We just raised one chick. A cock bird."

"Well, happens it's a cock bird I'm after. I've got two dozen hens that's getting mighty lonesome. Where is he!"

"That's him over by the well trying to pick a fight with that tomcat," Father said.

We boys caught Prunejuice and brought him to the man to examine. "He's got a crooked leg!" our visitor exclaimed.

"I was going to warn you about that," Father said. "I ran over him once."

The man in the Packard lit a cigar. "Well," he said. "I was hoping to find a bird I could take to the shows, too, and this one would only be good for breeding. Oh, I could offer you, say, $15, if you're interested. . . ."

"Under the circumstances," Father said quietly, "I doubt if I could refuse." He ran a hard but loving hand through the magnificent mahogany sheen of the rooster's hackle, and then bent over to nuzzle him against his cheek. "Good-bye, Prunejuice!" he said.

And when Prunejuice was ours no more, we thought that even the tomcat seemed a little sad. "Anyhow," Father said, "it's nice knowing he's going to a good home. And he's squared his account now, too. Let's see—we're near $8 to the good, plus the first five. . . . I'll have $13 to put in when they pass that basket again."

But when camp-meeting time came round again, Father put in an extra five—just to make sure.

"... And All His Wealth Was Wandering"

By Harry J. Boyle

How well I remember the day Uncle Pete arrived. The mid-November sky had bellied out all morning like a gray ticking full of feathers. By early afternoon it exploded, and the soft flakes of snow tumbled down as if intent on smothering our valley. Walking home from school to the general store in St. Augustine, Ont., where we lived was like pushing through wet curtains. I was excited, sensing winter had come to lock up our valley for the next six to seven months. Father was still out, teaming the mail and Christmas supplies from the railroad, and Mother was fretting: it was already dark by five o'clock, and the 12 miles of road would be filling in rapidly.

I puttered about the kitchen for some slices of fresh bread, slathered them with butter and brown sugar, and eased back behind the stove. The store was wonderful on an afternoon like this, with my baby brother gurgling in the meat basket cradle on top of the clothes counter, the gas light hissing and the whole place rich in smells of old cheese, dry codfish, shoe packs and harnesses, oiled floors and enamelware. Winter had arrived but the store seemed like a fortress of comfort. It was my world along with the valley and the people who lived there, from the shy Indian trappers and woodcutters to the tanned, lean farmers who found excuses on long winter nights to squat beside the stove and gossip.

Under the influence of a full stomach and the warmth, I dozed. A comfortable reverie was shattered by a short, snow-covered man bellowing in a voice that sent the baby into a fit of screaming.

"Is this any kind of decent welcome for your own kith and kin who has come two thousand miles to see you? Come and kiss your uncle Pete."

"What do you mean?" demanded Mother.

His silvered tusks of eyebrows waggled. "I'm your father's brother Pete," he said. "Your uncle Pete."

Mother tried to shush the baby.

"How do you do, sir?"

It sounded so ridiculous she started to laugh and soon we were all laughing. Except the baby, of course. Then Father came in from putting away the team.

"I see you've met your prodigal uncle," he said to Mother. "Well, just wait until you see the stuff he has with him. That's why we're so late. The team could hardly make the river hill, pulling all that luggage."

So there he was. The legendary Uncle Pete in the flesh, a stump of a man with broad, powerful shoulders and a voice that seemed out of all proportion to his size. The man who'd run away from home at 15 and had scarcely been heard of since, except in vague and garbled messages from travelers returned from out West.

"Fifty years ago," Uncle Pete said after supper. "It's the 50th anniversary of my running away. I worked that winter in the lumber camp over near Bay City in Michigan and when the spring drive was over I headed West. Well, I've made a nice little pile now, and I'm going to enjoy myself. The past is behind. Going to settle down."

He turned earnestly to my mother. "Leona, you know about these things—how are my chances for getting married? I was thinking of a pretty widow or a good-tempered old maid who would put up with a jackdaw like myself."

My mother pretended to be shocked but she wasn't. Country women are born matchmakers, and what a prize this amazing uncle would be!

He had three trunks of clothes, shaved himself every day and used gingery smelling lotions. He had silver-topped walking sticks, a diamond stickpin and gold cuff links. He hired Gus Redman to drive him around and called on all kinds of relatives. Mother was soon begging off invitations to visit homes where there was a widow or unmarried relative.

The only one she took pity on was Milly Simpson, the piano teacher, a sad toothpick of a woman who for years had been vainly trying to give neighborhood children the basics of a musical education. While Uncle Pete was at our place, Milly was often an invited guest.

"A charming and cultured woman of great promise," said Pete. "She's the kind that could be a good influence on a wandering man like myself." Everybody was agog when they heard Milly had ordered a new dress from the mail-order catalogue for the Christmas concert.

In the evenings Uncle Pete held court in the store. He had an armchair within easy spitting distance of the stove damper. The older, regular visitors had boxes and bags to sit on. The younger ones lounged on the floor with their backs to the counters.

Each night started off with small talk.

"I see the doctor went to Hendersons."

"Tilly had a girl."

"Another girl! That makes five. Tom mustn't have the right kind of recipe!"

The laugh petered out and Uncle Pete lit his pipe with a cedar splinter.

"Birthing comes easy to Indian women, most times," he began. There was silence except for the hissing of the gas lantern.

"I always got along well with Indians. Fine people, if you treat them well. I remember taking up a homestead in Saskatchewan. That was a hard winter and I hadn't laid in too much grub. Wanted to have some money for spring. We had a blizzard one day that came up sudden and you couldn't see your hand in front of your face. That night there was a noise at the door of the sod shanty. I went to investigate and there was a young Indian woman."

He made a habit of pausing dramatically at points like these.

"She was half frozen, and she was going to have a baby!"

From the listeners came muffled gasps.

"Well, I didn't know much about it, but I gave her some warm tea and she had her baby without too much help from me. Told me afterward she was on her way to her parents and got lost. Just a miracle she found my shack. When the storm broke, she wrapped up that baby and piked out. Wouldn't even hear of me lending her a horse."

Somebody asked, "Did you ever hear from her again?"

"I was just coming to that. About a week later I go out and there's a quarter of deer hanging from a nail outside the door. And it went on that way all winter. Come spring a handsome big brave appeared one day with a chunk of antelope, a bag of corn which I was doggone glad to get and the nicest pair of buckskin moccasins you ever seen. Just gave it to me and said he was the father of the baby and they called the youngster Little Thunder."

His own booming laughter explained the symbolism.

He was full of stories of how the plains looked waist deep in grass, and the rivers full of fish, and game so plentiful a man hadn't a reason to starve. I heard about Sarcees, Crees, and Piegans, and the Blackfoot who were his favorites. He had seen gunfights and knew Bill Cody.

And then something happened. It began with teasing at school and accusations that he was only a storyteller. Although I was loyal, some seeds of doubt were sown.

"Has Uncle Pete really done all those things?" I asked my mother one day.

"Oh, well, most of them, I guess," she said guardedly.

He must have sensed a slackening in my idolatry. One evening when he was dressing to take Milly to a box social, he called me to his room. "Something troubling you?"

"No, not really."

He rummaged in one of the trunks and came up with a pair of well-worn moccasins.

"Are those the ones?"

"Surely. Now, you remember I told you about killing a black bear with a knife? Well, boy, I'm going to give you the knife."

I stood almost transfixed with the stag-handled knife in my hand. Then, almost as if sensing remaining shreds of doubt, he peeled off his shirt and turned to let me see his back. It was raked with old scars. They must have been the slashes made by the bear.

"You didn't have to show me," I said, but we both knew better, and after that I was back in the fold as a firm believer.

Christmas was a dream. Uncle Pete had presents for all of us. Grandfather beamed over a meerschaum pipe with a shiny lid, Father was given a new rifle, Mother had a fur cape and under the tree I had a new toboggan. He gave Milly Simpson a wind-up phonograph. Like Milly, we thought he was going to marry her. "Oh, no, I just felt sorry for the poor soul," he said that night as we sat around the parlor stove, the room warm and cheerful and smelling of cigars and rum punch. "She's had a dream all her life about good music and she's never had a chance. Everybody should have a dream come true. Just like my dream of coming home."

I went off to try my toboggan the next day. When I got home, Uncle Pete was gone. For the first time in my life I knew what heartbreaking loneliness could be like.

We had one card from Uncle Pete, posted in Calgary. We never heard from him again.

Years later as I was traveling by plane over the prairies, it all came back to me. My seat companion, a western journalist, began reminiscing about the West, and mentioned a story he'd heard from an old man who lived in the Alberta town where he grew up. I recognized the story, and realized he must be talking about Uncle Pete.

"Strange man," said my companion. "He was good to us kids and had all kinds of yarns about the early days. Great hunter and trapper. My father, who ran the local newspaper, said he was as good a character as Twelve Foot Davis or Kootenai Brown. But old Pete never wanted his stories printed."

Casually, I asked if he knew what had become of the old man.

"Yes, I do," he said. "One day he went East. Said he wanted to make one trip before he died. Went back to see his folks. He hadn't been home for 50 years. We thought he might stay, but he was back by New Year's. I guess he knew, or had a feeling about it, and he got in his trip before he died in the spring. My father was quite moved. He was a great one for quotations. He had one for Pete's obituary. It went, 'Adventure was his coronal, and all his wealth was wandering.'"

"It should have been on his tombstone," I said repeating, "and all his wealth was wandering."

"Tombstone! Pete didn't have a nickel. The only thing he had was an amazing collection of fine clothes. They probably thought back East that he was a great success."

"Well," I said almost reverently, "perhaps he was. Not many men realize their dreams."

To Suffer
and
Be Strong

Know how sublime
a thing it is
to suffer and be strong

HENRY WADSWORTH LONGFELLOW

So Much to Live For

By Ivan Cormier

Early one bright February Sunday in 1959, a few weeks before my 39th birthday, a paralytic stroke shattered my world. One moment I was a well man stealing a few extra minutes in bed while my wife took the baby downstairs for breakfast; the next I was a helpless cripple, paralyzed from head to toe, robbed of the power of speech, almost dead.

Today, still in a hospital and with no hope of ever regaining full use of my limbs or vocal cords, I've gotten over any feeling of bitterness. Every morning I give thanks for being alive. Little things I used to pay no attention to seem so precious now: the smell of fresh air, the warmth of the sun, the greenness of grass. I've learned a great deal in the past two years—about myself, about my fellow man, about life. I have ended one life and begun another. I am telling my story in the hope that it may help other stroke victims.

I lived then at Edmundston, N.B., with my wife, Jessie Ann, and our three small boys. I was deputy registrar of deeds, and was studying by correspondence toward a law degree.

That Sunday I was lying in bed, thinking that in just two minutes I'd get up, when the bedroom suddenly jerked upside down. The furniture assumed grotesque proportions; the bed swayed sickeningly. For a split second I thought we'd been hit by a bomb. I called for help, then passed out.

For the next two weeks I was in a coma. Yet consciousness must have returned occasionally because I can remember the faces of people who peered at me curiously as I was wheeled on a stretcher along a hospital corridor; and I can recall the misty figure of a priest administering the last rites. I'm dying, I thought, but it doesn't matter. I was too tired to care.

I remember an ambulance. I didn't know it then, but I was being taken to Presque Isle, Me., to be flown to Montreal. Aboard the plane at Presque Isle, I heard the engines being revved—a familiar and vaguely comforting sound after my eight years as a Royal Canadian Air Force mechanic.

The flight seemed endless. Finally, Montreal—the mournful wailing of the ambulance siren, street noises, the reception room of the Montreal Neurological Institute where a team of doctors was standing by to fight for my life.

A few days later I woke up to find my wife at my bedside. Bottles hung at my head and feet. Needles were stuck into my arms and legs. A breathing tube had been inserted through a puncture in my windpipe, to help my defective breathing apparatus provide air to my lungs; another tube, for getting food into my stomach, hung from my nose. I wanted to tell Jessie Ann not to worry, that I wasn't as bad as I looked, that I loved her very much. I couldn't say anything. I could only look at her and hope she understood.

I had entered a strange and frightening world of complete helplessness. My arms and legs hung like weights, refusing to obey the commands my brain gave them. I had no control of my tongue or larynx; when I tried to talk I sounded like a drunken Donald Duck. I couldn't nod my head. All I could move were my eyelids.

"Fortunately for me, the cerebral cortex— the thinking part of the brain—escaped."

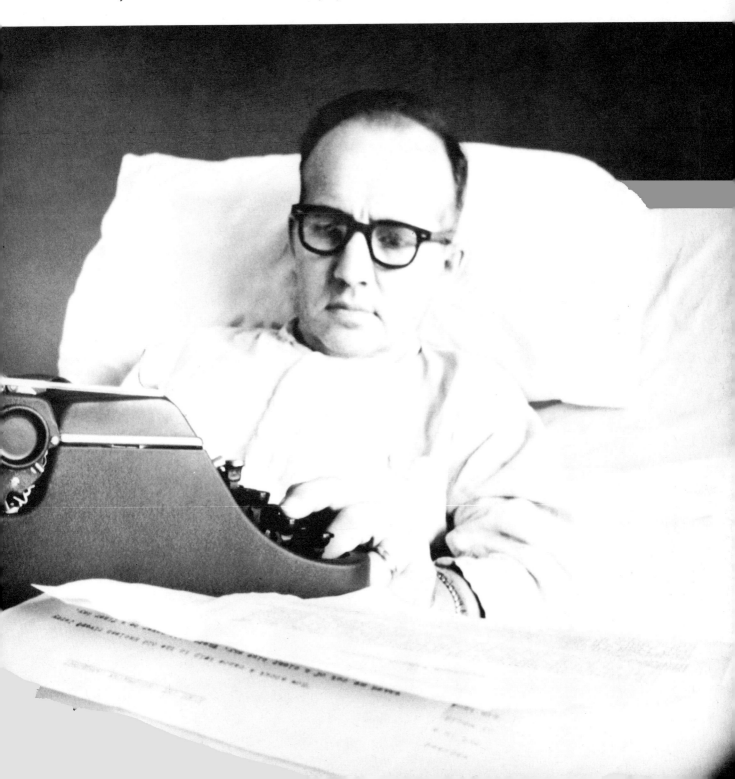

"...a familiar and vaguely comforting sound after my eight years as a Royal Canadian Air Force mechanic."

I comprehended everything that was said to me. The frustrating part was my inability to communicate in reply. I wanted to scream, "Can't you see that I understand you? Can't you see that my mind is all right?" There were moments in those early days when I was afraid that perhaps no one would ever realize I was sane, that I would spend the rest of my life being treated as an idiot.

At no time was I in any serious pain, but I was often extremely uncomfortable, a result of being unable to change my position in bed. Partly to ease my discomfort and partly to promote circulation and prevent bedsores, I was turned every hour. I came to look forward to being turned the way a small boy looks forward to Christmas.

Small changes in routine became events of great importance. For example, there was my bath. To keep me from drowning, the nurses corked off the tracheal tube in my throat. Then I was rolled into a sling, hooked to a crane, hoisted out of bed and lowered into the bathtub. The performance was so smoothly carried out that I was asked to repeat it for a group of visiting nurses.

By now I had a rough idea of the nature of my illness. As far as the doctors could learn, I had a blood clot in the basilar artery near the brain. This blockage of a major line of blood supply caused damage to nerve connections and short-circuited the communication system between my brain and my muscles. Fortunately for me, the cerebral cortex—the thinking part of the brain—escaped.

In March 1959 I was judged to be out of danger. I had learned to nod my head and to move the fingers of my left hand a little. Sometimes I had trouble untangling my little finger. It infuriated me. I hadn't yet accepted my helplessness. I kept thinking: What a terrible waste of time this is! I was haunted by thoughts of what I could be doing if I were "outside."

But I made progress. On February 27, 1960, a year after I had entered the hospital, I ate my lunch by myself—a painful business that took close to three-quarters of an hour and involved a good deal of spilling. A week later I managed to hold and drink a cup of tea—a thrilling accomplishment.

Now I was moved out of my single room into a ward with 12 other patients. Most were walking patients, and every time they passed my bed they offered words of encouragement. One who had been paralyzed by an auto accident said to me, "You'll be on your feet again soon." It was important to me to hear such words from someone who had endured what I was going through, who *understood.* One night I was allowed to watch the National Hockey League play-offs on television. I could stand it for only 20 minutes. The excitement exhausted me.

Then I was transferred to Queen Mary Veterans' Hospital in Montreal. But after three months Jessie Ann, realizing how much I missed the children, arranged for a transfer to the veterans' hospital at Lancaster, N.B., a suburb of Saint John. As the train carrying me hooted through the New Brunswick countryside, a lump formed in my throat. I was still alive, and I was going home. I wanted to cry.

Jessie Ann found a modest apartment in Saint John where she moved with the children. At Easter I spent six hours on a reclining

114

chair there, celebrating my 40th birthday while Philip, our eldest boy, celebrated his tenth. I was happy beyond description. The boys tried so hard to keep me amused—and I must have seemed so different from the father they used to know.

Back in the hospital I settled down to work in earnest. From here on, I knew, it was up to me—me and my physiotherapist. Between us we had to re-educate the muscles that had atrophied through disuse. My program was, and is, a rigorous one. After the morning bath I do arm exercises with wall pulleys. Every afternoon I am given exercises on a special table with an overhead frame and crossbars; while the therapist works on the resuscitation of my leg muscles, my arms and hands are given limbering exercises. This is followed by a standing period: I am strapped against a vertical board, tilted backward slightly, for an hour. Usually I play checkers or chess at the same time.

Every afternoon my speech therapist works with me. Try as I do, I'm still self-conscious about the way I talk. The explosive consonants like P bother me most. I couldn't count the number of times I've tried to recite "Peter, Peter, Pumpkin Eater"! Because of a lack of diaphragm control, I talk better lying down than sitting up.

Gradually, I'm making headway. I tell my children this is like a tree—the growth is so slow you can't see it, but the tree *does* grow.

To show off, I plan little surprises for Jessie Ann. One day I waited until she was in the room, then reached up a hand to turn on the light. More recently I managed to stand by myself without the retaining straps of my tiltboard for almost ten minutes—a major triumph. I can now clench my left fist. The doctors say that once I get back control of my right hand nothing can stop my progress.

The right side of my face is paralyzed, and I have trouble smiling. To acknowledge something only mildly amusing, I have to laugh —which makes me a good audience for my wardmates' jokes.

Trying to talk for long periods tires me, and it's probably pretty hard on the listener, too. Realizing how desperately I wanted to communicate, my wife brought me an alphabet card soon after I arrived at Lancaster. By using a pointer to spell out words on the card, I could express myself clearly for the first time since my stroke. No one who hasn't experienced a loss of all communicative faculties can understand what a relief this was.

For recreation and as part of my therapy, I weave wool doilies and scarves—not a very manly occupation, perhaps, but excellent for my hands. I have learned to use a typewriter, and I spend a great deal of time pecking away with my one good finger, putting down random thoughts and recollections of past experiences. I read voluminously, and my radio, of course, is a boon companion.

My physician says I will soon be able to go home for a week at a time. Even so, it will probably be a long time before I say a final good-bye to the hospital. I need therapy which only the hospital can provide if I am to regain the use of my limbs.

If my story has any message, it is that one must never lose hope, never give way to discouragement. A stroke victim does not want pity; he wants encouragement and understanding. I have had both from many people—nurses, doctors, orderlies, therapists, relatives and, of

"... not a very manly occupation, perhaps, but excellent for my hands."

course, my wonderful wife. Without her love I don't think I could have made it.

And every day I thank God for giving me the strength to get through my ordeal. I have so much to live for.

So wrote Ivan Cormier in 1960.

He could not talk, nor even use sign language. But, by painful effort over many weeks, he had managed to type—with one finger—a 22-page account of his ordeal. It was sent to *Maclean's*. Derm Dunwoody, asked by *Maclean's* to get more detail, visited Cormier. For three days he asked questions and Cormier spelled out the answers on his alphabet card. Left with more questions each evening, he pecked out the replies on his typewriter and had them ready the following morning.

His story was carried by Reader's Digest in 19 editions with a total circulation of almost 24,000,000—and letters of concern and encouragement came to Cormier from many parts of the world.

He never did manage to "say a final good-bye to the hospital." But he never lost hope either, never gave up.

During long years at Lancaster Hospital, he worked painstakingly at making wallets and eventually was realizing a profit of two dollars a day—"no small accomplishment," said one doctor, "considering his disability." He got home most weekends and for ten-day visits at Christmas and other special times. He worried about the extra effort his disability required from his wife and he longed to be able to ease the load Jessie Ann carried. He once wrote to a hospital welfare officer:

"One thought and one thought alone, next to that of my wife and kiddies, has predominated these past three years: progress, improvement, bettering my condition, getting better, partial recovery of a once active self . . . put it, spell it the way you want. It all means the same thing: gaining enough independence to rejoin my beloved, to walk again! If my mythical deadline of seven years in which to WALK could be shortened by 24 hours, I think I'd shout for joy!"

But he did more than just dream: "From a living hulk just a few years ago, a hulk that could move its eyes only, I've 'achieved' among other things the ability to stand on my own two feet (not strapped to the tiltboard), eat, drink, type, shave, brush my teeth, open my mail, put on my glasses, blow my nose. Not awe-inspiring but a far cry from the time when I couldn't utter a sound."

He learned to talk, although never clearly—only family and close friends could make him out. But the words that came slowly and laboriously from his typewriter were unmistakable. He wrote hundreds of letters—to newspapers, the Royal Canadian Legion, the hospital administration, political leaders, anyone he thought might join him in battling for veterans' rights and maintenance of veterans' services. He was particularly concerned about any dispersal of veterans' hospital administration to provincial jurisdiction. Wondering what "secret" plan the federal government might have, he wrote to Opposition Leader Robert Stanfield in August 1969: "What, in your opinion can this latter be up to? . . . How could we arrange to have the prime minister questioned in this regard at his next press interview?"

Cormier minced no words: hospital staff cutbacks, he said in a letter to one newspaper, were "cruel, brutal, unreasonable, short-sighted, arbitrary, destructive." Another time he wrote: "If the quality of a society is judged by its compassion for less fortunate citizens, then . . . someone must accept a scathing indictment." And: "The words 'We will remember them' should apply to the living as well as to our gallantly fallen comrades."

"Anyway," he wrote to the president of the Legion in August 1969, "while I have a living breath in me, I'll fight—in my own little way."

No letter from Ivan Cormier was signed. Formal letters that called for a signature ended with these typewritten words: *Still unable to write legibly—stroke '59.*

He was active until July 21, 1970, when he suffered a second severe stroke. Two days later he was dead.

"Ivan Cormier Dies At 50" said one newspaper headline. Another said more: "*Ivan Cormier est décédé laissant le souvenir d'un courage héroïque.*" The Saint John *Evening Times Globe* declared in an editorial, "Ivan Cormier's Great Fight": "There are few more moving examples of quiet courage . . . than the lonely battle against hopeless odds that Ivan Cormier waged for 11 years . . . 'Veterans do not request the impossible,' he said in his last published letter to the editor of this newspaper. Ivan Cormier didn't ask the impossible of anyone but himself. More than most, he achieved it."

His final letter to the editor reached the newspaper a few days after his death. Ivan Cormier's body had been buried in the Field of Honor at St. Joseph's Cemetery in Saint John when for the last time he was heard in the "Voice of the People" column. His plea was the old one: don't mess about with veterans' hospital services.

"If my story has any message, it is that one must never lose hope, never give way to discouragement."

The Vision
of Eddie Baker

By Judge Frank G. J. McDonagh

Before we drove him home from a meeting in Toronto one night in 1931, my wife Mary had heard much of Eddie Baker but had never met him. A tall, ruggedly handsome man with a warm smile, he spent the ride recalling the fun we'd once shared at a reunion of Canadian war veterans. Suddenly, Eddie touched my arm. "We've just passed my house," he said. "It's number 412." I stopped the car and backed up. As Eddie got out, strolled to his door, waved and went in, Mary stared in astonishment. "But Frank," she protested, "he can't be *blind*!"

Her reaction was natural. Blinded at 22, in World War I, Eddie had succeeded in overcoming his handicap so well that he often seemed to over*look* it. He could feel someone's height in a handshake; hear the size of a strange room by its echoes; or home in on a familiar place—even the time *I* missed it—with an uncanny sense of direction. But Eddie Baker's greatest faculty was still, paradoxically, his vision.

Half a century ago, when beggars with tin cups personified the plight of the blind, he saw their need for special help—*self*-help. With a dream, a few Braille books and six companions, Eddie founded the Canadian National Institute for the Blind, then built it into the broadest rehabilitation service of its kind on earth. Thanks to him, thousands of other sightless people have learned to make their own way—proudly and productively—at home, in business, in the arts. "Eddie Baker not only led us to a brighter world," a blind economist has said, "he also opened the door."

As a close friend for 48 years and CNIB president for two, I watched him do just that. In rising above his own blindness, which he lightly called "my new outlook," Eddie acquired clear insights. "The worst problem," he once told me, "is the feeling that you're hopelessly dependent on others." And so, through what became a $13,000,000 network of CNIB training centers across Canada, Eddie spent his life helping the blind to help themselves. By proving that they could master useful skills—as typists, factory hands, even lawyers—he also won far wider opportunities for *all* handicapped Canadians. "You can't judge anyone by what he's lost," he insisted, "—only by what he does with what's left."

The best proof was Eddie Baker himself. Cheerful, vigorous, almost fiercely self-reliant, he achieved a full, fruitful life—in his work for those who couldn't see him, and in a happy family that *he* never saw. With his vivacious wife Jessie, whom he met after his sight was gone, Eddie raised three sons and a daughter. On camping trips, he taught them to swim and fish. He even devised a way to pitch in their ball games—by aiming at the catcher's voice.

When sighted people marveled at his abilities, Eddie always referred to some of his CNIB "clients"—a girl who'd led her class in college, or a young man who ran complex computers—to show what the blind could do with a fair chance.

I met Eddie in 1920 when both of us joined a military-hospital committee made up of war veterans. A strapping six-footer without cane or dark glasses, he *strode* into our first meeting, stopped, "looked" around by listening, then made straight for a man who had greeted him. It was all so strikingly *normal*. After we became friends, I asked

Eddie Baker examines safety glasses at the 1961 inauguration of the Wise Owl Club of Canada, sponsored by the CNIB's Prevention of Blindness Department. The club honors workers whose use of safety glasses prevents eye injury in industrial accidents. At BakerWood, the CNIB's Toronto headquarters (opposite), pedestrians use a bridge to cross busy Bayview Avenue.

In its search for new careers for blind persons, the CNIB set up a computer course at the University of Manitoba, training programmers for industry and government. At the Winnipeg YMCA, blind youngsters find athletics are an important part of their adjustment training.

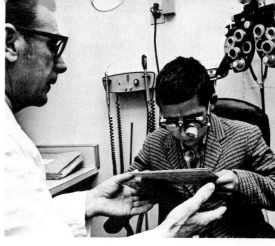

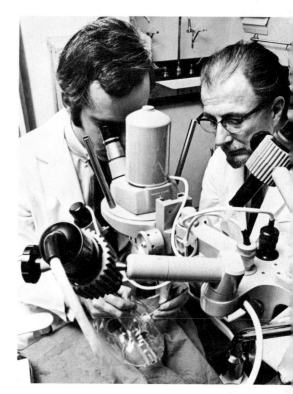

Eddie how he'd learned to walk with such a confident step. "By falling down," he casually replied, "and getting up."

Totally without self-pity ("It corrodes the soul"), Eddie was at once the toughest and the most tender person I've ever known. When a Toronto surgeon phoned him after an unsuccessful operation to save a patient's sight, he hurried to the hospital so that he could be present when the man came out of anesthesia. "My name's Baker," he said, taking the patient's hand, "and I want to help you."

Eddie's concern for all blind persons—some 27,000 in Canada alone—knew no national bounds. In 13 years as president of the World Council for the Blind, Eddie spread the CNIB's self-help techniques from Trinidad to Tokyo. For this service to sightless millions around the globe, U.S. colleagues voted him the first Helen Keller Award, in 1960. "It is good to give the unfortunate a living," that great lady once said of him, "and better still to raise them to a life *worth* living."

Edwin Albert Baker knew it, from bitter experience. Reared on a farm near Kingston, Ont., he worked his way through Queen's University and graduated as an electrical engineer in 1914. At the outbreak of World War I, he joined the army, rose to captain and went into the muddy trenches of Belgium. There, one night in 1915, a German sniper's bullet creased the bridge of his nose and destroyed both eyes. "The last thing I saw," he later told me, "was the bright burst of a star shell."

But even in his first dark days in the hospital, Eddie displayed two shining qualities that never grew dim: a firm will to fend for himself and deep concern for others. Instead of dictating a letter to his parents, he slowly wrote it in his own familiar scrawl, breaking the news to them as gently as possible. "Now," he wound up, "don't *worry* about me."

After being fitted with blue-gray artificial eyes, Eddie took up Braille, typing and some business administration at St. Dunstan's rehabilitation hostel in England. From its sightless founder, Sir Arthur Pearson, he adopted a tough-minded philosophy. "Nothing should be done for a blind man," Pearson held, "if he can possibly do it for himself." Eddie agreed from the start. At his first meal back home in Canada he found his meat already cut up. "Please, Mother," he begged, "don't *ever* do that again."

Eddie was now determined to live a normal life, and he applied for a job with Ontario's hydroelectric commission in Toronto. "I'll make good in a month," he swore, "or fire myself." Hired as a dic-

The CNIB battles blindness in many ways on many fronts. A CNIB-designed course graduates 60-word-a-minute typists (top left) for office typing pools across the country. Research into the causes and prevention of blindness never ceases. Top: a low-vision aid enables a boy to use his residual vision. Above: doctors at the Maisonneuve Hospital in Montreal do research associated with the Eye Bank of Canada. Much research is sponsored by the E. A. Baker Foundation for Prevention of Blindness, established by the CNIB in 1962. Among its first contributors was Baker himself. "I belong to a rather select little group," he said, "and I'd like to keep it that way."

Eddie Baker, in a photograph made shortly before his death in 1968, chats with friends after the placing of the cornerstone for a training and vocational guidance center named after Arthur V. Weir, CNIB general manager from 1923 to 1965. Baker seized every chance to open doors for the blind. One night, on the way home with friends from a Masonic meeting, their car had a flat tire. Trying to change it without a flashlight, the others fumbled pitifully. "Let me do that," Baker offered. "I don't need a light." Astounded by his swift success, his lodge brothers repaid the favor by finding work for three blind auto mechanics. "Part of my job," Baker once said, "is to open society's eyes."

taphone typist, Eddie was soon promoted to more demanding work.

He won friends just as fast. Among them were J. R. Robinson, editor of the Toronto *Telegram*, and his young daughter Jessie—Eddie's future wife. At their home he also met financier Lewis Wood. "If you ever need help," Wood told Eddie, "let me know."

Before long, Eddie found that Toronto's tiny Braille library—the only service for blind adults in Canada—was folding for lack of funds. With five friends, all sightless but one, he talked local clubwomen into raising $7,000 to save it. Next, he recruited Lew Wood as financial adviser on a bigger project—a rehabilitation agency for *all* blind Canadians.

At first, in 1918, the CNIB consisted of only two small shops largely bankrolled by Lew Wood, where men made brooms and women sewed clothing for sale. Then, with government backing, Eddie opened the CNIB's Pearson Hall training center, teaching other war-blinded veterans how to walk and work in an unseen world. "By a twist of fate," he observed, "I've turned from electrical to *human* engineering."

Besides enlisting staff and public support for a network of CNIB's rehabilitation centers, Eddie designed training programs to help thousands of other sightless Canadians make the most of their remaining faculties. Through them the blind learned to read and write Braille; to "navigate" on busy streets; to swim and dance (for coordination, exercise and fun). Housewives were taught to cook, sew and care for their children—all by touch, sound and smell. Before long, hundreds of blind men and women were employed in CNIB workshops, producing furniture, brushes, leather goods and handicrafts, or running CNIB food canteens in office buildings and factories. Others, anxious to get out on their own, had qualified as professional musicians, piano tuners, masseurs, stenographers or mechanics.

As a "leader" of the blind, Eddie took great pains not to be "led" himself. When George V named him to the Order of the British Empire in 1935, Eddie called at the governor-general's residence in Ottawa and paced off the ballroom where his formal investiture would be held. Receiving the honor next day, he walked its length alone—shoulders back, head high—while VIPs watched in open admiration. Behind this lay more than personal pride. Eddie felt a special duty to uphold the dignity of all the blind people he championed.

With the coming of World War II, Eddie became the source of help and inspiration for a second generation of blind young Canadian servicemen. In accepting an LL.D. degree from the University of Toronto in 1945, he praised their "fortitude in the face of adversity"—at a time when his own was sorely tested. For he'd just learned that his son David, a navy pilot, had been killed in action.

Though Eddie's hair rapidly whitened after David's death, he spurred the CNIB to develop a full range of free services for the blind: vocational schools, home teaching, seeing-eye dogs, family counseling, low-interest housing loans, a lending library of 8,500 titles and 46,000 Braille and tape-recorded units, 21 modern residences for the sightless aged and homeless as well as public clinics where more than 100,000 cases of serious eye disease have been treated. Eddie campaigned for and won free university tuition for all blind students in Canada, welfare laws assisting most handicapped persons, and aided in the establishment of the Eye Bank of Canada from which more than 3,000 Canadians have received corneal transplants—and the precious gift of sight.

Not least of Eddie's accomplishments was the building of a $3,500,000 CNIB headquarters complex in Toronto. Named Baker-Wood, it's a lasting monument to his lifetime of service to others.

There, in 1962, Eddie resigned his position to Arthur Magill, a skillful executive who, like most CNIB leaders, is blind. "I'll take the job," Magill told him, "but no one can take your place." Before he left, the Institute created an E. A. Baker Foundation for Prevention of Blindness, a fund to support medical research.

In retirement at a country house near his birthplace, he kept as active as ever. On one visit I found him pruning branches—40 feet up a tree. "I only do this when Jessie's napping," he explained. "It makes her nervous."

The last time I saw him was in March of 1968, at a dinner marking the CNIB's 50th anniversary. By then, his Institute was operating training centers and offices in 50 cities, serving Canada's blind from coast to coast. But most pleasing of all to Eddie, who was still looking ahead, was the fact that the Baker Foundation had already collected $980,000 for the battle to save others from his own fate. As the Toronto *Star* pointed out a week later, when this remarkable man suddenly died, "Both those who see and those who do not should be grateful that Edwin Baker saw things as he did."

Guide dogs—also called seeing eye dogs —are the invaluable companions of many blind persons. Here Newfoundlander James Noseworthy strides along with Ona.

Rehabilitation
Is Good Business

By Jeannine Locke

Gardiner Griffiths of McAdam, N.B., had just turned ten on that fateful Easter Sunday in 1924. Hiking home from a woodland camp, he and a couple of pals tried to hitch a ride on a passing freight train. Gard slipped and fell under the wheels; that night his left leg was amputated just above the knee.

For months, Gard hobbled about on crutches, until his father could afford to buy him a wooden leg. School became a struggle and after the seventh grade he quit. During the next 20 years Gard worked at odd jobs, married, fathered three children and managed to save a little money. In 1950, he bought a small grocery store—just as hard times hit McAdam. A rail junction, the town slumped when the Canadian Pacific began scrapping branch lines and automating its yards and shops. Within ten years, the grocery was bankrupt.

For Gard Griffiths, hampered by an unwieldy leg and lack of education, there was no work to be found. And so, still strong and vigorous in his late 40s, he was reduced to living on government welfare. "It's a terrible thing," he would protest to his wife, "when all a man has to do is to kill time."

Then, one day in 1962, Gard read a newspaper story about a chain of gas stations staffed with disabled men. The stations—called Rehab Showcases—were the project of Stanley Cassidy of Fredericton, N.B., a remarkable businessman whose avocation is rehabilitation of the physically handicapped. Besides helping the disabled to help themselves, Cassidy aimed at publicizing the cause of all handicapped workers. "The handicapped *can* do useful, full-time jobs," he maintained, "and the showcases are visual proof."

That very day Gard Griffiths wrote Cassidy, applying to run a Rehab Showcase station in McAdam. Six months later, he was boss of his own business, working hard and feeling fitter than he had in years. Before long he had paid off his old debts and was taking home about $7,000 annually. "Mr. Cassidy lets me run this station to suit myself," he said happily. "I make a good living and I'm my own boss."

Griffiths is but one among thousands of New Brunswickers whose human resources have been reclaimed, largely through Cassidy's efforts. Since the late '50s Cassidy has devoted his spare time, business skills and substantial sums of his own money to the task of rehabilitating the province's handicapped citizens. His thrust and industry were behind the building of Fredericton's Forest Hill Rehabilitation Center, a treatment and occupational training institution serving the whole province. Says Dr. David Hall Brooks, at one time the center's medical director: "Stan is responsible for making New Brunswick move with the times, both in physical medicine and rehabilitation."

Some two million Canadians—about ten percent of the population—are physically handicapped by such disabling illnesses as arthritis, multiple sclerosis, cardiovascular disease or accidents. Their rehabilitation is a challenge to the most sophisticated skills in medicine, psychiatry and sociology, and Stan Cassidy is an extraordinary example of what one layman can do to help.

A lean, breezy man, Cassidy is concerned with the social and economic aspects of rehabilitation. He sees himself as a "hard-boiled businessman who applies business principles to the work of helping

Harry Fowler, crippled by multiple sclerosis at 34, jobless and alone, had all but given up when Stan Cassidy put him to work at a Rehab Showcase in Fredericton. Cassidy, a hardheaded businessman who flies a twin-engine Beechcraft, has no use for coddling—anyone. His investment in rehabilitation has paid off handsomely, for him as well as the handicapped.

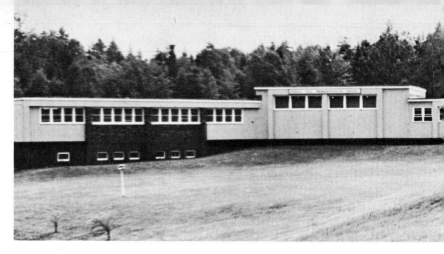

When the Forest Hill Rehabilitation Center (right) was opened at Fredericton in 1958, New Brunswick discovered how great was its backlog of untreated handicapped people. Below: a physiotherapist works with a patient at the center, known as "the house that Stan built."

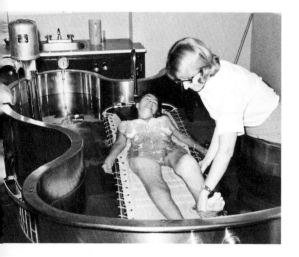

the handicapped." Having sponsored a treatment and retraining center in 1958, for example, he wasn't satisfied until he could see results. "But employers would not buy our product," he found. "They weren't willing to risk hiring handicapped workers." So Cassidy hit on the idea of Rehab Showcases, to demonstrate that putting the handicapped to work was sound business sense.

Cassidy himself is a self-made man. An engineer who worked his way through the University of New Brunswick, he built up a large electrical contracting firm from an original bankroll of $1,000. Accordingly, he has no use for the attitude that the world owes anyone a living. "I'm only willing to help people who want to help themselves," says Cassidy. "I don't believe in coddling."

What he does believe in is the marvelous ability of the human mind and spirit to conquer physical handicaps. "You restore purpose to a man's life," he says, "and he'll do a good job no matter what his physical liabilities may be."

To sell this approach to rehabilitation, Cassidy flies his twin-engine Beechcraft some 60,000 miles a year to address meetings. "I'm not suggesting charity," he emphasizes—"just a chance for the handicapped to earn their living." The chain of Rehab Showcases turns a tidy profit not only for the handicapped operators but also for owner Cassidy.

Selling rehabilitation involves a vast amount of service. When the budget of the Forest Hill center can't be stretched to send professional staff to an important conference, Cassidy usually provides transportation. And besides airlifting his Showcase operators to and from their annual dealers' meeting in Halifax, he regularly flies to Montreal, Ottawa and Toronto to "talk rehabilitation" with interested government agencies and citizen groups. He was invited to Washington for meetings of the President's Committee on the Employment of the Handicapped, which was highly impressed by his Rehab Showcases.

It was through the Masonic Lodge, in which Cassidy rose to become a Shriner in 1944, that he became involved in the problems of the physically handicapped. Visiting Shriners' hospitals for crippled children, he was impressed by the marvels achieved by physical medicine. But he began to wonder: "What happens to these kids when we send them home?" He discovered that, because public funds were lacking, no facilities for rehabilitation existed east of Montreal. With a small, scattered population and with personal income well below the national average, New Brunswick was hard put to provide even

Dorothy Clark, disabled by poliomyelitis and confined to a wheelchair, runs a magazine subscription agency in her home in Stratford, Ont. She also works as a driving-school receptionist and is campaign secretary for the Ability Fund (March of Dimes). Bob Peebles, whose injuries in a car accident in 1955 caused paraplegia, is office manager for the Rehabilitation Foundation for the Disabled, in Toronto.

adequate general health services. Convinced that a program of post-hospital rehabilitation was essential, Cassidy spent the next several years trying to gain support for the idea.

By 1956 he had a blueprint. On vacation in Mexico he had visited a rehabilitation center which, although small and modestly equipped, was a model of efficiency. On his return to Fredericton, he called on the provincial minister of health and social services, the late Dr. J. F. McInerney, and G. Wilfred Crandlemire, coordinator of rehabilitation. Because Cassidy's three teen-age children would soon be grown up, he offered his own 15-room home for conversion into a small rehabilitation center for crippled children. Crandlemire countered with a more challenging plan. What the province desperately needed, he said, was a center equipped to provide special medical treatment and occupational training for *all* age groups, not children alone.

"Well then," Cassidy quickly replied, "let's build one." Within three months the eight-man board of directors of the Forest Hill Rehabilitation Center, Inc., a non-profit enterprise, was calling tenders for construction of a one-story building on four acres of land outside Fredericton. Fully equipped, it would cost about $300,000.

Federal and provincial government grants covered about two-thirds of that amount. Board Chairman Cassidy promised to "beg, borrow or steal" the rest. By car and plane he canvassed New Brunswick for money and free building materials.

In May 1958, just a year and a half after the first meeting between Cassidy and Crandlemire, Fredericton's 20-bed treatment and rehabilitation center was officially opened.

From the beginning its facilities were strained. "So many handicapped people had gone without help for so long," Cassidy recalls, "that we couldn't begin to cope with the backlog." One patient referred to the center was a man who had got along for 23 years on crutches; his artificial leg had never fit properly. Another patient had grown to womanhood with a neglected clubfoot. Such cases appalled Cassidy. "We still have ahead of us the tremendous job of educating the public to rehabilitation," he told Forest Hill's board.

To fellow businessmen, Cassidy kept repeating: "Unless you hire handicapped workers our whole rehab program fails." By July 1960, Cassidy was ready to practice what he preached. His first Rehab Showcase, staffed by Herman True, a young local man who had lost a hand in an industrial accident, opened for business in a Fredericton suburb.

Three years later, explaining his enterprise to the President's

Committee in Washington, Cassidy disavowed any motives of charity. "I much prefer to see a handicapped man given a chance to earn his living, either in his original occupation or a newly acquired one. I'm trying to make this point with my Rehab Showcases.

"In my own case they're gas stations," he went on, "because I've had some experience in that field. But it could be any enterprise—a dry-cleaning depot, for example—that does not involve heavy work. The basic idea is that interested businessmen invest in such enterprises and continue to own them. Handicapped persons operate them on a lease basis. Where the arrangement doesn't work out, the operator can be changed. At worst, the business can be sold at no loss to the original investor."

Cassidy made sure that his investment of $125,000 in five showcases was no more speculative than the $1,000 he had put into his own business 20 years before. From the start, he had full cooperation from Imperial Oil, the company whose products he would sell. On the basis of Imperial Oil market surveys, he picked locations, beginning with two stations in the Fredericton area. Later, he added McAdam and St. Stephen to his chain, moved into Cross Pointe, Que., and opened a sixth station at Keswick, N.B. He remained responsible for maintenance and property taxes. In return, his operators paid him a percentage of their markup on gasoline sales. The business was thenceforth theirs to run productively.

All stations are thriving, according to Cassidy. "My top operator now nets between $8,000 to $10,000 a year and I get a good return on my investment," he says. In human terms, however, Cassidy's Rehab Showcases are paying much richer dividends.

Take the case of Harry Fowler, who runs a Fredericton Showcase. Like Gard Griffiths, Fowler had almost abandoned hope by the time he met Cassidy. At 34, just after being demobilized from the army, he had fallen victim to multiple sclerosis, the mysterious crippling disease of the nervous system. "One day," Fowler recalls, "my legs just gave out."

But Fowler kept working, first as a house painter and then as a helper on a poultry farm until 1953 when, as he puts it, "I finally ran down." For the next nine years, except for an occasional summer job, he was unemployed. Meanwhile, his two sons and a daughter married and set up homes of their own and his wife died of polio. Left alone, Fowler lost heart. In 1962, when Herman True gave up Fredericton's Water Street Showcase to go into business on his own—he had proved his ability to himself as well as his customers—Fowler applied for the job. Unable to walk without a cane, he had no real hope of being accepted.

"Mr. Cassidy took a big chance on me," he says now. "But it worked out fine all around. I'm a bit slow, and so I pay a helper—he's handicapped too, by heart trouble. Between us we keep the place open seven days a week, from 7 a.m. until 1 a.m. We both make a decent living. And we're as independent as the birds."

Cassidy's ambition is to expand his chain of Rehab Showcases, to keep on selling rehabilitation to the public, to accomplish even more in helping the handicapped to help themselves.

128

"Yessir, I Sure Would!"

By David MacDonald

The call for help came at 12:30 a.m. It was an icy night, February 26, 1963, and a gale was howling across the Bay of Fundy. The Seal Cove telephone operator first roused a dozen able-bodied fishermen. Then she thought to ring Vernon Bagley, a bandy-legged little man of 46 who doubled as game warden and village wag. Vaguely mindful of the wind outside, Bagley stumbled sleepily to his phone. But the operator's words shook him awake: "Someone's over the cliff at South West Head!"

Bagley shuddered. Like most folks on Grand Manan, a small island just off the New Brunswick coast, he well knew that rugged, rocky precipice—200 feet above the sea—and he could almost feel the fury of wind and waves lashing at it.

As Bagley dressed, his wife tucked spare mittens into his hip pocket. Then he slid into his beat-up car and set out for South West Head, six miles away. The twisty road was slippery, swirling with snow. Being a prudent person, a former fisherman who'd taken a safer job ashore, Bagley drove cautiously: no sense taking unnecessary risks.

In the black of night, as a February blizzard battered Grand Manan Island, shipwrecked Billy Jones battled his way to this lighthouse atop South West Head and gave the alarm: his brother was trapped 200 feet below, barely beyond the grasping surf.

The night's events, shaped by the raw forces of nature and human need, had actually begun the morning before. Fifteen miles across the bay, at Haycock Harbor, in Maine, two men had cast off in a leaky motorboat. Billy Jones, 42, and his brother Floyd, 36, who eked out a living from odd jobs, were hoping to gather periwinkles to feed their families. But a gale struck from the north, the engine failed and they were swept out to sea. For 12 hours, in thrashing seas and a blinding blizzard, both men bailed, vomited and prayed. After dark, the storm drove them toward a winking lighthouse on the southern tip of Grand Manan, then flung them aground below towering South West Head. The brothers managed to drag themselves up beyond the surf. Floyd, numb with cold, could go no farther. Billy started climbing up the cliff. "I'll make for that light," he yelled. Floyd didn't answer.

Three hours later, lightkeeper Ottawa Benson and his wife heard a thump at their door. Mrs. Benson opened it—and shrank back. Crouched on hands and knees, covered with snow, a man stared up with half-crazed eyes. "My brother . . ." he stammered. "Me and my brother's been blown ashore. I got up, but he's still down there."

Benson was dumbfounded: other storm victims had perished beneath that steep cliff, but no one had ever scaled it before. So he quickly rang the phone operator at Seal Cove, nearest of the island's seven fishing villages.

Floyd (left) and Billy Jones, both "tougher'n tripe" . . .

On Grand Manan, a close-knit community of the sea, 2,500 strong, any cry for help is a command. Soon the Seal Cove men began arriving, 17 in all, including Vern Bagley. They conferred briefly with Benson, then tramped a mile through the snow to the place where Billy Jones had come up the cliff and begun crawling to the light. Far below, roaring breakers slammed at the ink-black bluff, hurling spray high into the night. Searchers yelled Floyd Jones' name, but it was hurled back in their teeth by the 50-mile-an-hour gale.

"It's murder to send anyone down there now," one man shouted. There was a rumble of agreement. "Let's wait till daylight."

"No!" came a high-pitched protest. "That'll be too late." Out of the crowd stepped Vern Bagley, his face grave, his manner untypically firm. "Tie a line on me."

The others stared in awe. A short but wiry man with rumpled features and crinkled eyes, Vern Bagley was regarded as the local "character," always joking and good for a laugh. "That Vern," islanders often observed, "he'd poke fun at his own grandmother."

But tonight wasn't for fun. Bagley secured a nylon rope around his waist and began inching down toward the Hog's Back, a ridge of loose rock sloping sharply to the sea. He'd gone only a few yards when slabs of stone slid out from under him and went hurtling down the bank. In panic, Bagley clambered back to the top. "No use," he panted. "I can't do it."

With the line still knotted at his waist, he walked slowly away. Sensing his embarrassment, the others quietly resumed debating what to do. And then a strange thing happened. Bagley suddenly looked up. "Yessir," he said aloud—though no one had spoken—"I sure would!" He went to the brink of the bluff. "I'm going down again."

This time, clutching a flashlight in one hand, Bagley swung wide of the treacherous Hog's Back. Beside it ran a steep gully, the quickest way down—for him, or for a rockslide. Edging across the top of the gully, he vanished behind another almost perpendicular ridge, hesitated, then began to feel his way down the cliff's jagged face. Some 150 feet down the crag, he paused on a flat rock and flashed a light to either side—no sign of Jones—and then up the bluff. High above, to his horror, he saw that his lifeline had hooked over the gnarled root of a fallen tree. Instead of running straight down, it slanted across the gully to the snag, and then down, in the shape of a figure 7. If he moved any farther, his weight could unsnag the line from the root, and the sudden slack would drop him to the cliff's bottom.

Frozen with fear, Bagley pondered his precarious position. His only hope, he saw, was to flick the rope free, so that the resulting slack could be noticed and pulled in. "More line!" he yelled. In the thunder of wind and sea, no one above could hear him.

But somebody else did. From off to Bagley's left, beyond the Hog's Back, came a feeble cry: "Over here!" Floyd Jones was alive.

Bagley now faced an agonizing choice. If he went on, trying to save Jones, his rope could pull loose at any second. If he held back, Jones would surely die. "Oh, God!"—the wail was weaker—"Help me!"

Up on the cliff, a bonfire cast an eerie glow on the weathered faces of the rope-handlers. Bagley's cousin Horace lay at the very edge

...and Vern Bagley, with the award he received after his heroic rescue attempt.

of the precipice, "reading" the line. It quivered in his hands, and he saw a flash of light far below. "Pay out more line," he called. "He's going into the gully!"

Vern Bagley had made his choice. Crossing the gully, he slipped on ice-crusted snow. But the lifeline—his sole hope and greatest fear—held fast. To keep his mind off it, Bagley concentrated on Floyd Jones as he crept up the flank of the rocky Hog's Back. Atop the ridge, he lay flat and shone his light over the other side.

About 25 feet below, just out of reach of the surging sea, Floyd Jones knelt on a narrow ledge, arms and face pressed into a crevice. His clothes were stiff with ice. Only his blond hair moved in the wind. Now Bagley completely forgot his own predicament. While the men above felt his motions and released more rope, he backed over the edge. Hanging over the sea, arms and legs pressing out from the rough rock, he made his way downward.

Suddenly, atop the cliff, Horace felt the line go limp. "We've lost him!" he screamed. Frantic, he hauled in the rope—30, 50, 70 feet of it. Then, just as suddenly, he again felt his cousin's weight and a reassuring yank on the line.

Far below, trembling from a brush with death, Bagley crouched beside Jones. At the very instant that he stepped onto the ledge, his slender lifeline had finally jerked loose from the snag. Over and over he told himself, *I'm alive!*

But Floyd Jones appeared to be dead. Bagley removed a glove and touched the man's frigid, bare head. "Can't move," came a hoarse rasp. "I'm froze from the belt down."

"Don't worry," Bagley replied. "We'll get you up in no time."

Brave words. For the problems ahead were as large as the cliff itself. The semiconscious Jones couldn't be hauled up alone; the savage winds would batter him against the rock. There was only one possibility. With the rope still tied to himself, Bagley got Jones to his feet and eased his hands into the extra mittens his wife had given him an eternity ago. Then he wrapped Floyd's arms around his own waist, from behind, jammed them under the rope, and tightened it securely.

131

After three sharp tugs—the haul-up signal—the lifeline strained. The two men dangled in space, then began to rise. Jones, a 180-pounder, clung to his rescuer with the strength of desperation. For Bagley, shielding him from the rock, the ascent was agony. The rope cut into his back and Jones' clutching fingers tore at him like talons.

As he neared the Hog's Back, Bagley felt Jones slipping. He caught him by the neck and wrestled him over the hump. There they lay, Jones unconscious, Bagley gasping for breath and trying to figure out his next move.

The little man was now too tired to make a wide detour, the way he'd come down. And on the Hog's Back itself were tons of loose rocks, flung down by an earlier landslide; one false step there could be fatal. That left only the steep gully, where the lifeline might dislodge stones and start an avalanche.

Bagley retied his line around Jones and signaled to the top. Buckling under the inert body's weight, he descended into the gully and began the long climb. Clinging to the rope with one arm, using the other to protect Jones, he pushed and pulled up the slope. At times, he had to lift Jones over fallen trees. Other times, he dragged him.

About 25 feet from safety, Bagley's tortured legs gave out. Wedging the unconscious Jones behind a boulder, he crept on up the rope alone. Ninety minutes after he'd left on his impulsive mission of mercy, Bagley was hauled back over the clifftop. "He's just below," he gasped to the waiting men. "But I'm all done in."

As assistant lightkeeper Sid Guptill went down on another line, Bagley dropped into a snowbank and lay there, waiting. Within half an hour, Floyd Jones was pulled up, still alive. Gently, he was covered with coats and rushed to the hospital.

Exhausted, aching in every fiber, Vern Bagley stood at the cliff's edge and gazed down in silent disbelief, a man tested and proved solid. As he trudged away, two fishermen linked their arms through his, supporting him. "Vern," said one, "we're mighty proud of you."

Next day, at the hospital, the Jones brothers tearfully thanked the little man who'd risked his life. Billy couldn't remember how he'd scaled the cliff, except that the wind at his back had helped keep him from falling. All that Floyd recalled of his rescue was the touch of Bagley's hand waking him. "It felt," he said, "like a hot flatiron." Doctors doubted that Floyd could have survived another 15 minutes of his ordeal. Though both men were pain-racked from exposure—even Floyd's tonsils were frozen—they quickly recovered.

A year later, 300 islanders packed the Grand Manan high-school gym to see Vern Bagley awarded a rare honor—the Carnegie Silver Medal for heroism. (Sid Guptill received a bronze medal.) After the ceremony, Bagley was asked about the strange remark he'd made—"Yessir, I sure would!"—before he went to Floyd Jones' rescue.

"Wal," he replied, "I'd been tellin' myself all the reasons why I couldn't go back over that cliff. But then this idea hit me so hard—*Would you go if it was your own brother?*—that I answered out loud. Then I just had to go. 'Cause, when you get right down to it, we're *all* supposed to be brothers."

Trademark
Canada

You are a new nation,
the raw nugget;
the untempered blade,
the uncontrolled flame . . .

DICK DIESPECKER

Without Fear or Favor

By Paul Friggens

At Montreal International Airport, one day in February 1964, a crack drug squad of the Royal Canadian Mounted Police secretly observed the arrival of Uruguayan diplomat Juan Carlo Arizti. Tailing Arizti downtown to Montreal's Central Station, the detectives watched as he stored four pieces of luggage in two lockers. Later, searching the lockers, they verified their suspicions: the suitcases, which had cleared Canadian Customs under diplomatic immunity, contained a huge shipment of heroin—enough to supply 60,000 addicts for three months.

Next morning, Arizti nervously checked his luggage before making reservations for the New York train the following day—and was obligingly assisted in closing the difficult locker doors by two constables disguised as floorsweepers! That night the RCMP drug squad replaced all but a few bags of the powdery heroin with similar-looking dummy bags of flour. ("We left some heroin in order to make a case in the United States," an RCMP officer explained later.) Then, hoping to trap others in the smuggling ring, they let the suspect pick up his luggage and proceed to New York—under the surveillance of both RCMP and U.S. narcotics agents. A few hours after his arrival in New York, detectives arrested Arizti and his accomplices—the Mexican ambassador to Bolivia, Salvador Pardo-Bolland, and René Bruchon, one of the biggest French traffickers in the business. Thus the books were closed on one of the biggest heroin seizures in history: 138 pounds of nearly pure stuff, worth more than $52,000,000.

This coup typifies the care and vigilance that goes into the work of the world's most versatile police force. Officially organized as the North-West Mounted Police in 1873 to keep the peace on Canada's western frontier, the RCMP today patrols the biggest beat on earth: 3,852,000 square miles that span seven time zones—a vast domain reaching from the great urban centers of Canada to the ice-locked lands and waters rimming the North Pole. "The Force," as it is always proudly called by its more than 15,000 members, performs more functions than any other police unit in the world. Its mission today includes all of the duties which, in other countries, are normally handled by separate criminal investigation services, national security agencies, intelligence and counterespionage networks, and border patrol forces. In addition to these national duties, the RCMP upholds the law in eight of the ten provinces (Ontario and Quebec have their own police) and in about 150 municipalities.

Most RCMP members discount the romantic Nelson Eddy/*Rose Marie* image and the myth that the Mounties "always get their man."

The Mountie that most Canadians know is a well-equipped, highly-trained man in a cruiser. In eight of the ten provinces he is a *provincial* policeman or one of the local force in some 150 communities. RCMP men work also in the air and at sea and—a few—in the stirring "Musical Ride" for which the Force is world-famous.

136

Today, for example, the RCMP no longer uses horses—except in the world-famous cavalry troop which performs the "Musical Ride" at exhibitions in Canada and abroad. Gone also are the faithful sled dogs of the Arctic Patrol. In place of these relics the RCMP today operates 16 highly technical modernized divisions at home with computers, laboratories, aircraft, fast marine cutters and snowmobiles.

There's no glamour, either, about the Ottawa headquarters of the Force—a steel-fenced, gray stone building originally intended as a seminary. The RCMP is run with the kind of quiet devotion to duty that has filled history books with stories of heroic RCMP feats.

These stories began, perhaps, on the morning of July 8, 1874, when a cavalcade of dashing mounted police, rattling field pieces, lumbering oxcarts, wagons and cattle, moved out of Dufferin, Man., and, with bugles blowing in the wind, headed westward to proclaim law and order. Before long, the Force had made Canada's western frontier safe for settlement, and won the Indians' goodwill and respect. After signing the Blackfoot Treaty in 1877, Chief Crowfoot testified: "If the police had not come to this country, where would we all be now? Bad men and whiskey were killing us so fast that few of us would be left today. The police have protected us as the feathers of the bird protect it from the frosts of winter."

Even in those days, the growing Force faced repeated challenge. It secured the frontier for the influx of homesteaders, fought prairie fires, searched for settlers lost in blizzards, carried the mails and arranged funerals. During the great Klondike Gold Rush, scarlet-clad troopers brought law and order to the rip-roaring gold camps, guarded bullion and patrolled the treacherous Chilkoot Pass to the goldfields. Paid only 75 cents a day, the courageous troopers carried the law to remotest Canada. In 1904, in recognition of its exemplary service, King Edward VII gave the Force its Royal prefix.

The semimilitary force first known as the North-West Mounted Police was set up in May 1873, the month that American whiskey traders massacred 30 Indian men, women and children in the Cypress Hills of Saskatchewan. Three hundred men trekked west, put the whiskey traders out of business, built police forts, learned the ways of the plains, rode countless patrols. Word spread among the Indians: these men had brought good law and treated white and Indian alike.

Today the RCMP combines traditionally fine police work with modern criminology. Regional crime laboratories use the most scientific techniques, from the electron microscope to neutron activation analysis, in a remarkable record of crime detection. When nine of the ten members of a family in Shell Lake, Sask., were slaughtered in one of the most brutal mass murders in Canada's history, brilliant ballistics work in an RCMP crime lab led to a recently released 21-year-old mental patient. With a grinding compound, the killer had altered the rifling of his .22 repeater which would have identified the marks on the fatal bullets. The police were not foiled. They proved that the firing pin of the rifle was homemade—and matched exactly the impressions on the cartridges recovered at the scene of the crime. Prints on the rifle positively pinned the murders to the chronic schizophrenic.

A few years ago in New Brunswick, a 90-year-old man was found robbed and murdered in his cabin. One suspect had a bloodstained bill with a single minute hair attached. Analysis showed the hair to

be from a bumblebee's leg! Once more, detectives searched the crime scene. Sure enough, in an old chest, where the victim kept money and personal papers, were the dried-up remains of a bumblebee. Along with other evidence, this bizarre bit of detection helped the RCMP clinch its case.

Wherever possible in such criminal identification, the RCMP speeds fingerprints and "mug" shots from the crime scene to Ottawa headquarters by wirephoto or facsimile, for cross-checking against more than a million prints and photos on file. In its most exhaustive cross-checking job, the RCMP helped solve one of the most sensational murders ever.

About 12:15 p.m. on June 1, 1968, after examining close to 250,000 passport applications, an alert RCMP team in Ottawa pounced on the photograph of one Ramon George Sneyd. The photo bore a marked resemblance to James Earl Ray, alias Eric Starvo Galt, wanted for the assassination of Dr. Martin Luther King, Jr. When subsequent investigation revealed that Sneyd had left for England, photographs and fingerprints were rushed to London. Booked on a flight to Brussels, Sneyd/Ray was captured at London's Heathrow Airport just as his plane was about to take off. Diligent, painstaking work by the RCMP put the finger on Ray and helped bring him to trial.

From snowmobile to ships to this Twin Otter aircraft, all kinds of modern transportation are used in the many aspects of RCMP work: criminal investigation, national security, intelligence, counterespionage and border patrol.

The Force fights fraud with the same unrelenting zeal. In a model piece of police work, it smashed one counterfeit ring in 72 hours! In Montreal, on the evening of September 21, 1962, a new series of counterfeit $5 Bank of Canada notes began appearing. Working through the night, RCMP mapped a block-by-block surveillance of an area under suspicion. Next day, observation led to Clifford Roberts, who had concealed 22 counterfeit bills in his bedroom. Roberts refused to talk. But through the Montreal underworld, the "Horsemen"—as criminals call the RCMP—learned that a one-legged character driving a Cadillac could be involved. Police located Liguori Lacombe in his car and made a search. They found one puzzling item: an ignition key which didn't fit the Cadillac.

After vainly trying to unlock some 150 cars in the vicinity, detectives found the key fitted one parked on a side street. A search of the trunk produced 1,521 counterfeit bills in a shopping bag. Shown

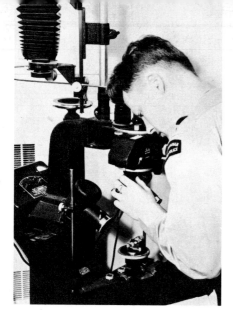

In the identification branch at RCMP headquarters in Ottawa a constable works with a comparison microscope . . . in a toxicology laboratory young Mounties learn about distillation apparatus.

this evidence, Lacombe directed police to a Montreal nightclub where they learned that a bartender was suspected of counterfeiting. Police found a counterfeit $5 bill in the bartender's home and a further 6,433 bills in his summer cottage. Hot on the heels of the counterfeiter himself, the police made a door-to-door check of the area, uncovered an offset printing press, the counterfeit plates, a copy camera and other incriminating material. The counterfeiter was arrested and later convicted.

Today, roughly half the territory policed by the RCMP lies in the Canadian North. There in the summer of 1895 the Force established a 20-man police post with the responsibility of patrolling the whole of the Yukon. For this task the RCMP had to choose its men for their two-fisted courage, and ability to endure privation and utter isolation.

In the RCMP's musty archives at Ottawa can be found hair-raising accounts of Arctic adventure: the story, for example, of a young constable's nightmarish 400-mile journey by dog team to Fort Saskatchewan in the dead of winter with a dangerous mental patient lashed to his sled; and the history-making patrol of the tiny RCMP schooner *St. Roch*—the first ship ever to navigate the hazardous Northwest Passage in both directions. Then there was the remarkable adventure of Inspector Charles "Denny" La Nauze who traveled 3,000 miles by boat and dog team to track down Eskimos who had murdered two missionaries for their rifles. The killers had butchered the bodies and eaten the livers. After two years and four months on his unbelievable manhunt, Nauze finally brought the murderers to justice.

But the grimmest story members of the Force tell involves Inspector Francis Fitzgerald and "The Lost Patrol." On December 21, 1910, Fitzgerald left Fort McPherson in the Northwest Territories with three constables and 15 dogs to mush 500 miles across the mountains on routine winter patrol to Dawson, Yukon Territory. When the patrol was alarmingly overdue, a search party was dispatched from Dawson—and on March 21, in a camp on the Peel River, 35 miles from McPherson, they made a ghastly discovery. Beside long dead ashes of a campfire lay the emaciated bodies of two members of the lost patrol; bits of boiled moose skin hinted of death by starvation.

Ten miles down the trail, the search party found the bodies of Inspector Fitzgerald and his third man. Unable to cross the icy mountains to the Yukon, Fitzgerald had turned back 300 miles from his starting point. Faithful to regulations, the inspector had kept a diary:

"Tuesday, January 31st. 45 below. 62 below in p.m.," he wrote. "Skin peeling off our faces and parts of body and lips swollen and split. I suppose this is caused by feeding on dog meat. Everyone feeling the cold very much for want of proper food."

On February 3, he recorded: "Men and dogs very thin and weak, cannot travel far. Have still about a hundred miles to go. I think we will make it all right, but will have only three or four dogs left."

Just 25 miles from McPherson, Fitzgerald perished. Scratching with a charred stick on a piece of paper, he left this farewell message: "All money in dispatch bag and bank, clothes, etc., I leave to my dearly beloved mother, Mrs. John Fitzgerald, Halifax. God bless all. F. J. Fitzgerald, R.N.W.M.P."

Today the RCMP patrols the North with the aid of modern transportation, such as snowmobile and airplane, helped also by the best in radio equipment. In that part of the country, a member of the Force wears many hats. He's policeman, coroner, justice of the peace, postmaster, notary, veterinarian, game warden, Customs officer. He rations critical supplies, investigates old-age assistance claims, administers first aid and, in an emergency, can deliver a baby.

Although it is rarely revealed to the public, the work of the Force's highly secret Security and Intelligence branch is no less dramatic or significant than other functions. A 1969 report of the Royal Commission on Security is blunt: "Canada," it warns, "remains the target of subversive activities conducted by communist countries; in addition, Canada can be used as a base for operations against other countries, especially the United States."

It was just such communist espionage that defecting Igor Gouzenko, a cypher clerk in the Russian embassy in Ottawa, revealed in September 1945. The sheaf of 109 secret documents that Gouzenko handed over exposed an astounding Soviet spy network operating throughout Canada. The Communists had penetrated many departments of government and successfully recruited several Canadian citizens, one a member of Parliament. At once, the RCMP undertook to guard Gouzenko (he is still in hiding), while its investigators began checking the defector's massive revelations. In the end, ten Canadians were convicted of espionage. In recent years, the RCMP has turned up repeated evidence of continuing espionage and Canada has expelled several members of communist embassies as a result.

How has this remarkable force developed such versatility?

It begins with the training of recruits. Thousands of letters flood in from would-be constables—white, black, Indian and Eskimo youths. At the Regina training center, a sharp, 23-year-old university graduate from Newfoundland told me he was following his father; his younger brother would join too. "The Force stands for a lot of values we believe in," he said.

After passing a battery of tests, a recruit undertakes six months' make-or-break instruction, including rigorous physical training. It

Inspector Francis Fitzgerald and the three constables of what came to be known as "The Lost Patrol." All four perished on what was to have been a routine patrol in the winter of 1910-11. Fitzgerald's last words, in a message found by his body, were: "God bless all."

forges an esprit de corps which lasts a lifetime. The faculty are top police officers fresh from the field, who rotate every three years in order to keep trainees updated. Each year some 800 recruits study a variety of subjects, including police investigation, criminal law, riot and crowd control, self-defense, and community relations. "Remember, we are public servants with no right to push anybody around," trainees are told. "Always be firm, but fair."

Graduating, a recruit spends the next six months at an RCMP detachment. Following this field training, he has four years to serve to fulfill his five-year contract, after which he usually sticks with the Force. He cannot marry for two years and he must be financially solvent. Nowadays, as much college work as possible is encouraged, and many men are sent to university for further in-service training in the law, and in political and social science. All this pays off—the RCMP's annual turnover, including retirement, death and resignations, is less than five percent.

The extraordinary devotion to duty this training develops is exemplified by heroic Constable H. M. C. Johnstone and his part in one of the wildest gun battles in RCMP history.

At 10:30 a.m. on April 3, 1956, the piercing whine of a bank alarm sounded in the Burnaby, B.C., detachment. Then a terse radio message: "Burnaby to all cars and stations. . . . Bank alarm. . . . Royal Bank of Canada. Lougheed Highway and North Road."

Two young constables, Johnstone and A. L. Beach, were first on the scene. Johnstone leaped from the patrol car and entered the bank, while Beach parked in the rear. Inside, the situation appeared normal. "Everything okay?" Johnstone asked the bank manager. The banker shook his head. Hidden behind the counter, a masked bandit held a sawed-off shotgun at his back. Suddenly, one of two other bandits sprang from beneath the counter and fired a .38-caliber slug point-blank at the policeman. Falling to the floor, Johnstone was riddled with seven more shots. But for a button on his uniform deflecting a bullet from his chest, he would probably have been killed.

Bleeding badly, the wounded Johnstone pulled himself up to return fire. He shot one bandit in the shoulder, spinning him backward and knocking the gun out of his hand. He blazed away at a second who was leaping the bank counter clutching $10,000 under his arm. Then, staggering to his feet, the crippled constable chased the fleeing bandit. When the smoke had cleared, one bank robber was found shot cleanly through the heart. Another had surrendered meekly to Johnstone, who was found, when reinforcements arrived, sitting on the sidewalk covering a third bandit with his now empty gun.

"Outgunned but not outfought," said a news report of the episode which earned Johnstone a promotion and the coveted George Medal "for great bravery." He told me, "That shooting never affected my attitude about police work. I was eager to return to duty."

Such words echo throughout RCMP history, calling to mind the deeds of dedicated men in years past—men like the heroic constable who perished in a blizzard decades ago. Searchers found this tragic note scrawled on a notepad in his scarlet tunic: "Lost. Horse dead. Am trying to push on. Have done my best."

Corporal H. M. C. Johnstone, newly promoted from constable, receives the George Medal for his bravery in a gun battle with bank robbers in Burnaby, B.C. Johnstone receives the medal from B.C. Lieutenant-Governor Frank M. Ross.

Her Majesty From Ontario

By C. W. Harvison

The most unusual incident of my career as an RCMP officer involved a little old widow of considerable financial means who believed she was Queen Victoria.

She had stated publicly several times that she intended to travel from her home in northern Ontario to meet "the children"—King George VI and Queen Elizabeth —on their arrival at Quebec City for their Canadian visit in 1939.

We were advised that she had gone to Toronto to purchase a new wardrobe. There, it was learned, she visited a dressmaker and ordered three dresses, to be made from old patterns she provided—patterns from the Victorian era. Then she visited an art gallery and purchased two oil paintings for $300. These, she said, were to be gifts for "George and Elizabeth."

Two days before the scheduled arrival of Their Majesties, the little lady traveled to Quebec surrounded by old-fashioned luggage, with the paintings sharing her seat on the train. For this journey she had chosen to travel incognito, wearing a dress of fairly modern design. At the hotel, she hung the oil paintings out a window of her suite. Neatly written cards attached announced that the oils would be presented "to Their Majesties, my great-grand-children." They were signed, simply, "Victoria."

Though Their Majesties' ship wasn't to arrive until midmorning, I was at Wolfe's Cove with my troop of 25 men by about 5 a.m. The docking area had been roped off. At one end stood a dais on which a number of dignitaries were to be presented to the King and Queen. A red carpet stretched across the enclosure to the far end,

where His Majesty was to inspect a guard of honor of the Royal 22nd Regiment. Another red carpet ran at right angles to the dockside, where Their Majesties would disembark and be greeted by the governor-general, the prime minister, and other persons of high office. The decorations were magnificent. Everything was ready for the arrival of troops, guests and public.

About 6 a.m., a taxi made its way to Wolfe's Cove. The cab stopped a short distance from the rope barrier, and the driver rushed to open the door. Slowly and majestically, "Queen Victoria" alighted. After a brief conversation, the driver took a folding chair and the oil paintings from the cab and followed her to the rope barrier, which he lifted to

allow her entrance into the enclosure. Surveying her surroundings, she selected a spot at the end of the red carpet, at the precise point where His Majesty would inspect the guard of honor. The driver placed the folding chair in the desired position, put the oil paintings against the side of the chair, gave a smart salute and started back to the cab. At the rope he smiled sheepishly at me, shrugged his shoulders and took off.

I carefully scrutinized the little widow. She was wearing a black dress with the wide sleeves and voluminous skirts of another era. As a headdress, she wore a small round hat of the style I had seen worn by Queen Victoria in a number of portraits. A purple sash, sparkling with several "orders," completed her ensemble. Having recovered from my initial surprise, I took stock of the situation. Certainly the lady had to be moved—but gently. There was no threat to security here. Just an

elderly woman who wished Their Majesties all the good in the world.

I walked along the red carpet and, after saluting, presented myself to "Her Majesty." I then explained that, due to a regrettable error, the planning staff had neglected to advise her of last-minute changes in the seating arrangements—changes brought about by the King's desire to inspect the guard of honor. If she would consent to a place immediately behind the rope . . .

She was most understanding. I escorted her to a spot behind the barrier from which she would have a good view of the proceedings, got her comfortably seated, placed the oil paintings beside her, and saluted. She thanked me for advising her of the change in plans and, quite regally, gave me permission to leave. She was a marvelous little person. But, to be safe, I assigned a Mountie to stand behind her.

When Assistant Commissioner H. Royal-Gagnon arrived, I drew his attention to "Queen Victoria" and gave him details of the incident. He in turn presented himself to "Her Majesty."

The arrival of King George and Queen Elizabeth was a scene that I shall not soon forget. All the while, though, I was conscious of the little lady seated just behind the rope. I need not have worried. Throughout the ceremonies she sat quietly, not making the slightest scene.

I was not the only one impressed by that gracious little lady dressed in black and wearing her purple sash and "orders." After the Royal Visit was over, Royal-Gagnon told me that he had related the story to one of the Queen's Ladies-in-Waiting, who had repeated it to Their Majesties. Charmed and touched by the tale, they arranged to receive the little lady from northern Ontario at a private audience, during which they accepted the oil paintings.

Looking back, I realized that I should not have feared trouble. I should have known queens do not create scenes in public.

Whiskey Whiskey Papa

By Lawrence Elliott

On any given day, Whiskey Whiskey Papa may have nine pilots and some $2,000,000 worth of airplanes in action—ferrying mail, movies and civil servants to the Eskimo settlements, airlifting expectant mothers to hospitals, carrying drilling gear to oil survey teams and supplies to far-flung polar expeditions.

The world of Weldy Phipps centers on a gravel airstrip and a cluster of lonely red barracks buildings known as Resolute Bay. It reaches out over a million square miles of the Northwest Territories, across ice-burdened seas and barren, uncharted islands, its ferocity certified by place names such as Glacier Strait and Bay of God's Mercy. You could call Weldy a bush pilot except that Resolute, five jet hours north of Montreal and 550 miles north of the Arctic Circle, is a long way from anything that grows as tall as a bush.

The region assails pilots with 100-mile-an-hour winds, 24-hour nights and 60-below-zero temperatures. Magnetic compasses spin uselessly under the pull of the North Magnetic Pole, 100 miles from Resolute, and atmospheric conditions can black out radio reception for days.

Atlas Aviation Ltd. provides the only regular year-round flying service, and Welland Wilfred Phipps—whose initials make him Whiskey Whiskey Papa in radio code—is president, senior pilot and chief mechanic. From Frobisher to the northernmost weather station at Alert, Weldy Phipps is rated the best flyer in the Arctic.

The events of one spring day in 1970 show why. Low on gas, an F-27 with 13 passengers aboard became hopelessly lost in a slashing snowstorm on the approach to Resolute. "We could all hear the pilot on the radio," said Jack Austin, an Atlas man. "He was in a real sweat. Then we didn't hear anything at all and after ten minutes Weldy said, 'He's down.' With that, he puts on his parka and takes off in the single-engine Otter."

Flying 20 feet above the rugged hills of Cornwallis Island, Weldy somehow spotted the tail section of the downed F-27. He made six passes before he found a spot to land, then ran for the wreck to find passengers and crew, all dazed and two badly hurt, striking out on foot for Resolute—in the wrong direction. Weldy flew the two injured men in, then returned for the others in a Twin Otter.

A reticent, crew-cut, barrel-chested man, Weldy will land an aircraft on virtually anything short of a mountain peak. In 17 years and 17,000 flying hours in the North, he has made more landings on what is generously called unprepared ground—beaches, ice floes, hilltops—than any other living pilot. He has flown food to stranded explorers and parts to damaged airplanes, has plucked downed pilots off drifting ice and rescued reckless adventurers.

There are many who hold that Phipps is leading the way in the awakening of this fierce and infinitely promising land.

Fran and Weldy Phipps long ago decided to let *him* do the flying. But Mrs. Phipps is nonetheless a vital part of Atlas Aviation Ltd. A slender and attractive blonde, she sits imperturbably at a beat-up old desk in the 10-by-12-foot shack that is Atlas' operations office. She writes tickets, calculates payloads for the manifest and—first priority—tends the radio. Two hundred yards down the airstrip is the complex of house trailers where she lives, as do all the Atlas hands. Five of her eight children live there, too—the eldest are "outside," away at school. Besides looking after Atlas ground operations and the care and feeding of all the Atlas "family," with Weldy she is raising a substantial and close-knit family of her own. Phipps invented the Weldy Wheel—fat balloon tires with only a few pounds of air pressure—as an answer to the Arctic's shortage of landing strips. His doughnut-wheeled Super Cub can ride easily over rocks and ice hummocks, land on any reasonably level surface the length of a football field—and take off in less. Most important, on boggy tundra, the balloon tires' uncommonly high flotation—they put barely four pounds of pressure per square inch on the fragile ground—enables the plane to roll freely where a man would sink to his ankles.

The mountains and glaciers of Ellesmere Island (above) and Grise Fiord (opposite page) are typical of Weldy Phipps' High Arctic. It is a cruel land in which only the most rugged survive, a vast but thinly populated community where a neighbor's help can be the difference between life and death. Phipps recalls, without malice, that the RCAF opposed his operating alone in the Arctic islands in the early 1950s. "They were responsible for search and rescue. But they had no jurisdiction over civil aircraft and could not stop me. They said, though, that if I went missing they would not initiate a search. Ironically, in 1959 an RCAF Canso was forced down 18 miles from Alert, out of fuel—to the great embarrassment of the air force. They had to charter my services with a Super Cub to fly in fuel and a new nosewheel."

Says an oil geologist: "There's oil and all kinds of minerals up here. But how do you find them? Dogsled's too slow, helicopters too expensive. Then along comes Weldy and puts you and your equipment down within half a mile of where you wanted to be and you're in business."

Says a Mountie stationed at Arctic Bay: "Say you have a man who *has* to get to a hospital. You call Weldy. You say, 'Weldy, we've got weather right down to the ground.' Weldy says, 'Light a couple of flares. I'm coming in.' And he does."

Says an area administrator: "With regular service into every Eskimo settlement and weather station—winter and summer—teachers, nurses, technicians and their families aren't afraid to come up here anymore. You have to thank Weldy for that."

Weldy, who was born in Ottawa in 1922, settled on a flying career as a boy, and the local airport became his headquarters and haven. When he was barely 18, he enlisted in the Royal Canadian Air Force and was shipped to England soon after the outbreak of World War II. He was a flight engineer craving pilot training when, in April 1943, his Halifax bomber was crippled in a raid and he had to bail out over Germany. He spent 15 months in a prisoner-of-war camp before, as he casually puts it, "another chap and I got away."

After the war he quickly won a commercial license. Supporting himself by barnstorming and parachute-jumping at fairs in Ontario, he learned all there was to know about the whole wide range of airplanes that he rented, borrowed and bought. He also gave flying lessons and acquired one student named Frances whose blond good looks impressed him more forcefully than her aptitude as a pilot. "We weren't getting anywhere," Weldy recalls, "until finally I said, 'Listen, why don't we get married and I'll do all the flying for the family.'"

Weldy, meanwhile, was being drawn irresistibly north. Working for Spartan Air Services out of Ottawa, he flew summer surveys and photographic missions in the sub-Arctic. More and more he was struck by the promise of light aircraft in opening the vast locked land. In 1953 he went to Resolute and spent the summer flying prospectors

146

and medical evacuations. The next two summers he was back. Criss-crossing endless miles of soggy but essentially flat tundra, Weldy fretted about being limited to a random handful of stony landing strips. It took him five years to work out that problem, but when he did the result was nothing short of a transformation in polar flying. The secret was the redesigned undercarriage that came to be known as the Weldy Wheel—fat balloon tires a yard in diameter with only five pounds of air pressure.

Between June and September 1958, flying two Department of Mines geologists on an Arctic survey, Weldy made 400 landings on unprepared terrain. The geologists mapped 30,000 square miles of mineral-rich territory. The following summer, there were seven Super Cubs probing the Canadian northland. The Arctic islands were open to commercial exploration and the great oil rush was on.

The ultimate test of Weldy's oversized wheel—and his gifted audacity as a pilot—came in 1960. Back in Ottawa one November night, he was awakened by a call from a federal health officer: an epidemic of whooping cough was raging at Grise Fiord at the tip of Ellesmere Island, northernmost Eskimo settlement in the world. One child was already dead, and attempts to drop a paramedical team had been turned back by weather. Would Weldy try flying a doctor in? After taking a special flight to Resolute where his own plane was disassembled and stored for the winter, Weldy toiled through four hours of sub-zero cold, refitting the Super Cub's wings, tail and tires. Then, shivering in the unheated cabin, he and the doctor took off.

The arctic night blanketed every landmark, but Mounties at Grise Fiord lit flares along what they hoped was an adequate landing stretch on adjacent sea ice. Three nerve-racking hours later, Weldy spotted the flares and swooped down for a look. What he saw was about 250 feet of lumpy ice and, at the end, a huge pressure ridge promising disaster. Hoping for the best, he plunged down and, brakes groaning, bounced to a safe halt in little more than 200 feet. A few days later, the epidemic was under control—and Weldy had decided that there was nothing to keep him from operating out of Resolute the year-round.

Phipps is proud of all his pilots, but perhaps a special corner of his heart is reserved for this young Eskimo, Markoosie. He started with Atlas as a mechanic's helper but his innate flying skills—and Weldy's encouragement—won him a commercial license. Markoosie is the author of the book *Harpoon of the Hunter*.

147

For his pioneering work in developing light aircraft to meet the rigors of polar flying, Weldy was awarded the historic McKee trophy, Canada's highest aviation honor, for 1961.

Next year, he organized Atlas Aviation Ltd., with headquarters at Resolute. When Fran came up for a summer visit, she was captivated by the North and said to Weldy, "Why do I have to go back?"

"Only to get the kids and sell the house," he replied with a satisfied grin.

It was bitterly hard going at first. Weldy and Fran went into debt to buy a twin-engine Beechcraft which, in those fierce winters, required 15 hours of preparation for every three hours in the air. Working on it in 56-below weather, Weldy's fingers went numb with frostbite and thickened with blisters.

But business boomed. Weldy re-invested nearly every cent in new planes and new equipment. He gradually attracted pilots able to cope with the violence and vagaries of Arctic flying. They earn up to $6,000 a month during the summer rush. But they work for their money. Through the long nights, and when fog and storm shroud the land, they must steer a course by stars or sun, juggling sextant and astrocompass with one hand while flying with the other. In freezing drizzle, enough ice can quickly build up on their wings to force them down through the murk to a blind landing.

Prime Minister Trudeau, touring the Northwest Territories, asked Weldy to fly him to Grise Fiord. Trudeau, who had done some flying himself, sat in the co-pilot's seat as the Twin Otter homed in on the red cliffs of Ellesmere Island. Then, all at once they were aiming straight at a towering mountain. The prime minister's face went white and the newsmen in the cabin behind tightened their seat belts. In the last split second of safety, Weldy banked sharply, dropped the final 100 feet and set the Otter down on the tiny Grise Fiord strip, hewn from the rock at the very foot of the mountain. The newsmen broke into spontaneous applause, and Trudeau, smiling weakly, said, "I wouldn't try to park a Volkswagen on this strip."

It is hard to conceive of Resolute without Weldy Phipps. He is a natural community leader, a fact which voters in the High Arctic recognized in 1970 when they elected him to the Council of the Northwest Territories. In times of crisis, his almost stoic calm provides a ready antidote. One time a nervous pilot, trying to land in a fog, missed the runway. Back up in the soup, he radioed that he was low on gas, couldn't see a thing and didn't know what to do. Somebody ran to the Arctic Circle Club to tell Weldy. "Tell him to swing out over Barrow Strait and turn due north," said Weldy. "I'm going to build him a fire he can see for 100 miles."

With that, he went off and found an RCAF truck loaded with seven drums of gasoline. At the end of the runway, he dumped the gas and lit it with a thrown wad of burning newspaper. Then he went back to the club.

Twenty minutes later the young pilot came to thank him. "If there's anything at all I can do for you . . ."

"No, nothing for me," said Whiskey Whiskey Papa. "But you owe the air force for seven drums of high test."

Somebody Buried *Something* Here

By David MacDonald

Just off the rugged southern shore of Nova Scotia lies a tiny island shaped somewhat like a question mark. The shape is appropriate, for little Oak Island is the scene of a baffling whodunit that has defied solution for almost two centuries. Here, ever since 1795—not long after pirates prowled the Atlantic Coast and left glittering legends of buried gold in their wake—people have been trying to find out what lies at the bottom of a mysterious shaft dubbed, hopefully, the "Money Pit."

Using picks and shovels, divining rods and drilling rigs, treasure hunters have poured about $1,500,000 *into* the Money Pit. To date, they have taken precious little out—until recently only three links of gold chain and a scrap of ancient parchment. Despite more than 20 attempts, no one has yet reached bottom: each time a digging or drilling crew has seemed close to success, torrents of water have suddenly surged into the shaft to drown their hopes. It's now known that

The expensive business of hunting for Oak Island's elusive treasure—if there is one—was taken over in 1969 by a Canadian-American group with $500,000 to spend. "No matter what happens," said project coordinator Kerry Ellard of Montreal, "we're going to clear up this mystery for good." The Money Pit, believed connected with Smith's Cove (foreground) by flood tunnels, is inland at approximately the center of this aerial photograph.

149

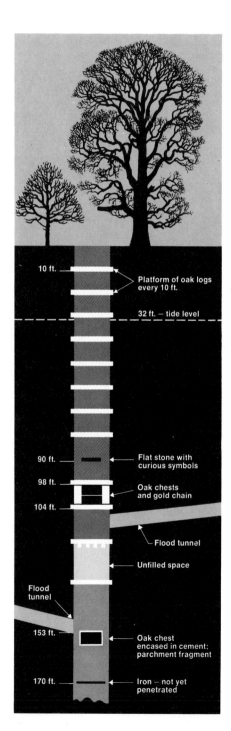

10 ft.

Platform of oak logs
every 10 ft.

32 ft. – tide level

90 ft.

Flat stone with
curious symbols

98 ft.

Oak chests
and gold chain

104 ft.

Flood tunnel

Unfilled space

Flood
tunnel

153 ft.

Oak chest
encased in cement;
parchment fragment

170 ft.

Iron – not yet
penetrated

the Money Pit is protected by an ingenious system of man-made flood tunnels that use the sea as a watchdog, but to this day no one knows who dug the pit, or why.

One legend makes it the hiding place for the plunder of Captain Kidd, who was hanged for piracy in 1701. Other theories favor the booty of Blackbeard and Henry Morgan, both notorious buccaneers; or Inca treasure stolen by Spaniards; or the French crown jewels that Louis XVI and Marie Antoinette were said to be carrying when they attempted to flee during the Revolution; or Shakespeare's missing manuscripts. Whatever the pit may contain, few other treasures have been sought so avidly.

The long parade of searchers began one day in 1795 when Daniel McInnes, a 16-year-old boy from Chester, paddled over to uninhabited Oak Island to hunt for game. On a knoll at one end of the island he noticed an odd depression, 12 feet in diameter. Sixteen feet above it, on a sawed-off tree limb, hung an old ship's tackle block. McInnes' heart raced, for in the nearby port of La Have, once a lair for pirates, he had heard many legends of buried treasure.

Next day he came back with two other boys, Tony Vaughan and Jack Smith, and began digging. Ten feet down they hit a platform of aged oak logs; at 20 feet, another; at 30, a third. In the flinty clay walls of the shaft they could still see pickax marks. As the work grew harder, they sought help. But no one else would go near Oak Island. It was said to be haunted by the ghosts of two fishermen who vanished there in 1720 while investigating strange lights. So the boys gave up, temporarily.

Later, McInnes and Smith settled on the island. In 1804, intrigued by their tale, a wealthy Nova Scotian named Simeon Lynds joined them in forming a treasure company. They found more oak tiers every ten feet down the pit, to a depth of 90 feet. They also uncovered layers of tropical coconut fiber, charcoal and ship's putty, plus a stone cut with curious symbols that one cryptologist took to mean *Ten feet below, two million pounds are buried*. At 93 feet, the diggers drove a crowbar five feet deeper and struck a solid mass. Lynds felt sure that is was a treasure chest.

But next morning he was amazed to find 60 feet of water in the pit. Weeks of bailing proved fruitless; the water level remained constant. Lynds assumed that this was due to an underground freshwater spring. The next year, his hired miners dug 110 feet down, off to one side of the Money Pit, then began burrowing toward it. When they were only two feet from it, tons of water burst through. As they scrambled for their lives, the shaft quickly filled to the same depth as the Money Pit.

Beaten and almost broke, Lynds gave up. McInnes died. But Vaughan and Smith never lost hope. In 1849, they took another stab at the Money Pit, with a syndicate from Truro, N.S. The results were dramatic.

At 98 feet, just where the crowbar had hit a solid mass in 1804, a horse-driven pod auger (which picked up a sample of anything it passed through) pierced a spruce platform. After dropping through an empty space, it cut into four inches of oak, 22 inches of metal pieces, eight of oak, 22 of loose metal again, four more inches of oak and six of spruce, and then into deep clay. To the drillers this suggested an exciting prospect—a vault containing two chests, one atop the other and laden with treasure. Moreover, the auger brought up a tantalizing trace of it—three links of gold chain!

A second 110-foot shaft was dug in 1850. It also flooded. But this time a workman fell in and came up sputtering, "Salt water!" Then someone noticed that the water in the pits rose and fell like the tide. This discovery jogged old Tony Vaughan's memory; years before, he'd seen water gushing down the beach at Smith's Cove—520 feet from the Money Pit—at low tide.

The treasure hunters stripped the sandy beach, searching for a hidden inlet of the sea. Under the sand, to their astonishment, they found tons of coconut fiber and eel grass on a stone floor that stretched, 154 feet wide, the full distance between high- and low-tide marks. More digging uncovered more surprises; five rock-walled box drains slanted in from the sea and down, converging toward the Money Pit.

In effect, the beach acted as a gigantic sponge to soak up tide-water and filter it into a conduit. This conduit dropped 70 feet straight down, later exploration proved, then sloped back to a point deep in the Money Pit—all of it filled with loose rock to prevent erosion. This brilliant baffle was no natural obstacle; it was the work of a genius. As diggers neared the cache at 98 feet, they had unwittingly lessened the pressure of earth that plugged the mouth of the conduit.

Undeterred, the Truro crew built a cofferdam to hold back the sea. The sea promptly wrecked it. Next they dug 118 feet down and burrowed *under* the Money Pit. But the bottom of the pit collapsed into the tunnel, then dropped into a mysteriously empty space.

Though the Truro syndicate lost $40,000, its discoveries excited wide interest in Oak Island. A series of costly expeditions followed, all dogged by bad luck. One outfit gave up after a huge steam pump exploded, killing a man. In 1893, almost a century after the dig began, another syndicate was organized by Frederick Blair, a Nova Scotian who was to spend almost 60 years trying to solve the mystery.

His company was the first to locate the flood tunnel outlet, 111 feet down the side of the Money Pit. To block it at the source, dynamite was set off deep underground near the shore at Smith's Cove. After filling the Money Pit with water, well above sea level, Blair threw in red dye. Not a trace of it seeped back to Smith's Cove—proof of the dynamite's success.

But on the *opposite* shore of the island, 300 feet from the pit, red stains appeared at three places! This meant that there was at least one more flood tunnel to cope with. No one has yet found it.

Blair and his partners also resorted to core-drilling in the Money Pit. At 153 feet—the deepest yet—their bit chewed into seven inches of cement, five of oak, 32 inches of metal pieces, then more oak and cement. Finally, at 170 feet, it hit impenetrable iron.

To Blair, this indicated a treasure chest encased in primitive concrete, larger and buried deeper than the ones drilled through in 1850. This time, along with flecks of gold, the bit brought up a tiny scrap of parchment bearing the letters *vi*—written with a quill pen

Oak Island is pocked by pits that treasure seekers have been digging for almost 200 years. Many are hazardous and have been fenced. One shaft near the Money Pit was used as a refrigerator by the family of Bob Restall (above) during the years they lived on the island.

151

Bob Restall (with his wife Mildred and sons Rickey and Robert) spent an estimated $100,000 searching for the Oak Island treasure. He found little more than a stone (here held by Rickey) on which was chiseled the date 1704. Restall, his son Robert and two other men were killed in a treasure-hunting accident on the island in 1965.

and India ink, according to analysts in Boston. "That's more convincing that a few doubloons would be," Blair claimed. "Either a treasure of immense value or priceless historical documents are at the bottom of that pit." But the syndicate never found out. After spending $100,000, it folded.

Only Blair carried on. He obtained treasure-trove rights to the island for 40 years, then offered to lease them for a share in any bonanza that might be found. The first taker was engineer Harry Bowdoin, of New York. With several prominent backers looking on—including a young lawyer named Franklin D. Roosevelt—Bowdoin dug and drilled in 1909, to no avail.

Other syndicates from Wisconsin, Rochester, N.Y., and Newark, N.J., all failed. In 1931, William Chappell, of Sydney, N.S., a wealthy contractor who'd run the drill that brought up the parchment, sank $30,000 into the Money Pit before the Depression made him quit.

He was followed in 1936 by Gilbert Hedden, a New Jersey millionaire who spent $100,000 more. Hedden ran power lines over from the mainland to drive high-speed pumps, and hired a Pennsylvania mining firm to sink a 170-foot shaft. He finally concluded that all the digging and flooding had probably shifted the treasure as much as 100 feet—it was impossible to say in what direction.

At the time of Frederick Blair's death in 1951, Oak Island and its treasure rights were acquired by William Chappell's son, Mel, a Sydney architect and builder—who had worked with his father's expedition in 1931. Mel Chappell spent $25,000 on one excavation, then leased portions of his rights to a series of other fortune hunters. One was Bob Restall, of Hamilton, a former motorcycle stunt rider. Restall quit his $150-a-week steelworker's job in 1959 and moved to Oak Island with his wife, Mildred, and their sons, Robert and Rickey.

The family lived beside the Money Pit, a caved-in crater filled with sludge and rotting timbers, and Restall managed to clear a 155-foot shaft sunk in the 1930s. He added eight holes, trying to intercept the flood tunnels.

To finance his hunt, Restall sold about half of his half-interest in any treasure to people who wrote from as far as Texas. After five years Restall figured that his quest for Oak Island's elusive hoard had cost almost $100,000. Yet all he had to show for it was a stone chiseled with the date *1704*, which he found in one of the holes—that and a profound respect for whoever designed the Money Pit. "That man," he said, "was a hell of a lot smarter than anyone who's come here since."

One day in August 1965, while working at a 27-foot shaft on the beach at Smith's Cove, the 59-year-old Restall was overcome by carbon monoxide from a gasoline-powered water pump. His son Robert and two other men who went into the pit to help were also overcome. All four men died.

But the search for treasure went on. Mining experts say the elaborate safeguards of the Money Pit could have been built only by an engineering wizard with plenty of help—and plenty to hide. As petroleum engineer George Greene put it in 1955, after drilling on Oak Island for a syndicate of Texas oilmen, "*Someone* went to a lot of trouble to bury *something* here. And unless he was the greatest practical joker of all time, it must have been well worth the effort."

Late in 1965, a few months after Restall's death, a California petroleum geologist, Robert Dunfield, made a new try. He and some associates, including Montreal manufacturer David Tobias and Dan Blankenship of Miami, brought in a 100-ton digger, of the sort commonly used in strip mining. Their intention was to excavate a huge open pit, 50 feet across at the surface, which could be opened up to a depth of 180 feet if necessary.

The 148-foot level was reached in four weeks. Elated, Dunfield estimated he was only 50 feet from the treasure chamber. Then an unseasonable thaw threatened a cave-in.

"Even the thaw wouldn't have stopped us," said Blankenship, "but suddenly it was Christmas. Our crew refused to dig over the holiday. Every one of them went home. With the ground getting softer every day, we hunted everywhere for an emergency operator. Dunfield called Chicago and offered one guy $1,000 a day to run the crane. Nobody wanted the job. By the time our own crew came back, the pit had started to collapse. All we could do was fill it in to save the whole area from destruction." Dunfield had spent more than $80,000. He gave up.

Not so Tobias and Blankenship. They had a new plan. With owner Mel Chappell's blessing, they began a far-reaching drilling program in 1967.

"Documentation on the island has always been sketchy," said Tobias, "so our idea was to ignore all the reports of previous searchers and accept only the evidence of our own eyes."

The drilling yielded interesting results. Cavities were located in the Money Pit area—several below bedrock at 212 feet, a depth far greater than any reached by previous searchers. From one hole the drill brought up bits of wood and fragments of china. From another came a piece of brass which appeared to have been torn from a larger body and was embedded in thick, putty-like blue clay. When the clay

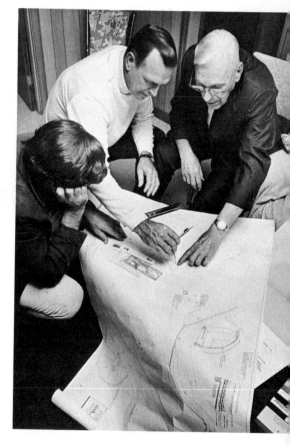

M. R. "Mel" Chappell (right), of Sydney, N.S., Oak Island's owner since 1950, studies treasure-hunt plans with Dan Blankenship (center), a Miami contractor who is operations director, and Kerry Ellard of Montreal, project coordinator for Triton Alliance Limited. Triton is pressing the search for an answer to the Oak Island riddle.

An excavator which puts a 27-inch hole through almost any kind of overburden was brought from Colorado in 1970 to help in the search near the Money Pit. Work at Smith's Cove (top) hopefully will rediscover box drains uncovered there in 1850. A new cofferdam (foreground) protects digging operations.

was washed off, the brass first gleamed brightly, then rapidly oxidized to a dull brown. Metallurgists said it was made by a process that was used for hundreds of years until new methods were introduced in the nineteenth century.

Encouraged, Tobias formed Triton Alliance Limited in 1969, with Blankenship and Chappell, and Donald C. Webster, a Toronto financier, and George Jennison, former president of the Toronto Stock Exchange. Convinced that undercapitalization, more than anything else, had led to the failure of previous attempts, the group raised $500,000.

"By now it was no simple matter of treasure," said Tobias. "We had come to believe that Oak Island was probably one of the great historical and archeological question marks in North America, and we invested as much in the hope of getting answers as we did in the expectation of finding immense treasure."

In 1970 Triton built a cofferdam at Smith's Cove, uncovered the remains of the 1850 cofferdam, and brought up a layer of coconut fiber—but found no sign of the box drains.

Buried in the seabed near the new dam were three 30-foot logs, each notched every four feet, apparently to hold a squared upright which had been doweled into place with a two-inch oak peg. At each upright position—pieces of upright remained—was a Roman numeral cut into the log with a saw. The three logs formed part of a U-shaped structure whose open end was toward the shore. The remains of a

Behind the 1970 cofferdam (top left) were found remains of a similar dam built in 1850. Also unearthed in recent years were unexplained notched logs with Roman numeral markings (top), pre-1790 oak pegs and iron nails, and a mysterious wooden box (above).

nail drawn from one notch was found to be made of wrought iron, forged prior to 1790, said a metallurgist. Carbon-dating showed the uprights and pegs were pre-1790.

Archeologists are baffled. A specialist in eighteenth-century naval construction believes it had nothing to do with ship-building, nor that it was a dike or wharf. Was it a land-based structure pushed into the sea for some reason? The Triton people believe it may have been a cofferdam, built to enable the original workers to construct the flood-tunnel drains. Seafaring men, without horses or machinery, might have built a wooden dam, similar to the hull of a ship, rather than one of earth and rocks. The discovery of a wide board running along the bottom of several uprights lends credence to this theory. So does a handmade, wrought-iron caulking iron found close to one of the logs and identified as of the same period as the nail.

Just as puzzling is a wooden box—two feet by 18 inches by six inches—found near two of the notched logs. Open on top and with a two-inch oak dowel in one side, it could have been used to haul heavy boulders out of a tunnel. But where is the tunnel? And why did the box not float away when the cofferdam (if that's what it is) was breached to let in the sea?

In the 1970s, as in the 1790s, each new discovery brings new questions—and the mystery of the Oak Island Money Pit grows ever deeper.

155

Canada's Wonderful "Wishing Book"

By Robert Collins

The best gift I've ever had was a $1.25 "Toy Typewriter That Really Works," purchased by mail from Timothy Eaton's in 1930. Pastel blue and smelling gloriously of oil and ink, it had a rotary keyboard on which I began one-fingering my way through original short stories and "news" items—something I have done ever since. For that alone, I claim, part of whatever I am today I owe to Eaton's mail-order catalogue.

Most of the worldly goods on our Saskatchewan farm came from that well-thumbed book. Like millions of other Canadians, my own life is chronicled in purchases selected from its pages. And Canada itself—events, customs, morals, economy—is mirrored in the collected editions of this "best seller."

Modern Eaton's merchandisers wince at my nostalgia. Proud of their catalogue's new image as *the* favorite shopping medium of sophisticated city folk, they would rather forget that it once sold Peruvian Ointment (15¢) and Pomegranate Root (5¢) and was known as The Farmer's Bible. Now, they point out, Eaton's publishes eight editions a year, each with more than 2,000,000 copies, plus several sales supplements, and has a bigger readership than any other Canadian book, magazine or newspaper.

But in its early days that quaint old mail-order book—preserved today on microfilm in our Public Archives as a prized source of our social history—was friend and helpmeet to millions.

Indians called it the Wishing Book.

Generations of immigrants learned English by matching its pictures and text, as did students of French after its French edition appeared in 1927.

In my prairie home it was far more than just our "private" department store. It was entertainment, instruction, a window on an outside world that we then knew only by newspapers and magazines. When a new edition was pried from the mailbox, redolent with the heady fragrance of fresh-printed paper, it was read from cover to cover, from "A" batteries to Zinc Ointment.

Night after night, wondering and dreaming, we wandered through its pleasant, perfect world of smiling people and unlimited clothes, toys, tools, appliances.

Ordering from the catalogue was a delicious evening ritual around the coal-oil lamp, my father carefully hand-lettering the order blank and wielding a tape measure, following Eaton's exhaustive instructions for measuring everything from heads to ring fingers.

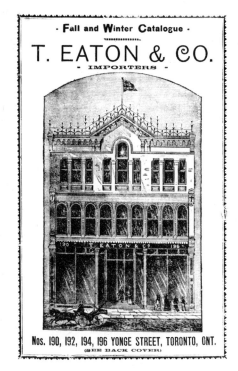

· Fall and Winter Catalogue ·

T. EATON & CO.
- IMPORTERS -

Nos. 190, 192, 194, 196 YONGE STREET, TORONTO, ONT.
(SEE BACK COVER)

The very first one (above) and the hundreds that have followed make Eaton's catalogues an important record of Canadian social history.

When another catalogue arrived, the old one might be used as a coloring book, for cutouts, for hockey shin pads (even Gordie Howe used catalogue shin pads in his early years). Folded and varnished, catalogues served as bookends; rolled, soaked in salt water and dried, they made excellent Yule logs; color illustrations boiled in water produced Easter egg dyes. And, more often than not, the book finally ended its career outdoors in the privy.

Timothy Eaton, a stern-eyed bushy-bearded Irishman, had founded his department store in Toronto, in 1869, with three revolutionary concepts. Instead of the prevailing retail techniques of dick-

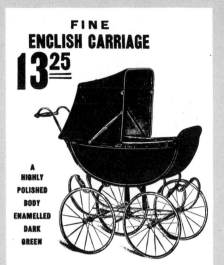

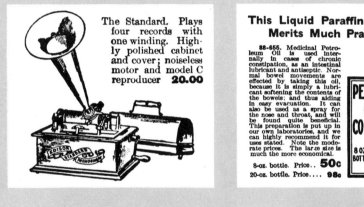

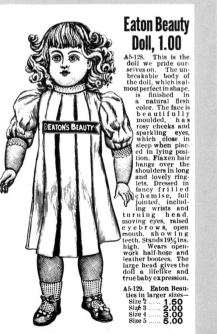

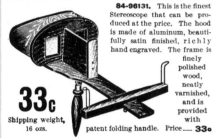

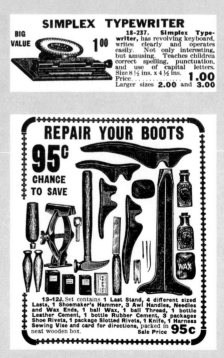

Our Medicine Outfit.

Every person going to the Klondike should have one. For **Five Dollars** we will supply an outfit containing—

¾ lb. citric acid, in bottle.
50 two-grain quinine capsules.
40 Lewis liver pills.
1 oz. chlorate of potash tablets.
6 mustard leaves.
3 belladonna plasters.
2 oz. Peruvian ointment.
8 " bottle white oil liniment.
2 " " instant relief liniment.
3 " " strongest essence of ginger.
3 " " of paregoric.
1 " " of laudanum.
1 " " tr. iodine.
8 " " pectoral balsam.
½ lb. vaseline.
1 drachm iodoform in bottle.
1 yard lint.
1 doz. bandages, assorted.
1 yard 7-inch rubber adhesive plaster.
4 oz. absorbent cotton.

Full directions and instructions for using with every outfit.

More elaborate outfits furnished for Ten and Fifteen Dollars. Lists furnished on application.

Any additions or changes to this list can be made at prices as given under heading of Drugs and Drug Sundries.

Provisions and Groceries.

This list conveys an idea of the amount required for one man for one year :

500 lbs. flour, $12.00.
200 " bacon, 19.00.
75 " sugar (brown), $3.00.
10 " coffee, $3.00.
10 " tea, $2.50.
10 " baking powder, $1.00.
1 doz. beef extract, $3.00.
1 " condensed milk, $1.50.
50 lbs. rolled oats, $1.04.
20 " corn meal, 29c.
25 " candles, $2.50.
100 " beans, $1.67.
10 " barley, 25c.
10 " split peas, 25c,
25 " rice, $1.05.
10 " prunes, 63c.
20 " evaporated apples, $2.20.
15 " " apricots, $1.43.
12 " " vegetables, assorted, $2.16.
5 tins assorted soups, $3.00.
20 lbs. salt, 20c.
1 " pepper, 15c.
12 " soap, 40c.
3 doz. yeast cakes, $1.44.
1 lb. mustard, 40c.
21 lbs. baking soda, 63c.
½ gal. lime juice, $2.40.
5 boxes matches, 50c.
Saccharine, 300 tablets in bottle, $1.10 each, $12.00 per doz. Each tablet sufficient for 1 large cup of tea.

ering, barter and long-term credit, he set a fixed and visible price on every item, sold for cash only and guaranteed satisfaction or money refunded.

Few could resist such a deal, once they got over the initial shock of handing over cash. In 1884, a mail-order department consisting of planks on packing cases was soon set up in one corner of his little store at Yonge and Queen streets. That year Timothy issued his first catalogue: a 32-page pink booklet which offered good brown wincey at 7½¢ a yard, men's cotton shirts at 45¢, carpet sweepers at $2 and, for 55¢, the Little Beauty Corset, available in drab, black or scarlet. (What kind of hussy would wear a *scarlet* corset! In fact, all sorts of respectable women secretly yearned for one and could now have it discreetly by mail.)

From that first edition, the catalogue was a homey, helpful document and Timothy soon had pen pals among mail-order customers across the nation. One appreciative customer sent Mrs. Eaton a basket of plums. Another asked if the Eaton family would try out a certain piece of sheet music "on your melodeon" before shipping it.

Promised that errors would be promptly rectified, the public was encouraged to "try to write us a good-natured letter but if you cannot, then write us anyway." A Saskatchewan homesteader reported grumpily that his new bathtub leaked. Not until he'd received a second tub and sent a second complaint did Eaton's realize that the troublesome "hole" was the drain.

And an Eskimo on Herschel Island, upon receiving a dress illustrated in the catalogue, wrote back peevishly, "Where is the girl that comes in the dress?"

Mail-order brides were about the only thing Timothy Eaton *didn't* have in stock.

Today, as I leaf through the editions since 1884, Canada's history files past me in little still-life portraits . . .

Here are the 1880s and 1890s, a leisurely half-forgotten time of one-cent china dolls, 25¢ steel-rim spectacles and ladies' imitation lace seamless Congress boots at $2.75. Remember celluloid collars and cuffs? Silk hats and 16-carat gold-headed walking sticks? And a choice of sweetbrier, honeysuckle, elder flower or morning glory soaps?

Now the Klondike rush of '98 is on, and Eaton's has prepared batches of supplies for greenhorns with gold fever: a $5 medicine kit, and a year's food supply for one man, from 500 pounds of flour and 200 pounds of bacon to a pound of pepper, all for $68.69.

A new century—and settlers are swarming into the West. Eaton's publishes special settlers' editions with everything from plowshares for the virgin sod to tar paper for cabin roofs. Doctors are scarce and undependable, so Eaton's carries every known patent medicine, including more than 30 varieties of Humphrey's Homeopathic Specifics, for such miseries as ague, grippe and Saint Vitus's dance.

Awesome inventions have come with this twentieth century. Here is Edison's Talking Machine for $16.50, or the horseless carriage, gingerly acknowledged at first with a few automobile robes, then openly with a line of auto accessories.

Yet for all the bursting-out around them, these catalogue Edwar-

1900

1914

1920

1929

1948

1967

Styles changed—and so did the *language* of fashion—but not Eaton's insistence on quality. "High Class Dressmaking by Mail," the catalogue said at the turn of the century, "is an Art with us. We delight our Lady Patrons in every province of the Dominion." A quarter-century later, both fashion and the fashion copywriter were still up to date; Eaton's offered for instance "a suit for the young fellow who likes 'dash and snap in his clothes,' yet nothing extreme." Always the catalogue expressed Eaton's pride in offering "the latest ideas procurable." They could confidently be regarded (said one issue in the late '20s) as "authentic guides to what is a la mode." And it's the same today.

For a book as modern as tomorrow, photo studios and everything else about the mail-order operation are as up-to-date as Eaton's can make them—a far cry from the original setup, as sketched for the fall and winter catalogue of 1890.

dians are as smug and self-assured as were their real-life counterparts, confident of endless prosperity, everlasting peace and the eternal might of the Empire. Lean, virile men with sculptured profiles and foppish moustaches gaze out indolently from under boater hats. Their women are stylishly frail, with nipped-in waists and bosoms that seem to advance a foot ahead of their derrières. Their small sons are trapped in effeminate high boots, hats that look like flying saucers, and Norfolk suits with buttons down the leg.

The Great War marches by almost unnoticed except by those with men in the distant trenches. But Eaton's welcomes the veterans back to the land in 1919 with a special catalogue of farm implements and plans for houses available through the Soldiers' Settlement Board.

Now, the catalogue's mood changes: bobbed hair framed in cloche hats, flat chests, and straight-line frocks that show the knees. Flappers! Midway through this singing, swinging decade a catalogue-cover Father in starched collar gathers Mother and son around a strange cumbersome box bristling with knobs and dials; it is one of Eaton's Minerve radios (cost $115). Voices, *music* came out of the air through this box—it was beyond belief!

Suddenly the colors turn sober and gray, as the Depression catalogues tighten their belts. Now my own childhood is rushing past. Such good books—well, they *seemed* good at the time—as *Slim Evans and His Horse Lightning* or *Sergeant Silk the Prairie Scout*, were offered for only 29¢. A "dressy" shirt for $1, a Pocket Ben watch for $1.75. Does anyone remember Eaton's Whoopee Pants? They were bell-bottoms with a triangular insert of red or yellow in each outer cuff—and who said there's a generation gap?

Into the 1940s; the catalogue and Canada are off to another war.

162

This time the war is real and immediate. The covers go red-white-and-blue. Everyone's favorite books are by "the inspirational British leader," Winston Churchill. Eaton's will ship special food parcels direct to British civilians or Canadian troops abroad.

Most of us of the Whoopee Pants generation did a term in blue or khaki. When we came home the catalogue paced us through the paraphernalia of adulthood—refrigerators, stoves and hi-fis. But Canada and the catalogue were changing. Small farms were vanishing. It was even suggested that Eaton's catalogue, by reflecting the well-dressed glittering urban life in its pages, lured rural youngsters to the city. Farmers who stayed on the land became mechanized and mobile. The catalogue's eight or nine pages of harness dwindled sharply.

Eaton's original illustrations dwindled too. Over the years the catalogue had employed some of Canada's finest illustrators, including Wyly Grier and Charles Comfort, FCA, William Winters and Duncan Macpherson.

Now, turning exclusively to photographs, Eaton's discovered a shortage of professional models in Canada. College girls and housewives, members of the Winnipeg Blue Bombers football team, and even passersby in the street posed before the camera.

Today, the book is as modern as a moon shot and although there are some 350 catalogue sales offices across Canada where customers may see samples, discuss problems and write orders, most housewives—even city dwellers living near one of Eaton's regular stores—still use the catalogue to "shop" in their own living room. In Canada of the '70s it saves time, baby-sitter fees, traffic frustration and parking problems.

Regular catalogue users receive all eight editions published each year, plus sales supplements. Newcomers to the list start out with only one edition but quickly graduate to the full set if they order regularly. Thus Eaton's woos new business yet restricts indiscriminate mailings of the expensive book, which can consume 1,300 tons of paper, 100 tons of ink and seven tons of glue at a production cost of $2 a copy.

Eaton's catalogue staff plans a year ahead, predicting future fashions, buying the 40,000 different items that are listed in any given year, and feeding a continuous flow of copy and illustrations to the presses. Meanwhile, orders from current catalogues pour in, and shipments go out from three main catalogue distribution centers across the land. The biggest, in Toronto, occupies an area equal to 56 hockey rinks, uses small trains to haul merchandise, has seven miles of conveyer belts, mechanized traveling clothes racks, and computerized order sorting and billing.

Yet for all this 20th-century automation, and although three-quarters of the business comes from towns and cities, Eaton's is still everybody's catalogue. Orders go out by boat, tractor and dogsled as well as truck, train and plane to customers as far away as Ellesmere Island in the High Arctic.

And millions of us still revel in the color, the Beautiful People, the sheer entertainment of the Wishing Book which, I'm pleased to notice, still sells a toy dial-a-letter typewriter (although it costs four times as much as in 1930).

Thousands of Eaton's employes work year-round on catalogues. As photographers select and shoot models, artists are busy at their drawing boards and copywriters find words to tell it like it is. Long under the ban in Eaton's advertising have been such advertising favorites as "amazing," "colossal," "ideal," "fabulous," "perfect."

A huge circus tent was the first home of the Stratford Shakespearean Festival. It was soon replaced by the 2,258-seat Festival Theatre, overlooking the placid Avon River.

Stratford on Avon— Canada!

By William French

Stratford—on the Avon River in Ontario—was a typical small industrial town distinguished for little save its name, which was the same as that of Shakespeare's birthplace in England. Then, in 1952, Tom Patterson got moving. And this lone man with his idea, launched by an impulsive telephone call, changed everything.

Once dependent on the railway repair depots of Canadian National for most of its employment, Stratford today is a bustling community with more than 50 diversified industries. It is a tourist mecca and a cultural center with a population so lettered that union pickets use quotations from Shakespeare on their signs. For the Stratford Shakespearean Festival, an annual four-month binge of theater and music set in the simple surroundings of rolling Canadian farm country, is thought by some qualified critics to have outstripped even its English predecessor as the most exciting and best-run such festival in the world.

And Tom Patterson started it all. He had lived most of his life in this town where streets, districts and schools bore Shakespearean names. At 32, he was plodding along as an editor on a business magazine in Toronto. Unlike most other men, he decided to shoot for the impossible dream he had had since boyhood: a Shakespearean Festival for his hometown like the original at Stratford on Avon.

Patterson knew a little about Shakespeare, but nothing about producing. He began asking questions and reading, and he learned that the English actor and director, the late Tyrone Guthrie, was the world's leading authority on Shakespearean productions.

It was then that Patterson made his fateful phone call to Guthrie's retreat in the Irish village of Doohat. Patterson? Guthrie knew no Mr. Patterson. And Stratford, Canada? Never heard of it! But the idea that some nobody from nowhere had the audacity to interrupt his seclusion aroused Guthrie's curiosity. He listened as Patterson spilled out his idea: a festival of Shakespeare under the Canadian stars. Out of the question, said Guthrie. Won't work. Too many distractions in an open-air theater; too many insects. And money? How much money did Patterson have? None yet? Ridiculous.

But Tom Patterson couldn't let his dream die. He kept bubbling on with enthusiasm, and Guthrie began thinking. He himself had been pondering some radical ideas about Shakespearean performances. He had even thought of placing the plays in a modern version of the old Globe Theatre for which they were originally written. These experiments would cost a fortune in London or New York. Maybe this wild place in Canada was the more practical testing ground.

The fanfare of trumpets that starts the festival each year is a salute not only to William Shakespeare but—in a way—also to Tyrone Guthrie (left), and to the dream and perseverance of Tom Patterson which made the festival possible.

And so Tyrone Guthrie flew to Canada to tell Patterson exactly what was needed in the way of cast and facilities to make the festival a reality.

Patterson formed a committee of business and professional men to get the festival going. Then, flying to London, he wangled a luncheon date with the eminent actor Alec Guinness. There, in a fashionable pub, he delivered the same enthusiastic spiel that had won over Guthrie. It worked again. Guinness agreed to star in the first production.

Thus encouraged, Patterson quickly signed up Cecil Clarke, for

Stratford festival programs have carried the names of many of the world's great actors. Alec Guinness and Irene Worth (center stage, as the King of France and Helena in *All's Well That Ends Well*) were the international stars the year the festival opened. Canadian William Hutt played the title role of *Tartuffe* in 1968.

many years production manager at London's Old Vic, and Tanya Moiseiwitsch, the talented stage designer. He returned home flushed with success. But now there was the little matter of raising the money. About $150,000.

The city council put up $5,000. Business firms, foreseeing a boost to Stratford's economy, gave $500 here, $1,000 there. The J. Arthur Rank movie organization, prodded by its scholarly Canadian president, Leonard Brockington, gave a whopping $15,000.

The festival was on its way, or so it appeared. The committee agreed with Guthrie that an outdoor performance was too risky, and ordered a huge circus-type tent from a Chicago firm. A local contractor was engaged to build the seats and construct the stage.

But with the opening performance just two months away, the committee had only half the $150,000 on hand, and the sources of donations seemed to dry up. The tentmaker got wind of the crisis and halted work on the tent.

It looked as if Tom Patterson had reached the end of the line. The committee chairman telephoned Guthrie in London to inform him of the crisis and to suggest a year's postponement of the festival, but Guthrie, by now as fired up about the project as Patterson, was against postponement. The project should proceed full blast, he argued, or be abandoned altogether. The committee members swallowed hard. Next day Guthrie received a cable: DECIDED PROCEED STOP ASSURE YOU FULL STEAM AHEAD.

The committee rushed back to work, and miraculously the money turned up. The Perth Mutual Fire Insurance Company gave $25,000. Governor-General Vincent Massey gave $10,000. With a month to go, donations reached $157,000—enough to put them over the top.

There were still problems. The tentmaker had lost considerable time, and there was doubt that the big top would arrive soon enough. Rehearsals had to be held in a wooden shed with an iron roof; the

acoustics were terrible, and sparrows fluttered overhead. Proper costumes simply weren't available in Canada. Armor had to be made from stiffened felt by students recruited from art schools, period footwear fashioned by a shoemaker who ordinarily made work boots.

Yet on July 13, 1953, the Stratford Shakespearean Festival opened right on schedule. The play was *Richard III*. The prospect of Alec Guinness and Irene Worth playing in rural Ontario had lured the top critics of Canada and the United States to attend. Brooks Atkinson, the *New York Times* drama critic, called it "a spectacular production." Herbert Whittaker of the Toronto *Globe and Mail*, lauding Guinness' portrayal of the hunchback king, called it "the most exciting night in the history of the Canadian theater."

Opening night each July is a particularly stirring scene. Stratford's super-wide main street suddenly becomes an avenue of glamour, and famous faces dot the crowds thronging the sidewalks.

There's an air of carnival: bands play; pennants fly; fireworks streak in gaudy colors across the sky. Old friends renew their bonds at tinkling dinner parties. Oglers peer in anxious hunt for celebrities. Young autograph hounds scamper along the walks. Suddenly, just as in Shakespeare's time, there is the boom of a cannon and a fanfare of trumpets. All Stratford is abruptly hushed. Then, in the gaily pen-

Michael Langham (left) and Jean Gascon were Tyrone Guthrie's successors at Stratford. Festival stars have included Zoe Caldwell, Tony van Bridge and Frances Hyland (above, left, in *The Merry Wives of Windsor*) and Christopher Plummer (above, with Miss Caldwell in *Anthony and Cleopatra*).

As the Shakespearean festival prospered, Canada's own Stratford on Avon became a major tourist and cultural center. Not far from the great Festival Theatre, amateurs perform in the open-air Theatre-in-the-Park.

noned theater, located on a gentle rise overlooking a lovely landscaped park that borders the broad Avon River, the magic starts.

It's still in large part Tyrone Guthrie's magic. He had come to Stratford to test a major innovation—a stage unique in the modern theater. He and Tanya Moiseiwitsch had designed a wedge-shaped multilevel structure that jutted out into the auditorium. It is bare of props and curtains. The spectators sit in tiers on three sides of it, with no seat more than 65 feet from the stage. Placing actors close to the audience created a new, dynamic relationship.

But the stage was not Guthrie's only innovation. He took an unorthodox approach to Shakespeare, sometimes verging on the slapstick. Once he gave *The Taming of the Shrew* a Gay Nineties flavor to prove that the play could be performed against any background. He brought in such stars as James Mason and Julie Harris, to give the productions glamour; and he also started a resident company which now has a winter home at the National Arts Centre in Ottawa. These young actors provided a verve and exuberance which were, and are still, infectious across the footlights. Guthrie remained three years at Stratford, and made a lasting mark. He was succeeded first by Michael Langham and then by Jean Gascon, founder of Quebec's famous Théâtre du Nouveau Monde.

Although Stratford was an artistic—and financial—success from the start, it had growing pains. For one thing, there was the tent. In wind and rain it made an awful racket, occasionally drowning out the voices of the players. It also leaked a bit and knowing spectators were careful to bring umbrellas. On one occasion, during a poignant love scene, the whistle of the Toronto train howled an intrusion. Faces turned to stare at Donald Gordon, president of Canadian National, who was in the audience. From that night on, no train whistles sounded in Stratford on festival nights.

The townspeople watched the influx of strangers with marked suspicion in the early days. They were skeptical of visitors with fancy togs and fancy manners—and especially of actors, because everyone knows what *they* are like. Siobhan McKenna still recalls vividly the town's careful scrutiny when she first played Stratford. "I was aware of the lace curtains parting as I walked down the street," she says. "Finally, I decided to give them something to stare at. One day I climbed the telephone pole back of my house and just sat there so that lots of them could see me all at once."

Today the people of Stratford are proud of their festival and the celebrities it attracts. Prime Minister Trudeau was wildly cheered when he visited the festival and ran the country from a railway car.

For the first years, while there were still only six hotels and motels in all of Stratford, there was an acute shortage of accommodation. Playgoers from Detroit and Toronto frequently stayed in Stratford homes as paying guests rather than make the arduous round trip in one night. Now hotel and motel space has tripled but rooms in private homes are still in demand. The rates are reasonable (about $7 a night for a room with a double bed), and the informal atmosphere often produces lasting friendships.

Although Shakespeare is the backbone of the Stratford season, the festival now presents a varied program. There is Molière, Chekhov, Ben Johnson, Petronius. There's also, during the course of a season, opera, ballet, recitals, concerts, contemporary drama, jazz, folk music, even rock groups.

The old circus tent is, of course, long gone. By 1955 it was already evident that the festival needed permanent quarters, and this time there was no great struggle in raising funds. The festival now operates a $4,000,000 complex that includes the 2,258-seat Festival Theatre plus the Avon Theatre, a refurbished vaudeville house used for musical events and contemporary plays.

The festival has sent many of its players on to international stardom—Christopher Plummer, Kate Reid, Zoe Caldwell, Lorne Greene—and it has produced its own Canadian favorites. William Hutt, Bruno Gerussi, Barbara Chilcott, Frances Hyland, Eric Christmas, Tony van Bridge and many others have made the festival a success year after year.

But the greatest beneficiary of the festival's success has been the city. Tourists spend an estimated $9,000,000 a year in Stratford. The festival itself has an annual payroll of $1,700,000, employing up to 570 persons at the peak of the season. In addition, new industries employing more than 4,000 people have moved to town, all attracted by the festival's publicity or atmosphere. Tom Patterson has now left the festival. After 16 years as its public relations director, he resigned to form his own production company with Duke Ellington—whom he met, naturally, at a Stratford concert. But he still maintains his home in Stratford where, like the proud father he is, he can watch the continuing progress of the rambunctious youngster he brought into the world.

It was just an idea in 1952. But it worked. Patterson's inspired telephone call put Canada's own Stratford on Avon on the map.

Other cultural attractions have been developed in Stratford in the wake of the festival's success. The old Public Utilities Commission building, erected in 1883, was restored and redesigned by Rothmans as a centennial project and in June 1967 was opened as the Rothmans Art Gallery. It is run by the Stratford Art Association and is open year-round.

CUSO:
A Word for Partnership

By Janice Tyrwhitt

When Judy Pullen joined the Canadian University Service Overseas in 1963, she volunteered to teach for a year in India. Tall, strong and pretty, a 22-year-old physical-education graduate, Judy was sent to a refugee camp for Tibetan children at Kangra, in northern India. Since 1959, when the Chinese invaded their country, Tibetans had been fleeing across the border in droves, and hundreds of homeless children were waging a pathetic battle against hunger and sickness at the Kangra "transit school."

Judy mothered the children, romped with them and taught them—using twigs to scratch letters on wooden boards smeared with dirt. She helped another CUSO volunteer, nurse Lois James, to tend those children who were riddled with worms and dying from vitamin-deficiency diseases.

"But the school wasn't a grim place," she insists, "because the Tibetan kids were so full of spunk and laughter."

After nine months, Judy was asked to help full time in the most important task of the Tibetan government in exile: training teachers to help their people survive in a new country without sacrificing their ancient culture. Her new pupils at Dharamsala were Buddhist monks, schooled only in religious philosophy yet so intelligent that she had to read far into the night to keep up with their questions. Soon able to dispense with an interpreter, she taught in Tibetan, which she had learned from the lamas and the children.

Year after year, Judy renewed her CUSO contract because she was so badly needed. When at last she returned to her home in Oakville, Ont., it was for only a brief rest. She returned to India to work on a book and to help her husband Tsewang Choegval Tethong, a member of the Dalai Lama's staff and head of a Tibetan resettlement project for 5,000 persons in Mysore State, south India.

Judy's story is a striking example of the kind of work done by the more than 3,000 Canadians who in the last decade have gone to serve and learn in the emerging nations. These volunteers have special skills that the struggling young nations need and their own peoples can't yet supply. Pharmacist James Thorkelson taught Tanzanian pharmacy students, town planner Albert Denov worked on a master plan for Dar-es-Salaam, his wife as a librarian, and chartered accountant Paul Duchesne trained a Tanzanian town councillor to run his city's finances. The CUSO volunteers are trained to share local wages and working conditions and the local way of life.

Though CUSO has been called Canada's answer to the Peace Corps, it actually predates the U.S. program by three months and its aims and methods are very much its own. Founded on June 6, 1961, by several university groups concerned with overseas aid, it remains a private organization in spite of a contribution of just over $3,000,000 from the Canadian International Development Agency. Overseas governments and agencies have contributed a further $3,000,000 in salaries and housing supplements to CUSO personnel. Another $500,000 from the Canadian private sector includes money raised in "Miles for Millions" marches. Support by Canadian universities and colleges in the form of staff time, offices and equipment is valued at $200,000. Support from advertisers, the news media and pharmaceutical and other com-

The spunk and laughter of homeless Tibetan children surprised Judy Pullen, the Canadian girl who "mothered" them in a refugee camp in northern India. Like Albert Denov (above, with Tanzanian town-planners) and some 3,000 other volunteers, she was chosen by CUSO for her maturity, initiative, adaptability — and common sense. CUSO stresses partnership. Tanzanian President Julius Nyerere said of the Canadians: "What really matters . . . is that they loyally and efficiently carry out the decisions made by our government and our people."

Under the hot Indian sun, agriculturist Hans-Henning Mundel of Oliver, B.C., instructs farmers in the growing of new kinds of safflower and wheat.

panies, and the Department of National Health and Welfare in the form of free services and supplies, totals $500,000.

Unlike Peace Corps members, who often work in teams supervised by their own officers, CUSO volunteers are hired for two years as individuals and are paid by governments or institutions in the developing nations. Thus the host countries are in control and have a financial stake in each person and each job.

CUSO doesn't seek sentimentalists who regard overseas service as a noble sacrifice. "CUSO provides a practical focus for a young person's sense of uneasiness about the present," said its former executive secretary, Frank Bogdasavich from Saskatoon. "A Canadian going abroad under this program can involve himself, test his ability and take a hard look at his ideas when confronted with the 'Third World' in Asia and Africa. We can't ignore the fact that 18 percent of the world's population owns 80 percent of the world's wealth. Our sense of concern is not totally altruistic; it's very practical."

Canada's reputation as a neutral middle power in world affairs allows developing nations to accept CUSO workers without political commitment. Zambia, emerging from a long bitter struggle for independence and racial equality, welcomed CUSO volunteers. One yardstick of CUSO's success is the number of countries that want additional volunteers. In the fall of 1968, for instance, CUSO sent 120 volunteers to West Africa, but had requests for ten times as many.

172

Partnership—not charity—is the key word. Almost every volunteer finds himself plunged into a key occupation in a country that's growing excitingly fast. In Lima, Peru, geographer Bob Anderson worked for a government agency exploring the natural resources of the eastern slopes of the Andes, where a new road is opening up the high jungle for settlement. Hans-Henning Mundel is one of several CUSO agriculturists helping to develop new varieties of safflower and wheat and teach Indian farmers how to grow them. Nurse Wendy Marson, whose husband Brian was director of CUSO's Asian program, spent 1967 traveling through north India, working with hospital staffs to teach birth control to illiterate villagers. "Contrary to what many North Americans think, Indians *do* want family planning," she said. "The problem is to reach them."

Every volunteer must be flexible enough to learn local language and customs—and cope with local hazards. On the salaries of the country (for a teacher, $35 a month in India, $175 in Nigeria), volunteers learn to live on local foods: chilies, curries and rice in Madras; beans, rice and green bananas in Burundi. Working conditions may be primitive or extremely sophisticated. Before she went to Sarawak, physiotherapist Barbara Reid worked in two Jamaican hospitals: one a paraplegic rehabilitation center more advanced than most, another where patients slept three to a bed. Vancouver's Brian Bailey, district headmaster for a group of rural schools in Borneo, tore out the back of his riverboat on a crocodile and had to swim for his life. One CUSO worker who helped a tribesman with a sick relative was startled by a Dayak custom for saying thank you. Her hands and face were slapped with soot. Once she had to feign sleep to avoid another tribal gesture of hospitality: a male partner for the night.

CUSO ordinarily sets no age limits, although most volunteers are in their 20s. The oldest so far was Donald Lowe of Vancouver, a civil engineer. In his late 70s, he supervised all roads, bridges, water supplies and government buildings in a 75,000-square-mile district of western Uganda. Dr. Frederick Shippam, a pediatrician, left the staff of the Montreal Children's Hospital at the age of 67 to work in Our Lady of Lourdes Hospital in eastern Nigeria. Evacuated by CUSO in June 1967, just before civil war broke out, Dr. Shippam insisted in serving out his full term at a hospital in Ghana.

Dr. Ross Ford, former director of CUSO's Caribbean program, estimated that fewer than four percent of CUSO volunteers fail to do a good job—thanks in large measure to its rigorous selection program. Candidates are quizzed by faculty who have served abroad, and by returned volunteers, as well as by students from developing countries. In these conversations, candidates reveal not only the skills but also the temperament that will—or won't—fit them for two strenuous years. As a Ghanaian cabinet minister once told CUSO, "Underdeveloped people aren't much use in underdeveloped countries."

Working in multiracial, multilingual societies gives volunteers a new slant on Canada's own two cultures. One in four CUSO workers belongs to the thriving French-language program in Latin America and in 15 French-speaking African nations.

Normand Asselin, former director of the French West Africa

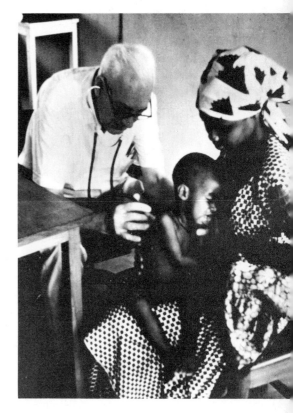

A Nigerian child cries at the touch of a cold stethoscope during an examination by Montrealer Dr. Frederick Shippam, who was 67 when he volunteered for CUSO duty. Age is not in itself a limitation: CUSO's oldest volunteer was almost 80, the youngest 19.

program, says: "People grow up quickly overseas and come back really alive to social and political problems. They are more willing to take part in the affairs of their own country, too. French Canadians have tended to ignore Canadian foreign policy, for example. Now CUSO is preparing them to make a contribution to it and to shake off its reputation of being 'British.'"

I spent a summer weekend at a farm outside Toronto, where newly chosen volunteers met others who had come back from overseas service the previous fall. Though they can't define it, the returned volunteers claim that a community of spirit keeps them going when they're lonely and frustrated overseas. Brief as it was, that weekend saw the birth of CUSO spirit among the newcomers. The bond is strengthened during orientation, a tough six-to-eight-week session. Volunteers for each area train together, first in Canada and then abroad. Latin America's group, for instance, spends ten weeks at a special training school in Cuernavaca, Mexico, before proceeding to Colombia, Peru, Ecuador, Bolivia and Chile. Everyone gets an intensive course in the language and customs of his new country—usually from people of that country—and extra training in his own specialty.

Returned volunteers are already beginning to change and challenge many Canadian institutions. All seem to have gained fresh insight into themselves and their country. They're using their overseas experience in government agencies like CIDA. They're going into the Canadian North to work with Indians and Eskimos. They're seeking a voice in politics.

The more returned volunteers, the more the CUSO spirit spreads. A service club invites a CUSO speaker and winds up sponsoring a volunteer. A businessman whose daughter has joined CUSO offers to serve on the local committee. Colleges and universities ask CUSO how to plan courses that will fit their students for overseas service.

To meet the changing needs of the developing nations, CUSO keeps experimenting and growing. In 1961, it sent 17 volunteers to India, Ceylon, Sarawak and Ghana. Ten years later, more than 1,200 were working in some 40 countries. The trend in overseas requests is for persons with high qualifications and extensive work experience, with a strong demand for technical personnel. Responding accordingly, CUSO finds specialized workers such as Gordon Bernius, a geologist whose years in British Columbia and the Yukon prepared him to do mineral prospecting for the Tanzanian government. John Bielby programmed computers in Tanzania, Mary Jo Murphy was an X-ray technician on the Caribbean island of St. Lucia. CUSO helped to establish Canadian Executive Service Overseas, an agency that sends business executives on short projects to advise on industry. (In socialist countries, capitalists may find themselves playing an unlikely role: Clifford E. Soward, the former president of Maple Leaf Mills Ltd., helped nationalize milling in Tanzania.)

What *all* the emerging nations want is workers who will help their people carry on alone. Working together, CUSO volunteers and their hosts are truly learning, as one volunteer puts it, that "teaching others to help themselves requires a special generosity of the human spirit."

174

New School
for Old Values

By David MacDonald

Thirty-eight teen-agers and five teachers of St. John's Cathedral Boys' School in Selkirk, Man., were trucked to the banks of a roiling river deep in the wilds of northern Ontario. There they launched five big war canoes, climbed in and, for an offbeat entrance exam, began to paddle back to the school—400 miles away. "On this trip," history master Ted Byfield warned them, "you'll find out what kind of kids you are." One 15 year-old lad answered for all. "Oh, man!" he moaned, "we'll *never* make it."

Nine days later, those same youngsters rounded a bend in the muddy Red River, saw the tall white cross of St. John's on its west bank and burst into a rousing French voyageur song that they'd learned along the way. They had paddled daily from dawn to dusk, in rapids and rain, hefted 220-pound canoes over rugged portages, slept in the open, survived their own campfire cooking and made an exciting discovery: they were stronger, gamer kids than they'd ever imagined. For after trooping back into St. John's, bone-weary but beaming, the newcomers blithely mapped out a *longer* trip. "Now that we know we can hack it," the 15-year-old explained, "we're not afraid of hard work."

In short, they were ready to face life at one of North America's toughest, most remarkable little prep schools, which prepares boys for manhood by subjecting them to the rigors of intensive study, Spartan living, manual labor, hickory-stick discipline and enough athletic demands to daunt a decathlon champ.

Opened in 1962 in an abandoned Indian hospital, St. John's is based on the old-fashioned belief that the only way to draw forth a boy's best is to tolerate nothing less. For its more than 100 students, aged 13 to 18, this means a regimen designed to stretch them to the limit in mind, body and spirit. "We never demand the impossible from kids," says headmaster Frank Wiens, "—just one hell of a lot more than they *think* is possible."

Besides swotting over their books for nine hours a day, St. John's boys must scrub floors, clean dishes, collect garbage or pitch hay, shovel manure and tend 10,000 chickens a year on a commercially run school farm. They also stuff sausages, cure hams and bacon, then peddle them in nearby Winnipeg to help pay expenses. Once a week, in season, they're either off on grueling sub-zero snowshoe treks or training for 1,500-mile canoe trips. Furthermore, the school's firm rules are enforced with a wooden "paddle," applied sternly.

Far from a collegiate sweatshop, however, St. John's is a lively,

Teen-agers at St. John's are *voyageurs*, students, pig farmers, sausage makers . . . "learning how to lump it through to the end."

175

The first St. John's, overlooking a bend in the Red River, is in a one-time Indian hospital at Selkirk, Man. The second is at Genesee, Alta., near Edmonton. Youngsters learn to *enjoy* learning, whether about queen bees (with teacher Dave Thompson) or from books (or chess) in the library.

stimulating place where students gain satisfaction and confidence in shaping up to tough demands. "We all gripe about the grind," said a husky senior of 17 from Saskatchewan. "But it's never dull—we're too busy to be bored—and it gets great results."

Indeed so. Despite the heavy work load on St. John's boys—many of them dropouts, kick-outs or "under-achievers" from other schools —their passing rate in final exams is over 80 percent compared to 70 percent for Manitoba's public schools.

"The difference is in the demands," claims Frank Wiens, who left public-school teaching to run St. John's. "Since mass-education systems are geared down to the so-called 'median' student, they're often stuck with a standard of mediocrity. Even when teachers know that's beneath most kids, they can't push them up higher—to reach for their full potential. But at St. John's, outside the system, we can and we frequently do."

For example, while most high schools use just one history text, St. John's seniors routinely work through 20—including four fat volumes of Churchill and two in French. Logic, normally a university subject, begins in Grade 9. St. John's pupils have written sonnets, composed a folk-rock Mass, produced plays in French and German. "When kids find out that learning can be fun," says Wiens, "there's no holding them back."

For all its academic industry, a breezy air of informality flows through St. John's, a cluster of rustic old buildings and barns in the verdant Red River Valley. Teachers and students dress in jeans and T-shirts. Though boys must "Sir" all masters, the fact that they eat, hike, paddle and do chore-duty together results in a spirit of camara-

176

derie that bridges the generation gap. It also sustains the school in time of need: when St. John's recently built a $125,000 addition, for only $70,000, almost all the work was directed by teachers and cheerfully done by student-power.

While such economies help to hold down tuition fees—under $1,500 a year—the greatest saving lies in the coolie wages paid to St. John's 16 staff members. Banded into a semireligious community called the Company of the Cross, they receive room, board, clothing—and $1 a day. Except for Rev. Philip Sargeant, an Anglican priest, all are laymen (of many denominations) who've given up far more comfortable situations to work at St. John's.

Typical is Fred Parr, from the University of Western Ontario, who turned down a $7,500 teaching post at another school. "This place offers something better than money—satisfaction," he said.

Ted Byfield, who resigned as a Winnipeg newspaper reporter to go to St. John's with his wife Ginger, feels the same way. "Some people around the Press Club still think we're nuts," he says with a chuckle. "But then, the whole idea of this school has been wonderfully crazy all along."

It began in 1957 when Byfield and Frank Wiens, both parishioners at St. John's Cathedral in Winnipeg, were asked to start a club for its choirboys. They repaired two old navy cutters and took nine lads for a 400-mile rowing trip on Lake Winnipeg. "I learned more about kids in those two weeks," says Wiens, "than in ten years of teaching."

A German immigrant's son who'd grown up in the Depression and worked his way through college, Wiens felt that modern schools were too soft to challenge the ability of most youngsters. Byfield readily agreed, as did other parents in the St. John's congregation.

So they bought an old house, and began weekend tutoring classes in Latin, Greek, physics, even basic economics. The student body grew steadily and, between long boat and snowshoe trips, St. John's pupils were soon designing their own slide rules for higher math, building ham radio sets and winning province-wide elocution contests.

Unpaid instructors included a member of parliament, prominent businessmen and a lawyer named Hugh Parker, who put three sons in the part-time school. "One was a regular 51-percenter," he recalls, "the kind of kid who's content just to scrape by. But St. John's pushed him over *80* percent."

As word of such successes led to overcrowding, backers leased the century-old Indian hospital at Selkirk, 25 miles north of Winnipeg. From 12,000 personal letters, students raised $10,000 to renovate the ramshackle building that became a full-time, nonsectarian boarding school in 1962.

Since then, many young grads have seemed to breeze through college on sheer momentum. "The great thing about St. John's boys," says a University of Manitoba professor who has taught several, "is their attitude to learning. They really *enjoy* it."

One reason is that teachers use imaginative means to rouse their interest. Instead of merely memorizing history-book facts about the British conquest of Quebec, for instance, St. John's pupils conduct a courtlike probe of the event—with student "witnesses" being grilled

Newspaperman Ted Byfield (top) and teacher Frank Wiens saw the choirboys' club they formed in 1957 grow into one of the continent's best little prep schools.

Pigs at St. John's graduate as sausages, chops and bacon. Along with honey collected by student beekeepers, they produce a tidy profit for the school.

by classmates—and then relate it to contemporary unrest in French Canada.

French, an option in most Canadian schools, is a must at St. John's. Starting in Grade 8, pupils study bilingual Hansard reports of parliamentary debates, get news and NHL hockey games only from French-language TV. Among other activities, St. John's classes have joined in archeological digs, worked in francophone parts of Quebec, bred pigs, gone backstage at the ballet, interviewed survivors of Buchenwald for insights into World War II. Because the school is small, students get the advantage of individual attention. "If a boy is weak in chemistry, we cater to his needs with special help," says one master. "And if he's just lazy, we cater to that too—with extra chores."

Athletics at St. John's are intended to develop stamina and spunk. After weekly workouts on the Red River all able-bodied pupils must spend part of each summer paddling the routes of early Canadian fur-traders, from the Rockies to Manhattan Island. Toughest test of all is the 800-mile Grand Portage, a hard-slogging journey over eight rivers, 36 lakes and 55 trails, between Lake Superior and Winnipeg.

On such arduous outings, teachers get a rare opportunity to assay their students' mettle. After lake storms once turned back a ten-day boating expedition, just hours short of its goal, Frank Wiens found 13-year-old Ian Parker sobbing in his tent. "We came this far," the boy complained, "and then we *quit*." With that tenacity, Wiens later commented, "I thought he'd tough his way through any studies we piled on."

Right. Young Parker went on to compile the best high-school average in Manitoba, then won the coveted Woodrow Wilson National Fellowship.

The school farm doubles not only as a handy source of revenue but also an extra means of instruction. Under teacher Dave Neelands,

178

Salesmanship, too, is on the St. John's curriculum, as youngsters peddle the school's food products door to door in Winnipeg. So is hard-hat construction. Teacher Wayne Cooper (foreground, left) helps students lift trusses for the roof of a building which now houses the school's academic wing, dining room, kitchen, laundry room, common room and offices.

students raise chickens, honey bees and geese. "When boys are entrusted with chicks worth thousands of dollars, they learn more than poultry farming," Neelands observes. "If someone fouls up their feed or leaves the barn door open in winter, the whole school's a loser. So they learn to shoulder their responsibilities, and they never let us down."

The same is true when pupils go knocking on doors in Winnipeg to sell their frozen chickens, sausages and pork products. On annual sales of $90,000, they turn a $20,000 profit for their school. "Even if we didn't need the money," says Frank Jones, who runs St. John's meat program, "we'd still want our boys selling in the city. It's the best experience they can get in dealing with people."

A former stock salesman from Vancouver, Jones first read about the school a few years ago. "The article made it seem like a prison," he remembers, "yet all the inmates in the pictures were *smiling*." So he went to St. John's with his wife Diane, to see about enrolling their own son. "In talking to the students," he says, "we were really impressed by their mature sense of values—good, 'square' old values like honesty, perseverance, achievement. To us, giving that to boys seemed pretty worthwhile, so we came to work here."

Although it's a tough school with a predictably high dropout rate, St. John's has a long waiting list. Moreover, its rugged regimen has proved so successful that the Company of the Cross recently opened another school in Alberta, with plans for a third in Quebec or Ontario. While some educators regard it as a throwback to the past, many parents see it as hope for redeeming the future. So, in fact, do some of its students. "One day I'll send a son of my own to St. John's," a young senior told headmaster Frank Wiens. "The kid may not like it here," he said, grinning, "but he'll sure learn how to lump it through to the end."

The Cats That Conquered Winter

By Ronald Schiller

Snowmobile racing, like snowmobiling itself, is a popular new winter sport. But, demanding judgment and dexterity at high speeds, it's not a sport for everybody. Successful racing is no matter of power alone; there must be expertise, a feel for the vehicle and the terrain. Races provide important testing for "improvement of the breed." Machine stress in a weekend of racing is probably equal to a full season of ordinary use.

Not many years ago, it took Awa Taka'uga four "sleeps" in the arctic night to tend his 40-mile-long trapline by dogsled, and he could make the trip only twice a month. The rest of the time he was forced to spend fishing and hunting to feed his ten ravenous huskies.

Now, scooting over the frozen tundra of the Northwest Territories at speeds up to 25 miles an hour by snowmobile, Awa can do the trip in less than two days.

Halfway around the globe, Finnish reindeer herder Jouni Jomppanen faced economic disaster. Twenty men on skis and eight dogs took two weeks to round up his 4,000 animals, and the work was so grueling that labor was almost impossible to find. Today, Jouni's worries are over. With the aid of motorized sleds, he too can cut down his work drastically; now, four men and two dogs can round up his herd in two days.

In the brief existence of these frisky mechanical cats, they have revolutionized life in the snow belts of the north. They can rocket down twisting mountain trails with the agility of goats, plow straight up 45-degree slopes, surfboard over the surface of 30-foot-deep snow. On the flat, they can run for an hour on a gallon of gas, attain speeds of up to 50 m.p.h., and draw sleds weighed down with 1,000-pound loads.

Professional fishermen, loggers, telephone linemen, oil prospectors and missionaries use snowmobiles to reach areas that were once impenetrable. Nurses in Labrador visit isolated cases or bring patients back to the hospital in them. Western ranchers use snowmobiles to haul feed to starving cattle, and the Royal Canadian Mounted Police and Scandinavian troops employ them to patrol their arctic regions.

But recreation is the basic purpose of 95 percent of all snowmobiles. On a good winter weekend, close to a million people flit around the snowfields of our continent, reveling in what has become the hottest chilly-season sport ever to hit North America.

Snowmobiles are so intrinsically simple, safe and effortless to operate that they can be driven by eight-year-olds. Basically, the vehicle consists of a narrow steel frame, seven feet long, mounted on a 15- to 24-inch-wide flanged rubber track, propelled by a two-cycle, air-cooled motor, generating from ten to 65 horsepower. Sitting or kneeling on a padded seat, which can hold two people riding tandem, you steer the vehicle by a bicycle-style handlebar which turns two miniature steel skis mounted on leaf springs in front. Your left thumb controls the brakes, your right thumb the throttle. There are no gears.

1922-23   1927-28

1931   1932-33

1942   1958

Joseph-Armand Bombardier's first experimental machine, forerunner of the Ski-Doo, was built in 1922-23. It had four sleigh runners powered by a propeller and a four-cylinder Ford Model T engine. By 1927-28 he'd gone in part to wheels, joined by a steel belt. In 1931 he rebuilt a Model T into a snowmobile with a closed body. Next he experimented with a four-runner vehicle shaped like an airplane body and powered by a Ford engine and—again—a propeller. At mid-war some snowmobiles were armored and joined the army; others did postal duty. Postwar models included the Muskeg tractor of the 1950s and the world-famous Ski-Doo. Right: Bombardier on an early model in 1957.

The motor is revved up by squeezing the accelerator, and stops the instant your hand leaves it, eliminating the danger of runaways in spills. The only trick a driver must learn is to lean into curves and shift his weight on side slopes to maintain balance.

To snowbound families of the north, the versatile little vehicle is a blessed antidote to winter doldrums. "We used to go stir crazy in winter," recalls farmer Joe McGuire. "All we did was watch television, play cards and snarl at each other." Now, while Joe and his oldest boy are out ice fishing or hunting on one of the family's two snowmobiles, Amy McGuire whips the younger kids around on a sled in the other. In the evenings, they frequently join neighbors on moonlight rides, often ending up at a wienie roast. "No outsider can appreciate how much the snow buggies mean to us," says McGuire.

Joseph-Armand Bombardier, the shy, self-taught French-Canadian mechanical wizard who perfected the Ski-Doo, would have understood Joe perfectly. He spent 40 years devising ways of breaking through the icy shackles that imprisoned his village of Valcourt, in the Eastern Townships of Quebec, for six months each year. His first attempt in 1923 at the age of 16, which resulted in a rickety sled driven by a Model T engine and homemade airplane propeller, was sheer disaster. When the explosive racket burst on the calm of Valcourt's main street, villagers crossed themselves, horses bolted and huge icicles crashed from the eaves of nearby buildings. Armand's scandalized father packed his son off to a Montreal garage where he might put his mechanical talents to better use.

Bombardier might have forgotten his ambition had not tragedy intervened. Back in Valcourt during the winter of 1934, his infant son, Yvon, was stricken with appendicitis. Although the nearest hospital was only 15 miles away, the boy died in the sled while Armand frantically flogged his horse through the six-foot snowdrifts. Determined to conquer the enemy that had taken his son's life, Bombardier in 1936 perfected his first practical snow vehicle, a seven-passenger, enclosed cabin on half-tracks and skis costing $7,500, which he called the "Bombardier Snowmobile." Several thousand are still in use as winter buses, trucks and ambulances, in Canada, Alaska, Greenland and Europe.

During the next 20 years, while designing other large snow vehicles for industrial purposes, Armand remained on the lookout for an engine small and light enough to power the one- or two-man snow scooter he had first envisioned. On a 1958 trip to Austria, he found it—a two-stroke, single-cylinder engine, weighing less than 30 pounds. By the following winter he had built the first 250 of the little vehicles which he called Ski-Dogs, since he expected them to replace the husky. But buyers referred to them as Ski-Doos, a name which has since entered dictionaries as a synonym for snowmobiles.

By the time Armand died in 1964, 7,000 Ski-Doos had been sold. By 1970, production exceeded 200,000. Bombardier Ltd., run by Armand's son André and two sons-in-law, has become one of the largest enterprises ever founded and managed by French Canadians.

With acquisition of Industries Bouchard Inc. of La Pocatière, Que., makers of Moto-Skis, Bombardier in 1971 controlled 50 percent of the snowmobile market. But some 70 other manufacturers still com-

Joseph-Armand Bombardier (top) remembered the winters of his youth in Valcourt, Que., as sentences of imprisonment. There were places to go and things to do but no way to get there and do them. His efforts to overcome winter earned him the affectionate name, "the indomitable snowman." His nephew, Jean-Luc Bombardier (below), was the first Canadian to reach the North Pole by snowmobile.

The snowmobile: just the ticket for telephone linemen, ski-slope first-aiders, policemen ... firemen, farmers, fishermen ... all who must navigate in winter.

pete for a share of the industry's $600,000,000 annual sales of snowmobiles and related products. Prices for the most popular models range from $700 to $1,000 or more.

The snowmobile picture isn't entirely snow-white, of course. Their low-slung silhouettes, which make them hard to see, and the carelessness with which some of them are driven have resulted in many fatal accidents. A snowmobile can carry a man farther into deep snow in 15 minutes than he can flounder back through in a day. Yet people who know nothing about repairing breakdowns or winter survival take off alone into the wilderness. Officials recommend that snowmobilers travel in pairs or groups, carry extra gasoline and tools for repairs, as well as food, hatchet, map, compass and a flare gun to signal their location in distress. Some snowmobilers harass animals, even chasing foxes and deer to exhaustion and death.

The good deeds performed by snowmobilers, however, considerably outweigh the bad. Snowmobile clubs have rescued lost children, hunters, fishermen and victims of airplane crashes. During the blizzards of 1966-67, which brought traffic to a standstill from Illinois to Quebec, they rescued stranded motorists, rushed doctors to patients and sped expectant mothers to hospitals. Ski-Doos and Fox-Tracs, airlifted from their Quebec and Wisconsin factories to Window Rock, Ariz., in December 1967, saved the lives of hundreds of Navajos marooned for days in a blizzard without food, fuel or medicine.

Snowmobile races, of which more than 100 are held annually, are soaring in popularity. Longest is the 490-mile marathon from Winnipeg to St. Paul, Minn., a 13-hour run which relatively few complete. Most famous is the five-day World Championship Snowmobile Derby, held in northern Wisconsin. Contests include flat racing around a banked cloverleaf, where the souped-up machines hit speeds of 70 miles an hour; obstacle courses and jumping events in which vehicles soar off a two-foot-high ramp.

The most spectacular snowmobiling exploit to date was the North Pole trek in four Ski-Doos in the spring of 1968 by Minneapolis insurance man Ralph Plaisted and a party of friends, including Jean-Luc Bombardier, Armand's nephew. The explorers groped their way—in 60-below-zero temperature—from one ice floe to the next, gunning their machines and sleds across the narrow open water leads between them, chopping roads up and down pressure ridges three stories high. For six days, trapped in their sleeping bags by a blizzard which cut radio communication, they were feared lost. The last 50 miles were made at top speed over thin ice. "If we had slowed down, we would have broken through," said Jean-Luc.

Once their mission was accomplished, a ski-plane picked up the weary adventurers. But there was room in the cabin for only three of the four Ski-Doos. Somewhere on a floating ice cake in the Canadian Arctic they left a yellow and black snowmobile in good condition. It is free to anyone who cares to go get it.

Jean-Luc Bombardier, the first Canadian to reach the North Pole by snowmobile, died of a heart attack less than two years later. He had been a public relations officer for Bombardier Ltd.

184

But . . .

By Jack Olsen

In the early days of snowmobiling, accidents were considered rare and freakish. Now they are common. So many snowmobilers have died in collisions with cars and trucks that most areas have banned the snow vehicles from public ways. But snowmobilers manage to die anyway. According to the Ontario Safety League, "Snowmobiling may have the highest fatality rate of any recreational activity in the world." (There were more than 100 snowmobile deaths in Canada in the winter of 1970-71, about half due to collisions with cars.)

One part of the problem is the lack of restrictions on the age of snowmobile drivers. If a child can see over the windshield (or even if he cannot), he is eligible.

Another part of the problem is power. The first seven-horsepower snowmobiles whisked over the snow at speeds below 30 m.p.h. But the industry soon found itself in a horsepower race. Today the average family snowmobile will go 50 to 60 m.p.h., and the world's snowmobile speed record is 114.5 m.p.h. The cliché advertisement has become an airborne snowmobile, its goggled driver crouched over the windshield, his knees flexed and his clothes rippling. "Many amateur drivers try to emulate these stunts," the Royal Canadian Mounted Po-

lice *Gazette* reported, "with the result that the average production-line machine, not equipped for such sport, ends up smashed and the driver seriously injured or killed."

Great damage is done by well-meaning snowmobilers who roar into the woods in winter for a single reason: because they love the outdoors and the animals and the snow. They may love them, in fact, to death. The first unnatural ingredient they add to the forest is noise—earsplitting, pounding, reverberating noise. Although conservationists say that we don't know how badly wildlife needs the dead silence of winter, they are certain that most animals cannot accommodate to noise during the breeding season, particularly animals with high metabolic rates, like mink.

The snowmobile reaches its peak of mobility at a time when other inhabitants of the forest—animals, birds, rangers, wardens—are least mobile and effective.

The menace is both blatant and subtle. A well-intentioned snowmobiler packing down a trail in deep woods has no idea of the ecological destruction he may be wreaking. Philip Corbert, a wildlife expert who is director of the federal Department of Agriculture's Research Institute at Belleville, Ont., notes that snow is an excellent insulator, a natural protection for mice and other small animals. But it must be thick enough, and it must not be packed (it ceases to insulate when packed). Snowmobile tracks are permanent barriers in the brush for animals under the snow.

What is to be done? For the most part, conservationists are agreed that if the silence and sanctity of the woods are to be preserved, and if

nature's immutable laws are not to be flouted any further, authorities must consider legislation that would:

• Bar vast areas of public lands to snowmobiles, limit them to trails specifically marked for the noisy sport, and bar them flatly from public roads.

• Forbid hunting or trapping from snowmobiles, hunting or chasing game with snowmobiles, riding snowmobiles into hunting areas during game season, or indeed using snow vehicles in any way at all connected with hunting.

• In addition to registration and licensing of snowmobiles with motor-vehicle departments, require application of oversized numbers on front cowlings, and serial numbers embedded in the tread so that snowmobiles will leave an identifiable trail wherever they go.

The alternative to such rigorous legislation would seem to be the passive acceptance of another forest pollutant and the continued erosion of man's fundamental right to peace and quiet.

Vive le Canada!

By George Ronald

Too bad I didn't ask his name because *that* I'd likely have understood. Especially if he'd said it was Tremblay or Gagnon or Lefebvre or Paquette or any of the easy ones. Anyway, he was about my age (let's say early middle) and my build and height (average). Just a guy.

It was a hot summer evening. One of the children spied a-slide-with-bumps-in-it-Dad! I drove around the block and came back to this little park on the south shore of the St. Lawrence. He was there with his kids.

He nodded hello and then said in French that it sure was hot, eh?

"Pour sûr," I said.

"Quel pays!" he said.

"'Mon pays, mes amours'!" I said. He chuckled.

I was doing nicely and I felt pretty confident. *"C'est un beau parc,"* I ventured, *"n'est-ce pas?"*

Yes, a great park. Especially for kids. Then he took off in rapid-fire French and I'd had it.

"Ah, m'sieu," I interrupted, *"très lentement, s'il vous plaît!"*

Oh, sorry, he said.

"Je viens de Toronto," I told him. Not an apology; a fact, that's all.

But did I not speak French? Was I not doing so at this very moment?

I shrugged what I hoped was a reasonably *Québec* shrug and said, *"Ah, m'sieu, je ne parle qu'un peu de français."* And I stumbled on to explain that what little French I had I'd acquired 30 years ago in high school and . . . well, what I wanted to say (but it was too tough to translate) was that however good my French may once have been, it had withered through lack of use. Oh, I can get by in some stores if the clerks are really patient and *want* to help, and I can even read a *La Presse* editorial if I try and if I have a dictionary handy. But when it comes to a conversation in a park . . .

We were in danger of bogging down for good. If my French was poor, his English was all but nonexistent. Okay, this was Montréal, his country. *Mon pays* too, for sure, but *especially* his, just as Toronto is especially mine.

But we didn't bog down. We stuck with my Ontario high-school French and his good nature and our mutual good manners and when I failed completely I think he *pretended* to understand me. Anyway, we both *tried.*

Haltingly and always *très lentement,* we compared notes about his kids (four of them) and mine (six) and the high cost of kids. We talked about Apollo 11—it was the day after Armstrong and Aldrin walked on the moon—and agreed it was fantastic. *Magnifique!* Also that the kids weren't nearly as impressed as we old-timers were. And things such as did I like it here in Québec? *"Bien sûr,"* I said.

When it was time to go, my *"bonjour"* and *"bonne chance"* didn't seem adequate. I wanted to say I regretted our inability to understand each other better, that our problem of communication irritated and frustrated me. (Try translating *that!*)

I went back to this guy, this *Canadien* (this Canadian, like me), and I said again, *"Bonjour, m'sieu."* And then I said, because it sort of said itself, *"Vive le Canada!"*

The stranger whose name I didn't ask—this compatriot of mine—put his arm impulsively around my shoulder.

"Vive le Canada!" he said.

And we understood each other perfectly.

Two of the Greatest:

The Big Guy . . .

By David MacDonald

Hockey fans will be forever thankful that young Bobby Orr made it to the NHL before old Gordie Howe called it quits. Some of the luckiest, in Boston and Detroit, will remember having seen these two magnificent athletes in action against each other. Millions of others will recall having watched them only a night or two apart on television—the veteran Howe, his graying hair thin now, his face well lined with stitch marks, still one of the best after a quarter of a century at his trade; and Orr, a superstar while still a rookie, a player whose potential seems unlimited. There have been others at the happy overlap of the Howe era with the age of Orr—Phil Esposito, Bobby Hull, Jean Béliveau, Frank Mahovlich, among others—but Gordie Howe and Bobby Orr have been special superstars, a man and a boy cornering whole pages of the hockey record books. Howe was near the end of his second NHL season when Orr was born (on March 20, 1948). He was in his 21st season, and going strong, when Orr broke into the big league in the fall of 1966. These are stories of two of the greatest, men who will be compared as long as hockey lives: Gordie Howe and Bobby Orr, The Big Guy . . .

. . . and The Commando Raid.

One night in 1969, nearing his 41st birthday and the end of his 23rd season in the National Hockey League, Gordie Howe sat before his locker feeling very, very old. His stomach was upset. His bruised ribs ached. Worst of all, his legs were logy. Even so, as 15,000 fans packed into Olympia Stadium to see him lead the Detroit Red Wings against Chicago's Black Hawks, the six-footer they called "The Big Guy" slowly pulled on padded crimson livery and laced up his skates. "I'll try," he told coach Bill Gadsby. "But don't expect too much."

So saying, Howe clumped out to the floodlit arena and showed why he had long been widely regarded as the greatest hockey player—if not the most amazing athlete—of all time.

Shrugging off his miseries by sheer force of will, he seized command of the game. Gliding down the ice with easy grace, Howe stick-handled around a Chicago defender some ten years his junior, feinted the goalie out of position and whipped the puck past him. Next, on a pass from a teammate, he scored his 715th NHL goal. Then the old master clinched a 6-1 victory by netting yet another—his third within 15 minutes. While the crowd stood roaring in tribute, radio and TV stations flashed word that he'd topped "the magic 714"—*i.e.*, Babe Ruth's home-run total in *baseball*! "We had to reach into another sport to find any comparable achievement," one reporter later explained. "For in hockey, Howe's already beyond compare."

Coming off the prairies in 1946 as a rawboned rookie of 18, he rose to a singular position in the world of professional athletics. "No one but Howe," said *New York Times* columnist Arthur Daley, "has ever excelled for so long in such a fast, violent game."

A superstar for two full decades, Howe overcame an awesome assortment of injuries to be the NHL scoring champion six times (and to rank among its five top shots for 20 straight seasons). At the end of the 1970-71 season—his *25th* (if not his best)—he had amassed more goals (786), more assists (1,023) and thus more total points (1,809) than anyone else who ever hefted a hockey stick. (Montreal veteran Jean Béliveau was a distant second with 1,219.)

Away from the rink, Howe is gentle, mild, totally modest. With his long, lean countenance, his lazy sort of walk and his laconic way of saying, "Yep," "Nope" or "Gol*darn*!" he's the spittin' image of a bashful Gary Cooper cowhand.

But Howe on the ice has been something else again—a rough, tough competitor exciting the wonder of fans and foes alike. "Gordie does everything as well as it can be done," said Toronto star Dave

Keon. "He's the *complete* hockey player." A deceptively fast skater despite his loping, almost languid strides, he has tended to make his hard craft look easy, revving up to a fantastic 40 feet a second without even seeming to try. But Howe has been at his facile best when cruising in on a net-minder, not cocking his stick to slap the puck but snapping off hockey's hardest shot with a mere flick of massive wrists. "All you can do," said goalie Glenn Hall, "is turn and see if it's in the net."

Having mastered every facet of hockey, Howe is naturally well versed in its more violent aspects. He has been especially adept at wreaking revenge on all who slugged, slashed, tripped or otherwise

"I'm really just a lucky old farm boy," Gordie Howe has said of his hockey career—a quarter century of being handsomely rewarded for what he clearly loved to do. Few athletes have earned as much money—or admiration. On his 43rd birthday anniversary, the City of Toronto proclaimed Gordie Howe Day, citing him as "truly a man that the young people of today should aspire to emulate."

Gordie Howe on a ranch at Jackson, Mich., in the Hereford cattle business . . . in Saskatoon, for another Gordie Howe Day, with his wife Colleen, daughter Cathy and sons Murray, Marty and Mark . . . in New York in 1970, with Mark—an all-American junior hockey player—at the annual Lester Patrick Award ceremonies. Gordie received the Patrick award, "for outstanding services to hockey," in 1967.

molested him. "You do something to him, he won't even let on he noticed it," testified a Boston Bruin. "But after the *next* scramble, you've got a few stitches to prove he did." Howe's swift moves often escaped official censure. For checking him too forcibly in one melee, a veteran Philadelphia defenseman had his nose broken by Howe's elbow. "The funny thing is," the victim relates without rancor, "*I* got the penalty."

Though a rough customer, Howe has never been considered ruthless. Goalie "Gump" Worsley recalls a time when he lay helpless on the ice after a sprawling save—the puck loose in front of his face—while Howe swept in from right wing. Rather than rifle a shot that might have unhinged Worsley's head, Howe dropped on the puck to protect him. "Thanks, pal," said Worsley. "Forget it," shrugged Howe. "I'll get other chances." One reason he kept getting them was that his tough-guy reputation prompted most opponents to give him a wide berth. They seldom engaged him in fisticuffs, for example, because he was also the NHL's heavyweight champ. He won the title in 1959, after being mugged by big Lou Fontinato of the New York Rangers. As 16,000 Ranger partisans stared in stunned disbelief, Howe flattened Fontinato's nose, blackened both eyes, then knocked him cold. "I just came to play hockey," he said later. "But Louie wanted to fight."

If the threat of retaliation helped prolong Howe's career by deterring harassment, so did his striking ability to recover from injury. In spite of a near-fatal skull fracture, broken ribs, dislocated shoulders, twisted knees, concussion, a detached retina, the loss of a dozen teeth and facial cuts requiring some 400 stitches, Howe missed few games. For most of his career he played about 45 of the 60 minutes in every game—twice the average for forwards. By sparking the Wings' attack, then doubling as a defensive penalty-killer, he has been a one-man gang. "The best teams in the NHL," an opponent once declared, "are Montreal, Toronto, Chicago and Gordie Howe."

Born March 31, 1928, in tiny Floral, Sask., Gordie Howe grew up on the outskirts of Saskatoon, where his father odd-jobbed to support a wife and nine children during the Depression. At five, given a pair of cast-off skates, Gordie took to frozen ponds with a broken hockey stick. During long winters, often at 40 below, he played in after-school pickup games, then practiced at night. Unable to afford shin pads, he stuffed his stockings with fat catalogues from Eaton's, a company that later paid a handsome sum to put his name on its sporting goods.

At age 12, Gordie starred on five teams. At 17, he turned pro with the Red Wings' farm club in Omaha, Neb., then moved up to Detroit in 1946. Teamed with veteran center Sid Abel and cocky young Ted Lindsay—to form the famed "Production Line"—Howe compiled a so-so total of 35 goals in his first three years. His chief problem was a tendency to incur penalties for disorderly conduct. "Stop looking for fights," ordered his coach, the late Jack Adams, "and start playing hockey." Thus chastened, Howe took only one year to pot his next 35 goals.

Then, just hitting his stride, he fell into the boards during the 1950 play-offs and suffered a severe skull fracture. Rushed to a hospital, Howe awoke shortly before a 90-minute operation in which surgeons drilled a hole over one eye to ease pressure on his brain. "That got me a bit het up," he confesses. "I didn't know where they'd *stop*."

Detroit officials feared he'd never be the same again. But he came back to win four NHL scoring titles in succession. Seven times in the 1950s he displaced Montreal's fiery "Rocket" Richard as the All Star right-winger. By November 1963, Howe had tied Richard's lifetime total of 544 goals—hockey's most cherished record. Then, at home against the Canadiens, he uncorked a bullet-like drive that broke it. As 15,000 fans gave him a ten-minute ovation, Detroit police issued an all-points bulletin: "Gordie's new record is 545."

(Bobby Hull of the Chicago Black Hawks surpassed Richard's 544 early in 1971. By then Howe was within sight of 800.)

Besides ability and an iron constitution, Howe has tremendous drive, desire—and pride. "Gordie has simply *got* to be first," said Doug Roberts, an ex-teammate. "If you take the puck away from him, even in a practice, he'll always come right after you and get it back." At every sport he has tried, in fact, Howe has excelled. He once carded 67 on a championship golf course, and safely negotiated the longest run at Aspen, Colo., the first time he ever wore skis. "I try to do anything well," he explains, "so I won't make a darn fool of myself."

As for his first love: "To me, hockey's always been tremendous *fun*. Maybe that's what kept me going."

And for how long?

"I always said I'd go on playing as long as my legs held out and the game was *still* fun, but not one moment longer."

... and The Commando Raid

By Bill Surface

In the Stanley Cup play-offs in May 1970, the Boston Bruins and the St. Louis Blues were battling furiously in an overtime game. The first goal scored would decide it. Suddenly Bobby Orr of the Bruins left his own zone, skated up the ice and stole the puck. He passed it to teammate Derek Sanderson. Sanderson passed it back. Then, just as he swung his left arm to shoot, a hard-charging opponent bumped Orr so violently that he sailed ten feet through the air. Even so,

Howe works out with the Detroit Tigers, whose great star Al Kaline is a close friend. Deep-sea fishing is another of his favorite relaxations. Most of Howe's fan mail is from Canada, where his is a household name. When the CTV network tested 1,000 viewers with flashing photos of 12 VIPs, Howe was recognized by 88 percent—second only to the prime minister. "Ask a Canadian about Gordie Howe," a Los Angeles columnist wrote, "and the first thing he does is take off his hat and place it carefully over his heart."

propelled by his powerful swing, the puck went screeching past the Blues' lunging goalie and into the net.

When the red light behind the net flashed on, the Bruins—a team accustomed for three decades to losing—had become the champions of the NHL. In one of the wildest celebrations in Boston's memory, 15,000 hysterical fans squeezed onto the rink to acclaim their blond hero and wave signs saying "Score With Orr!"

Bumped hard just as he shot, Bobby Orr sails past the St. Louis net after scoring the goal that gave the Boston Bruins the Stanley Cup in 1970. Right: as a rookie, playing the Montreal Canadiens, he displays one of his "12 different speeds of fast."

A defenseman isn't really supposed to be in a position to score, any more than a lumbering football tackle is expected to score touchdowns. But, as an opponent once complained after losing the puck to Orr, "That's no defenseman. That's a commando raid!"

No other professional athlete has ever dominated any game so quickly and completely as young Bobby Orr. In his first five seasons in the league, the 5-foot-11-inch, 180-pound Orr accumulated a lifetime's worth of honors. By the end of the 1970-71 season, he had twice won the NHL's most valuable player award and had four times been named the league's outstanding defenseman. He was the 1969-70 scoring champion with 120 points. The next season, with a record 102 assists, he boosted his point production to 139 (second to the record 152 scored by teammate Phil Esposito).

Orr's most remarkable trait is his coolheadedness under hazardous conditions. Rocketing pucks, razor-sharp skates, swinging sticks and violent collisions have already left their mark: ridges on his slanting, oft-broken nose; frequent pain in a once-shattered shoulder; precious little cartilage in his knotty, surgery-scarred knees. His cheeks, eyelids and lips are so frequently swollen, discolored or heavily stitched that photographers despair of getting a shot of his "natural" face during the hockey season. He begins each game knowing he will be hounded. Bruising opponents will try to provoke him into a fight, so they both will have to sit in the penalty box—or even be ejected from the game. "What else can we do?" exclaimed Scotty Bowman, then coach of the Blues. "If we don't stop Orr, we don't stand a chance anyway."

With Bobby on the ice, the Toronto Maple Leafs have at times started only defensemen against him. In the 1970 Stanley Cup play-offs, the Blues replaced a high-scoring forward with a utility man whose only assignment was to "shadow" Orr, to trip, elbow and torment him. Though four freshly rested men were used in turn to harass Orr, he often managed to skate around them, either to shoot or to pass the puck to an unguarded teammate. He was the first player ever to get a goal or an assist in all 14 play-off games.

Aware that notorious hockey bullies are embarrassed if they conspicuously fail to bother him, Orr after a hard collision may gamely sniff blood back up his nostrils, clamp his teeth over a torn lip to camouflage the injury, pat the bruiser on the rump, and simply skate away. Yet many a ruffian has regretted it later. No outstanding player can long survive in this violent game unless it's known that he will avenge any deliberate blood-letting. Orr does so, but he gets his whacks in subtly—or waits for a moment when a penalty won't hurt his team. And he knows how to get results without being vicious. Forced into a fight with Ted Harris, then a Montreal Canadien and known as hockey's "best one-two puncher," Orr tossed his gloves into Harris' face and cocked his fist before Harris could shed both gloves. Made to look like the old gunslinger outdrawn by a young stranger, Harris subsequently showed less eagerness to challenge Orr.

For the most part, though, Orr avenges fouls against him by simply going about his job. Even when he is skating *backward* down the rink, his muscular legs enable him to crowd the fanciest forwards. Repeatedly they get away no more than hurried token shots.

Among Orr's business interests—one that provides a lot of fun and some off-season ice time—has been a summer hockey school at Orillia, Ont. He's an ardent fisherman and rented a seaside house near Boston so he could "toss out the fishing pole and haul 'em in." Neighborhood youngsters followed him wherever he went.

Bobby Orr serves dinner to Boston teammates in his house at Little Nahant, on
Massachusetts Bay.

Most defensemen, once they get the puck, quickly pass down the ice to the speedier forwards. Bobby has been known to control the puck for as much as *one-third* of the whole game himself. By the time his forwards have glided into position after a free-for-all at the Bruins' end of the rink, he has often brushed aside a foe with his right hand and skated up the ice, shepherding the puck with the stick in his left hand. Then, after a fake, he may rifle a shot at the goal. He slams the puck so hard (110 m.p.h.) that it sometimes knocks a goalie's stick backward and careers on into the net.

Orr's gait is so effortless that many opponents are deluded into slowing up. One Bruin claims to have seen him use "12 different speeds of fast—plus a passing speed." "You holler at him for loafing," recalls a former coach. "Then you see he is passing everybody."

He was born in Parry Sound, Ont., and at age three was skating aggressively into groups of older boys playing shinny on the thick ice of Georgian Bay. His father, a muscular munitions worker and former amateur player, gave him tips. Soon the boy was in the Minor Squirt Hockey League—for players under six years old. As Bobby advanced through peewee and bantam leagues, everyone thought he was far too slight for hockey. But, before long, professional scouts began to ask about the skinny No. 2 who was making a monkey out of everyone.

At 14, Bobby signed with the Bruins for a bonus of $2,300 and was assigned to an amateur farm team, the Oshawa (Ont.) Generals. Although he had skated so much that his leg muscles had grown out of proportion to the rest of his body, he weighed only 127 pounds, and he often found himself competing against men six years older and 70 pounds heavier. Bobby let his jersey hang outside his pants to disguise his frailty. And he skated so furiously that he made the all-league second team. Observers noted his instant acceleration, instinctive anticipation, and quick accurate shot. By his 16th birthday he had appeared on the cover of *Maclean's*.

In 1966 Orr went to the Bruins' training camp. As a green, crewcut 18-year-old known to be drawing the highest salary (reportedly $23,000) ever given a rookie, he was an automatic target for rough handling, and suffered injury after injury. Still he became the NHL Rookie of the Year and the Bruins' third leading scorer, and helped boost the Bruins' season attendance by 44,000. In the next three years the team finished third, second and first. Said one Bruin: "As long as we have Orr, we're a dynasty."

Late in 1969, teammate Ted Green, the longtime leader of the Bruins, suffered a skull fracture. Only when other teammates insisted did Orr move to fill the vacant leadership role. He began to stand in front of Green's empty locker before each game and cajole and encourage the Bruins to get them "up" for the struggle. He fired up his mates so effectively that they skated onto the ice as hockey's hardest-hitting team.

By 1971 Orr's skills were reputed to bring him nearly $70,000 a year in salary, bonuses and prize money. Commercial endorsements and investments reportedly earned him a like amount. "But I don't even like to think about money *and* hockey," he says. "I played just as hard when I only got a ten-dollar bill once a week."

City of the Future

By J. D. Ratcliff

Are cities doomed to be clamorous, dangerous places of filth, fumes and strangling traffic? Not this one! Here it never rains; the temperature never varies from a comfortable 72° F. There is pure air to breathe, and there are no screeching motor sounds. It's the city of the future: underground Montreal.

There may be 30 inches of snow on the ground above (Montreal averages 108 inches annually), but under the below-zero streets you may stroll, overcoatless, through several miles of attractive promenade. Choose among more than 300 shops, endlessly varied and strikingly attractive, a dozen cinemas and theaters, three-score restaurants, snack bars and sidewalk cafés. There is no sense of being confined in a tunnel—you wander on broad, traffic-free avenues up to 36 feet wide. Lighting is bright and imaginative. One plaza has leafless trees softly illuminated; another, a colorful, three-ton Murano glass sculpture—the largest in the world.

In this dazzling subterranean city, you can buy groceries, have a sauna bath, get a pregnancy test, purchase a suit of armor or a canary. You want to be married? A score of shops provide wedding dresses, and one can enter a church without setting foot in the snow. You could work and play here a lifetime—in connecting hotel, apartment and office buildings—and only have to surface to be buried (there is no mortuary).

As long as cities have existed, they have been associated with din, dirt, confusion. Leonardo da Vinci had a novel solution for big-city traffic problems: carts at street level, pedestrians on elevated walkways. Modern city planners have long agreed that traffic should be segregated: trains and subways at one under-street level, parking at another, and pedestrian concourses at a third. But costs and mechanical difficulties stood in the way. You could not, the experts said, build a new city *under* one already in existence. Then a unique situation arose in Montreal.

The core area of the city was a sad spectacle: aging buildings surrounding a seven-acre eyesore, the pit-yards of Canadian National Railways, known simply as "the hole." For a generation railroad officials had talked of developing this dismal tract, but until 1956 there was no action. Then they called in American developer William Zeckendorf, who proposed construction of a group of buildings featuring a 42-story, cruciform tower over the pit. Up to this point, Place Ville Marie, as it was to be called, was little more than a conventional real-estate development which would cost more than $100,000,000.

Traffic noise and polluted air are left behind as Montrealers head down into the other city that hums deep beneath the streets and skyscrapers.

"The hole" was a seven-acre eyesore in the heart of downtown Montreal—until its possibilities were recognized by developer William Zeckendorf, planner Vincent Ponte and CNR president Donald Gordon. The result was Place Ville Marie . . .

What made it unique was the fact that with Zeckendorf's chief architect, I. M. Pei, came Vincent Ponte, a Boston-born, Harvard-educated city planner. Ponte, 37 years old at the time, saw the situation for what it was: opportunity.

Here was the long-dreamed-of chance to collaborate with architects to achieve a weatherproof underground city that would be far more dramatic than the proposed skyscraper.

Ponte went into a sales spiel with the project sponsors: In all probability, Place Ville Marie would trigger a boom. As new buildings rose, they could tie into the underground city. Thus, it would eventually spread, rootlike, under most of the city's 200-acre core, linking four luxury hotels, two railroad stations, three giant department stores, and underground garages with space for 10,000 cars. It was a heady dream.

Naturally, there were objections. Critics thinking in terms of unattractive tiled tunnels asked: Wouldn't people shun under-street shops? They hadn't in the 17-acre area under New York's Rockefeller Center, Ponte replied. After all, people didn't like being splashed with salt slush in winter or seared in summer. Wouldn't people feel hemmed in, claustrophobic? Not, said Ponte, if "streets" were wide enough and attractively lighted.

As a clincher, Ponte reminded building managements who rented basements as storage space for $2 to $3 per square foot per year that underground shops would pay $8 to $12.

When Place Ville Marie opened in 1962, the popularity of underground living in weatherproof comfort was instant. Daily pedestrian traffic—still soaring—was estimated at around 100,000. Merchants clamored for space and almost without exception prospered. One haberdasher who turned down space at the outset ruefully notes now: "I want to cut my throat every time I pass that place."

Other giant complexes began to rise in the area. Ponte worked hand-in-hand with their architects, planning the monumental substructure that would connect each with his expanding underground city. Place Bonaventure, the second largest commercial building in the world (after Chicago's Merchandise Mart), was opened in 1967.

196

... a bright, clean, weatherproof complex of soaring skyscrapers and broad underground avenues.

The trade center offers display space to 1,200 manufacturers with a luxury hotel on top. Since it sits on a slope, the depth of the underground portion varies; in one place it goes down eight stories. Ponte provided two shopping levels—totaling five and a half acres—ramps and docks capable of handling anything up to 60-foot truck-trailer rigs, garage space for 1,000 cars.

As Place Victoria, Place du Canada and others hooked in to the underground city, the concept was catching on in surrounding areas. A mile from the city core, magnificent Westmount Square shot up—two apartment towers, and office building. And, of course, a below-street area for elegant shops, restaurants and a cinema.

This, in turn, connected with nearby Alexis Nihon Plaza, featuring three shopping levels, two towers, two parking levels and even a public "square."

At the outset it was feared that this vast expansion in Montreal's

Place Ville Marie was only the beginning. Five years later, in 1967, came Place Bonaventure (this page) . . .

center would bring on a transportation crisis—drawing tens of thousands of office workers and visitors into a limited area. In a curious way it *prevented* it.

For years Montreal had wanted a subway but lacked funds to build one. New taxes provided by the skyscrapers—more than $7,000,000 a year—sufficiently increased the city's borrowing power to enable it to build one of the world's finest Metros, with quiet, spotless, rubber-tired cars.

The spreading underground city, which thus helped get people and cars off the streets, is also adding new dimensions to living—not the least of which is safety. During the window-breaking and looting that accompanied the 1969 police strike, things remained tranquil below ground. Looters apparently don't like brightly lighted places where there is no place to hide and no safe place to park cars to transport stolen goods.

...then Place Victoria (this page) joined the expanding underground city. And soon this kind of development spread beyond the downtown core.

What is the future of this idea—a city offering safety, good air to breathe, an ideal climate? Ponte has projections up to the year 2000 for Montreal. As old buildings come down, new ones will tap into the underground—with an eventual six miles of concourse. Right now the underground has its Metro stations and links to two railway stations—a businessman in Place Ville Marie can board a Florida train without wetting his feet—and plans for underground bus terminals to tie into the new highway system.

Ponte sees the underground concept as the savior of cities everywhere. Controlled environment is as attractive in the tropics as in the wintry north. It appears that from now on any city can come in out of the cold—or heat.

Man, who emerged from the cave a few thousand years ago, may now be returning to it—but he'll do so with a quiet, attractive, pleasurable difference.

More than a mile to the west of Place Ville Marie, and linked to it by subway, is Alexis Nihon Plaza, three shopping levels surrounding its public "square." An underground walk (immediately below) connects this plaza with the supermarket, boutiques, restaurants, cinema and art gallery of elegant Westmount Square.

A Bridge
Across
The Gulf

Faith lights us
through the dark to Deity;
faith builds
a bridge across the gulf
of death . . .

OWEN D. YOUNG

That child's ten years
on this earth
are not all there is to it.
It can't be . . .

HER UNCLE BOB QUINN

The Triumph
of Janis Babson

By Lawrence Elliott

Her name was Janis. "With an 's'," she would gravely inform you. And that winter of 1959 she was eight years old. Her hair was darkening from the color of gold. She was slender and lithe. When she laughed, her eyes shone with an inner light of happiness, and life welled so strongly in her that sometimes it bubbled over.

"Gosh, Mom, it's *fun*!" she sang out one January afternoon as she flew into the house.

"What's fun?" Rita Babson asked.

"Oh—school and all the snow and playing with the kids. You know—everything!"

She had been born in Windsor, N.S. But when she was only a baby, her Mountie father was transferred to RCMP headquarters in Ottawa, and the family moved into a neat stucco house on a quiet street in the suburban area of City View, just southwest of the city. That house, that street, became Janis Babson's world, and she loved it exuberantly.

Down the street was the ten-room St. Nicholas Separate School, where she was in third grade—and in an earnest rivalry with Elizabeth Hayes for top spot in the class. Beyond stretched the farm where, long ago, she had been captivated by the hackney show horses. You could see her almost any afternoon, skipping down the hill with a gift of carrots swinging from her fist. Rita Babson said the only way she could keep carrots in the house was to hide them.

Also down the street lived Tricia Kennedy, her best friend; and next door, Suzie the beagle. There were books filled with the magic of faraway places; there was water coloring, and making up dances with her big sister, and knitting, and a boy with a crew cut named Ronnie who had smiled at her during Little League games the summer before. Each wakening day was a gift.

Sometimes, on her knees, she thanked God for all the good things in her world. She didn't feel spiritual. She wouldn't have understood the word. It was just that God was very close to Janis Babson, a part of everyday life. She knew Him. He was real.

Her feelings were special, but she was far from starchy or self-righteous about them. The fact is that a healthy curiosity and irrepressible spirit sometimes landed her in hot water typical of other life-loving children. One day, she and her elder sister Charmaine went to call for Tina Stanfield, a little neighbor friend. No one answered their knock, but finding the door ajar, they wandered in, feeling terribly adventurous—and only a little self-conscious—in the familiar house, now suddenly vast and hollow-sounding. Looking in the refrigerator, they oohed and aahed over fresh apples and homemade ice cream—succumbing, finally, and helping themselves to generous quantities of each. Wandering upstairs to the bathroom they found some lipstick, and inexpertly daubed their lips, noses and cheeks, accidentally dumping over a full box of bath powder in their enthusiasm.

It was at this critical moment that they heard the downstairs door open. They froze. Mrs. Stanfield was saying, "Who in the world left the refrigerator door open?" They dared not breathe.

Conscience-stricken, panic-stricken, desperately wishing themselves somewhere else, or at the least invisible, the girls fled to a bedroom, squirming behind the dresses in a clothes closet to hide. But they had plainly marked their every step with well-powdered footprints. It was only a matter of moments before, inevitably, they heard Mrs. Stanfield say, sounding like the voice of doom, "Well, well, and what have we here?"

Caught dead to rights, the young culprits were returned to their home, solemnly given a lecture, and sent to their room by their parents; but for a long time afterward, the older Babsons and Stanfields laughed themselves teary-eyed over the girls' real-life re-creation of the story of the three bears.

There were eight Babsons: Rita, pretty, with dark-red hair; Rudy, the tall Mountie; Charmaine, Janis, Roddy, Karen, Timmy and Sally. The babies, Timmy and Sally, were a special joy. Janis called them "the small fry." After church on Sunday she often persuaded her mother to prop them in the carriage and, her own head barely poking above the handlebar, she would push them from one end of Côte des Neiges Road to the other. She beamed with pride when neighbors stopped to admire her little charges.

"They're very naughty," she'd say solemnly, then burst into a sunny grin.

Her feelings ran deep. It made her sad, she once told her mother, to see Sally growing up. "She might be our last baby," she said. She worried about the birds getting enough to eat in winter, and about her grandmother in far-off Fort William. When she was stirred by a story, her eyes would mist over. Or she would ask, "Why do people have to be mean to each other? I wish I could be everybody-in-the-world's best friend."

One day during White Cane Week, Canada's annual effort in behalf of the blind, she was watching a television program. The announcer explained how the Eye Bank helped many blind people see again by arranging transplants of corneal tissue. Then a young mother appeared, to tell how she had lost her son in an accident, and how she had bequeathed his eyes to enable a stranger to see. She felt, she said, that in the restored vision of someone she would never know, her little boy lived on.

The TV program affected Janis deeply, and for a long time she sat thinking. Then she went to the kitchen.

"Mom," she said, "when I die, I'm going to give my eyes to the Eye Bank."

Looking at her daughter, Rita Babson quelled the impatient remark on her lips. For tears stood in the child's eyes as she told what she had seen.

"There are so many who need help, Mom," she said. "Thousands and thousands just waiting their turn! If only lots of people pledged their eyes."

Rita Babson was moved, but cautious. "I know how you feel, dear. But that's a very serious decision for a little girl. You might change your mind when you're older."

Janis' gold-dark hair rippled as she shook her head emphatically. "No," she said, "I'll always feel the same." Then she added, "And I'm not going to forget about it either, Mom."

There was a lot of snow that February, and for Janis it was an enchanted time. She was outdoors every afternoon, whirling down the hill on her "flying saucer," building great snow forts with Tricia Kennedy and the other girls. She came in reluctant and red-cheeked, still full of each day's adventure.

Then, all of a sudden, she ran out of steam. A few minutes of play left her spent. She yawned and sighed heavily, usually too tired to eat more than a few mouthfuls of dinner. Her mother thought she was coming down with a cold, but she had neither temperature nor sniffles. The great weariness did not go away.

As February slipped into March, shadows darkened under Janis' eyes. Her head ached, and the smell of cooking food sickened her. Then one night she snapped erect in her chair and cried out, "Oh, that hurt!"

"What hurt? What's the matter?" her mother asked, alarmed.

"My back. It's okay now, but it sure hurt for a second."

She wouldn't hear of staying home from school. "I can't let Elizabeth Hayes get ahead of me! Oh, please, Mom. I'm not *that* sick."

But on a particularly windy afternoon, when Janis hadn't come home with Charmaine and Roddy, Rita looked out the dining-room window and was chilled by what she saw. Arms loaded with books, Janis was battling up the slope of Côte des Neiges Road, pushing, one slow step at a time, through the snow, being blown almost to her knees by the force of the wind.

"Roddy!" Rita called. "Run out and help Janis home! Hurry!"

The seven-year-old threw on his coat and dashed out. He took his sister's books. Walking in front of her to break the wind's drive, he led the way home, while Janis clung to the back of his coat.

"Whew!" she gasped limply when they came in. "I don't know what happened. I just—I couldn't walk anymore." She slumped into a chair. "I'm so tired."

Rita slipped Janis' coat off, and looked closely at the child. She was suddenly frightened by Janis' pallor and the way her brown eyes seemed to fill her thin face.

When Rudy came home that night, he and Rita decided that a doctor should see Janis. So, the next afternoon, Rudy left work early and took the child to the office of Dr. James A. Whillans, the family pediatrician.

They sat in the waiting room, the big Mountie corporal and the pale child. It was to be the first of many such long times, of many waiting rooms for the two of them. And if Janis drew strength from the comfort of her father's calm presence, Rudy, in days to come, was to gain strength from his little girl's courage.

When they were ushered inside the examining room, Dr. Whillans, a young and enthusiastic physician, said, "Well, young lady, is this a new way of getting out of school?"

Janis grinned and brought a laugh to the two men when she answered, "No, it's a new way for Daddy to get out of work."

Rudy Babson remembers the moment vividly. "It was my last honest laugh for a long time," he has said.

He watched Dr. Whillans peer into his daughter's throat and ears and listen to the beat of her heart. Then, studying a blood smear through his microscope, he stiffened. "Will you let the nurse stick your finger again, Janis?" he asked.

When he'd examined the second smear, he spoke to her father. "She seems to have a pretty high white-cell count. I'd like to have some fancy blood work done at a lab."

The following Friday, Rudy drove Janis to a laboratory where a great many blood specimens were taken from her fingers and veins. The next morning, Dr. Whillans telephoned. "Look," he said to Rudy brusquely, "I'm not happy about this. I want you to get Janis up to the hospital right away. I'm arranging for a blood specialist to see her."

In the past days, neither Rudy nor Rita had speculated aloud, but both were much lost in thought. Now Rudy was alone in the kitchen. Softly he said into the receiver, "It couldn't be leukemia, could it, doctor?"

For a moment only distant electric whisperings filled the line. Then Dr. Whillans' voice came back. "It could be," he said.

Janis cried when her parents told her that she would have to go to the hospital. "But I'm not really sick," she pleaded. "Honest, I'm just tired."

She worried about missing school. But Rita explained that the doctors would make her better, and in the end Janis stopped crying and went up to her room to get her things. A few minutes later she came downstairs, having said her rosary, and murmured, "I'm ready to go."

The Ottawa Civic Hospital is a sprawling complex of red brick and glass. Janis felt little and lost there at first. But she was through with tears, and resolutely followed the nurse to the children's ward. When Rita and Rudy went in to say good-bye, she was wearing a white hospital gown and sitting cross-legged on her bed, studying the other children in the big white room. As her parents embraced her, she whispered anxiously, "You'll come back to see me, won't you?"

They came—Rita nearly every afternoon, together most evenings. They brought notes from Charmaine and scrawly drawings from Karen which Janis squealed over and displayed to her new friends. She passed the days playing with other young patients; sometimes she shaped funny animals from tissues and sent them home for the small fry.

She reported that the nurses took blood specimens from her fingers every day. "I'm beginning to feel like a pincushion," she laughed. "But if you look away and think of something different, it hardly hurts."

Janis was now in the care of Dr. Alexander English, one of Ottawa's leading hematologists. He promised a report as soon as possible.

It was a tense time of waiting and worrying.

At work, Rudy had to force himself just to perform his most routine tasks. During the drive home from RCMP headquarters in Overbrook each evening, he tried to imagine himself opening the front door and hearing Rita's voice, cheery and gay, the way it used to be before Janis became ill. "It's all right!" she'd be calling to him. "It was just a cold!"

Or an iron deficiency, or the flu—anything but that dread disease that was painful even to think about.

For Rita the hours were no less clouded. She made an effort to busy herself with the other children, household tasks, a magazine. But each time the telephone rang, it was as though she had lived all her life for that single electric instant, as she ran to snatch up the receiver. But it was never Dr. English.

Even Charmaine, now nearly ten, though she had been told only that Janis needed a "checkup," sensed the depth of the trouble. "Don't worry, Mom," she said toward the end of one particularly bleak afternoon. "Janis will be all right. I'm *sure* of it."

Rita clasped the child to her. "Of course she will," she whispered huskily. "You bet she will."

It was on Thursday night, only a little while after they'd returned from visiting Janis, that Dr. English did call. He asked Rudy and Rita if they would come back to the hospital. He was now able to give them a report, he said.

Rudy immediately began pulling on his coat, but Rita stood by the hall closet, fingers pressing her cheeks. Finally she said, "You go alone, all right? I can't. I'll wait for you."

"All right," Rudy said. He understood. He smiled encouragement, touched her arm, and went out.

After the children were in bed a neighbor came over to chat. "You're a good soldier," she said. "And it's going to be all right, wait and see."

When she'd gone, Rita flipped through the pages of a magazine.

Then she turned the television set on, but the images were blurred to her eyes and the words seemed tasteless, absurd. And so, at last, she turned the set off and just sat waiting in the new stillness. That was hardest of all, but there was nothing else she could do, not until Rudy came home.

"It's leukemia," Dr. English said, as soon as he'd closed the door behind the tall, tense Mountie. "There's no easy way to say it, is there? I'm sorry. We've done a thorough study and there isn't any question."

He was an intense, medium-sized man, but his eyes looked very tired, and Rudy remembers thinking that it was probably a terribly discouraging job, terribly hard for this fine doctor, to have to make that grim little pronouncement to different parents day after day, to have to get to know an unending line of children who must soon die. Rudy sank into a chair, for now—and all in a rush—it had come over him that his child, Janis, would die.

"I'm sorry," Dr. English said again.

"There's no—chance?"

The doctor shook his head. "Not for what you're asking," he said kindly. "It's always fatal. But she has what we call a subacute form of the disease, and I don't think she's had it too long. With good care and the medicines we now have, the prognosis is good. She can live a year, maybe more. You have to make the most of that."

Rudy nodded numbly. His first thought was to say something kind to this man who had such an awful job to do. But he could not find the words.

"You're free to take her anywhere you like," Dr. English was saying. "But I'm certain of the diagnosis, and there isn't a hospital in Canada, or the States, that knows more about treating leukemia than we do. It would only be needless expense."

He said that once they had worked out the exact medication and had brought Janis' blood into better balance she could go home. He would need to keep a continuing check on her white-cell count. For this, Rudy was to bring her to the cancer clinic in the hospital every week.

"Otherwise, she can do what she has always done—go to school, play. There's no need to tell her more than that she has something wrong with her blood and we're treating it."

Driving home, Rudy vainly sought a way to break the news to Rita. But as he walked in, he saw it was not necessary. She had guessed—and, after one look at his face, she knew.

Janis was in the hospital for more than a month. In that time, Rita and Rudy came to an intimate knowledge of leukemia. For some medically unfathomable reason, the bone marrow in Janis' body had gone berserk and was producing leucocytes—white blood cells—at a fantastic rate. A normal count would have been perhaps 7,500 per cubic millimeter. Dr. English's examination showed Janis' count to have been 100 times that. Worse, the cells were somehow flawed and would eventually spread through the body, invading healthy tissue, breaking it down.

The Babsons grew all too familiar with words like methotrexate and steroid. These were basic drugs in the battle to slow the inevitable course of the disease. Carefully administered—methotrexate is a nitrogen-mustard derivative and dangerously toxic—they would inhibit the wild leucocyte multiplication.

But soon Rita and Rudy learned the grim limitations of even these marvelous drugs. Gradually, they would lose their effectiveness. In the end, nothing would be of any use at all.

By mid-April, Janis had adjusted to the course of treatment, and was in nearly full remission. She could go home. It was one of those rare spring days, warm with the promise of summer, green stirrings everywhere. By the time the Babsons turned into Côte des Neiges Road, Janis was bouncing with excitement. When she saw Tricia Kennedy waiting in front of the gray-stucco house, she flew from the car.

"Tricia! I'm home! Oh, gosh, Trish!"

Rita Babson watched the two girls embrace. She saw lively new color in her daughter's cheeks, noted the spirit with which she bolted up the steps to greet her brothers and sisters. And she thought that it must all have been a bad dream. Janis was not really going to die. This awful thing could not be happening.

With the passing days, it seemed even more unreal. Janis was back in school and catching up on the work of the missed month. She played as zestfully as ever, and grumbled good-naturedly about the salt-free foods she was limited to. She had been passionate about things like pickles, relish and fish 'n' chips, and one day she improvised a doleful rhyme:

> *Oh, Mommy, please call a halt*
> *To French fries with no salt!*

But she ate well, drank milk in prodigious quantities and steadily gained weight.

On Dr. English's advice, Rita and Rudy had decided not to tell the other children. Janis was to live as happily and normally as possible.

Yet life was changed. Each day had its never-to-be-repeated significance. The things Rita and Rudy had always meant to do "sometime" with the children, they now did—for "sometime" had arrived. There were long automobile trips, games in the evening, a visit from Janis' grandmother. And always there was a persistent sense of disbelief that this sweet and vibrant child was going to be taken away.

Rudy took Janis to the clinic every Thursday morning. Dr. English had told him that if the "Cancer Clinic" sign upset Janis, he would treat her elsewhere, although he preferred the hospital because of the facilities. If Janis ever noticed the words, however, she did not mention them to her father.

She took to her new routine avidly. She rarely missed a chance to dash up to the children's ward and say hello to her beloved Freda, who managed the kitchen. She knew all the youngsters who came to the clinic on Thursday, and she became their guide, ally and champion. To first-timers, frightened by the alien smells and glistening tools of medicine, she was a veteran who could convincingly say, "One quick needle and you're all finished. It hardly hurts."

The hospital personnel were chary of deep feelings for patients they knew were going to die. Yet Janis quickly won over the nurses and technicians in the hematology lab, and flitted from office to office, greeting each one, chatting about school. If someone was absent, she tapped out a genial message on a typewriter: "Dear Miss Jessamyn, I am sorry I missed you today. Where were you? Love, Janis."

They never spoke about her when she was not there. But she could not be denied. "About eleven o'clock every Thursday," says one technician, "there was a sort of expectancy around here. And then she'd be here—like a burst of sunshine."

Steadily the leucocyte count fell.

Janis had a good summer. In September, for her ninth birthday, her parents gave her a new bicycle and, thrilled, she was off on an exploration of the nearby woods. On an even footing again, she and Elizabeth Hayes resumed their competition for the top of Miss McPhee's fourth grade.

But in October she had a setback. She was suddenly drained of energy. Dr. English reported that her leucocyte count had shot up again. The methotrexate had probably lost its effectiveness, he said. He prescribed transfusions, and switched to another drug. It would be well, he told the Babsons, if Janis were not quite so active.

"When will this old blood of mine get better?" she asked her mother. "I've been taking the medicine for so long. Will it ever get better?"

It was the first of many painful questions Rita Babson would have to cope with. Nor was she ever able to settle for a glib evasion. She took her daughter's hands and said, "It's a burden God has given you, sweetheart. Right now, all you can do is bear it. Someday I'm sure you'll know His reason."

Janis, whose faith was absolute, smiled. "I know, Mom. God couldn't make a mistake. I'm just grouchy."

So now she turned the rope for jumping games and handed out equipment during gymnasium periods and, when winter came, watched from the window while the kids went coasting down the hill. "I wish I could go out with them," she once told Charmaine, then added, "but I won't make it any sooner worrying about it."

Slowly she got better again. By March, when, according to Dr. English's prognosis, she ought to have been near the end, she had again

212

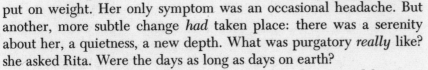

put on weight. Her only symptom was an occasional headache. But another, more subtle change *had* taken place: there was a serenity about her, a quietness, a new depth. What was purgatory *really* like? she asked Rita. Were the days as long as days on earth?

And twice she reminded her parents that she wanted her eyes to go to the Eye Bank.

She had always been anxious to please others; now this seemed to be her greatest happiness. Early Saturday mornings, to the accompaniment of, "Shhh, don't wake Mommy and Daddy," she would shepherd Timmy and Karen down to the basement and play school with them. She taught them to letter and color. Sometimes, lying awake in bed, Rita could hear Janis' small-girl voice in its grown-up cadences: "And now, children, because you have been so good, I am going to read you a story. . . ."

One Saturday, aglow with a new idea, she set out to prepare a truly grand surprise for her parents. While bacon fried and Roddy stood guard at the toaster—"Remember, it has to be golden-brown!"—she dashed out front and cut the summer's first roses.

Hearing the activity, Rita started to get out of bed. Rudy stopped her. "Whatever she's doing, she's having a good time," he said. "Let her be."

A few minutes later, carrying fancy trays, Janis and Roddy came up to present their offering with self-conscious smiles: a sumptuous breakfast embellished with two vases of roses. Rudy was speechless, and Rita could manage only a husky, "Well, what's this all about?"

"You two were so worried when I was sick," Janis said. "I thought this would be a nice way to say thank you. Roddy made the toast."

The Babsons were accustomed to no more than toast and coffee in the morning, but Janis hovered over them, urging them on. "Does it taste all right? Want another cup of coffee, Dad?" They ate every bite. Thereafter Saturday breakfast in bed became a standard offering from Janis to her parents.

By the end of the school year, her blood count was absolutely normal. She hadn't had a transfusion since spring. Unable to help himself, Rudy asked Dr. English one day if the improvement mightn't be permanent, if perhaps the miracle had happened.

"Be grateful she's all right now," the doctor replied. "Don't hope for more—please."

But the Babsons couldn't help it. A new drug, perhaps a

cure—scientists were finding such wonderful new things. "I knew it was wrong," Rita Babson has said, "and that it would only be harder in the end. But what could I do? I tried to make myself believe that Janis was only on loan to us, but it wouldn't work."

Soon it was September again, and Janis, now ten, began the fifth grade. She was delighted that Miss McPhee "got promoted, too," and was to be her teacher. This was the year, she promised her father, that she was going to pull up her lagging arithmetic mark. She did, and also turned her pixie humor loose in composition class. One paper, which Miss McPhee had her read aloud, was entitled, "Me, the Mayor of Ottawa."

In it Janis proposed, among other things, that the Mounted Police have their "salary doubled," and declared that "girls would get anything they wanted free." But she saved her most sweeping reform for the last: "Any juvinile deliquence," she wrote, "would be shot into space."

Her December report was one of her best: 100 in literature, and a new high of 82 in arithmetic. "Keep up the good work, Janis," Miss McPhee wrote on her card.

But school was almost over for Janis. There were unmistakable signs that the two-year battle was taking its final turn. Blood transfusions were necessary now—one every ten days. She had to resign as a captain of the Eucharist Crusaders, a school group, because she couldn't always get to the meetings. She was going to the clinic more often, and sometimes had to wait.

The examinations and tests grew more complicated. The ordinary finger pricks no longer yielded the detailed information Dr. English needed. From time to time it was necessary to do a bone-marrow aspiration—inserting a long needle into Janis' hipbone and drawing out bone marrow for study. It was a very painful operation.

Worst of all, the potent drugs she had been taking for 18 months were gradually changing her appearance. Her pert, slender face had darkened and grown heavy. The quick little body was pudgy now and awkward. In the beginning, Rita tried to pretend it wasn't so, as much for her own sake as for Janis'. But one day at school a child heedlessly remarked, "Hey, Fatty, you'd better go on a diet!" Janis came home crushed.

"Oh, it's *true*, Mommy!" she sobbed. "I'm changing. The kids are ashamed to look at me!"

Heart aching, Rita clasped the child close. No words came to her, and she prayed for guidance. At last she said, "Do you think it matters so much to God how you look, darling? It's what's inside you—what you *feel*. That's what He cares about."

This seemed to appease Janis for the moment. But her spirits weren't really lifted until Friday afternoon a week later when she came running into the house, then wheeled and peered excitedly through the curtain.

Lowering his newspaper, her father asked, "What are you doing, young lady?"

"I'm playing hard-to-get," she replied with her inimitable grin.

"Guess what! Ricky Lewis chased me all the way home from school!"

Rudy lifted the newspaper again and whispered, "Well, bless his heart!"

That December the St. Nicholas school sponsored a Christmas-card sale. The student who sold the most boxes would be awarded a copy of *Ste. Thérèse and the Roses*. Janis set her heart on winning. Thérèse was her favorite saint, and she had carried her tattered likeness for a year.

But by the time Janis got back from the clinic, the other youngsters had already canvassed all of Côte des Neiges Road. Except for her own family and a few close neighbors, there was no one on the street left to sell cards to.

Disconsolate, Janis started up to her room. She said, "If only I didn't have to go to that darn clinic . . . " She suddenly stopped. "That's where I can sell the cards!" she exclaimed. "Why, Miss Craig will buy a box! And Miss Jessamyn and Freda and—oh, Daddy, when do we go again?"

In one quick tour of the hematology lab and the children's ward, she sold enough boxes to win the contest hands down—and promptly came home to read her new book straight through. Beaming, she said to Charmaine, "Ste. Thérèse is my big sister in heaven, just like you're my big sister here."

In gratitude, she made a little Nativity scene of cardboard and cotton batting, and took it to the children's ward of the hospital. "Would you have room for this?" she asked the receptionist.

Touched, the woman said, "Why, we'll give it the place of honor." She swept clear a corner of the information desk and, with great ceremony, installed Janis' gift.

Just before Christmas, Janis' blood began to deteriorate again. Dr. English decided that it was necessary to do another bone-marrow aspiration. Janis turned white. "Please, Daddy," she begged, surrendering to fear for the first time. "I can't. I just can't!"

Rudy held her. "I think you can, Janis," he said softly. "All you need is courage and faith."

Slowly she straightened up. She asked Dr. English and Miss Jessamyn if they would leave her alone for a minute. Then, kneeling on the tile floor of the treatment room, she asked God for the strength to submit to the racking procedure. "I know it's necessary to make me better, dear Lord. But I do need a little extra courage."

Rudy turned away so she would not see his reddened eyes.

By Christmastime, the progress of the disease seemed inexorable. Janis refused to give in to her aches and her weariness, however. She plowed through the snow to school every day, although often Roddy had to help her get back home. Her Christmas shopping was painstaking: a manicure set for her mother, handkerchiefs for her father, toys for the small fry, a pencil case for Roddy, and barrettes glittering with sequins for Charmaine, who now fussed with her hair each night.

When the Babsons came home from Midnight Mass on Christmas Eve, Janis was awake and chatting with the baby-sitter. She was having such a gay time oohing and aahing over the newly decorated tree that Rita hadn't the heart to send her to bed. A few minutes later, though, nausea seized her, and she was content to take a pill and let her father take her upstairs.

Bright and early next morning, as though she'd never known pain in her life, she was down to open her presents with the other children; entranced with the pale-blue party dress her parents had given her, and with the coral pleated skirt and sweater set Grandma Babson sent. There was a battery-powered sewing machine for her; also, new paints, needlework and lots of books. As she sat on the floor, surrounded by wrappings and glitter, she said, "I'll never, never have another Christmas as happy as this one!"

A few weeks later, not long before the final bell of the school day, Janis jerked convulsively in her seat. Even as the pain in her back gathered full strength, she looked quickly around to see if anyone had noticed. She slumped back, trying to make herself inconspicuous, gritting her teeth in silent prayer for the dismissal bell. So, all unknowing, she walked out of St. Nicholas school for the last time. Roddy helped her home through fresh-fallen snow.

One morning a few days later, she had a severe attack of back pains that lasted longer than those at school. Janis was taken to the hospital the next day.

"I assume that the cell mass has spread through the spinal-nerve area," Dr. English said after the examination. "She'd better stay here. We'll see what we can do about that pain."

Janis made no protest when Rudy told her she'd have to be hospitalized again. Her face was drawn with pain and fatigue, but her spirit remained unvanquished. "I'm positive I'll get better sooner here," she said. "I'll be home in a week, you'll see."

An increase in drug strength soon brought her cell count into better balance. In three days she was out of bed and scooting from the kitchen and her great friend Freda down to see the girls in hematology. Feeling quite the old hand, she went from room to room cheering youngsters who were new to the hospital.

There was Betty, a blond girl just Janis' age. She had been operated on for cancer. She worried about missing schoolwork and was delighted when Janis volunteered to drill her in spelling and arithmetic.

One day a younger girl, Susie, whom she'd met on an earlier trip to the hospital, was brought to Janis' room. She seemed very ill. She was lonely and frightened, and Janis told her she would be her special friend. "You don't have to bother the nurses if you need anything. Just tell me." And so she brought Susie the bedpan and innumerable drinks of water and helped feed her at mealtime. Each day, before visiting hours, she straightened Susie's bed and said, "Now remember, no crying when your mother and father get here. They have plenty to worry about without *that*."

Most of all she loved to help the nurses look after the smallest children. She would fluff their pillows, read them stories and make funny colored pictures for them. One night she was awake until daybreak comforting Donna, a three-year-old who had been in an accident and was encased in a plaster cast. That afternoon the nurses solemnly appointed Janis "official unofficial nurse's aide."

But, for all her strength and depth of character, Janis was still a little girl. Despite her friendship with the nurses and technicians, the hospital had remained a thing of the adult world, and she had never suspected the real truth of why she was there. Now some intimation of what lay ahead may have brushed her mind. Sometimes she would walk downstairs to the clinic alone and sit on a bench, a silent, wide-eyed child in a pink bathrobe, and wait for children she had known through the two long years of her treatment there. They never came.

She asked the receptionist, "Doesn't Eddie come on Thursday anymore? And Gloria?" The woman told her no—no, they didn't come on Thursday anymore. Then she looked away.

Soon after that, Janis said to Rita, "Mom, remember Eddie and Gloria? They're dead, aren't they?"

"Yes, dear," was the softly given answer. "They are."

It was Janis who broke the long silence. Her gaze was no longer fixed on her mother, but seemed to have drifted off into the distance. "Don't be sad," she said. "They're in heaven now. They must be happy."

Miss McPhee came to see Janis, and brought letters from all her classmates. Janis was thrilled. She had to hear about each of them, and questioned Miss McPhee exhaustively.

Charmaine sent an eagerly awaited note with her parents each evening. Once, when she missed, Janis said sharply, "Tell Charmaine to get with it. I need to know what's going on."

Each word from Charmaine, each little trinket from Roddy or Karen, was tangible assurance that she was remembered, missed. More than anything else, the sense of closeness to her family sustained Janis through these days.

She busied herself making an elaborate Valentine card for Dr. English—and was enthralled when she got one from Ronnie, the Little Leaguer. "You were right, Mom!" she announced as soon as the Babsons walked in that night. "Looks are absolutely *not* everything!"

By the middle of February, she was able to go home again. But, because of the severe weather, Dr. English would not allow her to go to school. An ordinary cold could now have serious consequences.

Janis would sit by the dining-room window, watching until the last of the neighborhood youngsters had trooped down the hill to school. Then she'd turn to a book, or the mittens she was knitting for Sally. Sometimes, in the lonely afternoons, she grew restless and blue. "Mom," she'd call out, "forget the housework for a while and keep me company." Her favorite story, which she begged Rita to tell over and over, was how she and Rudy had met and married.

After school, friends came to visit. Invariably, from some deep resource, Janis rallied her energy to entertain them. Once, amid peals of laughter, Rita heard a girl gasp, "Oh, Janis, please stop! I'm suffocating with laughing." Her old rival, Elizabeth Hayes, brought some schoolwork, and the two chatted for a long time. When she left, Janis said, "They're learning to do fractions. I'll *never* catch up."

The pain grew worse. It was almost constant now, and though Janis hated to speak of it, her twisted face betrayed every spasm. Sometimes a sharp, uncontrollable cry rang through the house in the dark.

Rudy had to carry her to the car for clinic visits. To spare her further torment, the girls in hematology came out to the parking lot to take their blood specimens. Even that was agony, for they were now taking up to ten separate vials and smears each time, and Janis' arms and legs became pocked with wounds and scars.

"Always keep something in reserve," Dr. English had warned Rita in connection with the codeine doses Janis got. "Otherwise, at the end, nothing will hold her." But the vials emptied more and more quickly.

Early on March 15, Janis was struck with another racking session of pain in her back. It lasted into the late afternoon, her struggle with it so intense that Rita found herself desperately wishing that Janis would faint, anything to give her some respite from this unending torture. Finally, Rudy called for an ambulance, and Janis was sped to the hospital.

Dr. English promptly ordered a series of massive radiation treatments. It was an extreme measure, but he hoped that the X rays might shrink the rioting block of cells concentrated at the base of Janis' spine, relieving the pain and, perhaps, restoring some mobility to her legs.

But Janis never walked again. Instead, she was fitted with a back brace for support, and confined to her hospital bed. Still, she rarely complained and never spoke of any unhappiness. But one evening, when Rita and Rudy came to the ward for a visit, they found her dozing, a notebook open by her side. In it, she had just written this wistful record of her loneliness:

> At this moment I am crying for my dear, dear, dear mother and father as I am homesick in this hospital. I don't think I shall ever let myself think anything mean about them again in my life as right now I see how much I love them.

Rita put the notebook down. She and Rudy were badly shaken by what they'd read—and poignantly reminded that Janis' time was running out. That night they came to a decision and, in the morning Rudy telephoned Dr. English. If he brought Janis to the hospital as often as necessary, he said, if he and Rita followed instructions explicitly, couldn't they take Janis home?

"I suppose so," English said slowly. "It's—getting late, isn't it? There isn't very much more we can do."

Charmaine and Roddy made an enormous "Welcome Home" sign, but one of Janis' worst fears was realized: little Sally was strange with her. Lying on the living-room couch, barely able to move, Janis would call and call, to no avail. Once she intentionally dropped the little statue of the child Jesus that she had been carrying and begged, "Will you get that for Janis, please, Sally?"

The child permitted herself to be coaxed closer until, finally, Janis reached out and embraced her. "Oh, honey, I just want to hold you for a second. Don't you remember Janis?"

Sally began to squirm, then cry. Shattered, Janis let her go. "She doesn't even know me, Mom," she sobbed.

"You've been away so much, dear," Rita said gently. "And she's only a baby."

"But if I die—oh, Mommy, if I die, she won't *ever* remember me!"

Overwhelmed, Rita turned quickly away.

Janis read a little. As long as she was able to sit up, she could still knit, slowly and patiently. But mostly she just stared out the window and down the road. Pain was almost always with her. "It's as though someone were dragging a rough old tree branch through my back," Janis said. The rioting cells, massed at her spine, had begun to infiltrate her head, with the result that her teeth ached. She would bite fiercely on the little statue of Jesus, now seldom out of her hands. A vein in her temple throbbed, and often she grew dizzy. At last there was no choice: Janis had to go back to the hospital.

Later, Dr. English found Rita and Rudy, nervous and exhausted, waiting for him in the long corridor outside the children's ward. "There's nothing else we can do," he said. "I told you—I'm no miracle man. I . . ." He shook his head hopelessly, plainly in the grip of a very deep emotion, and walked away.

Soon afterward, Janis asked her father what was wrong with Dr.

English. "He used to stay and joke with me, and now he doesn't even look at me when he's here. Doesn't he like me anymore?"

"It isn't you, honey," Rudy assured her. "He's just—busy."

A remarkable camaraderie had sprung up between the little girl and the doctor in all the long months past; his face had lit up whenever the child marched into his treatment room at the clinic. Now the game was up. He could help her no longer, and it hurt more than he dared show.

Incredibly, Janis rallied. She was getting massive morphine doses now and, with the worst of the pain abated, her wasted little body found strength to fight back. Her uncles Jim and Joe came to see her, and Janis, who loved nothing better than company, responded with much of her old vivacity. She made them laugh with her complaints that she couldn't get a toe out from under the tight hospital sheets.

Next afternoon, due back in Kingston, Uncle Joe stopped at the hospital for a last good-bye. But Janis had been given some phenobarbital and was asleep. Later, learning that she had missed him, she was heartbroken. That evening, when the Babsons came to see her, she was dozing again, but this time there was a sheet of paper resting on her chest.

"If anybody comes and I'm asleep," it read, "don't go away!!!"

Slowly she began sinking again. Even morphine held her for only a few hours, and the end was plainly near. The day after she was admitted, the hospital chaplain had given her Extreme Unction, the final sacrament of the Roman Catholic Church.

The Babsons made up their minds that if there was one thing that would lighten Janis' last days—anything, no matter how much it cost—they would buy it for her. But Janis shook her head when they asked her.

"I've already cost you so much money," she said. "Besides, I really have everything." Then she worked her face into the shadow of a sly grin. "Anything?"

"Anything," Rudy promised.

"I'd like to see the kids again!" she said with a rush. "I know it's against hospital rules, but maybe you could sneak Charmaine up—just Charmaine. That wouldn't be so wrong, would it?"

Next evening, Charmaine between them, Rita and Rudy slipped up a back stairway to Janis' room. "Oh, oh, oh! You did it!" Janis squealed. She threw up her arms, and the sisters fell into a hectic embrace, kissing and hugging. Charmaine was wearing a brand-new yellow hat, and insisted that Janis try it on. They laughed and chattered away while the Babsons, who had closed the door, stood watching.

Janis was a parade of questions: "How's school? Do you ever see Ricky Lewis? Tell me about the small fry!"

Suddenly, the supervisor opened the door, and Charmaine drew in her breath. The woman stopped short, took in the scene with a glance, then strode briskly to Janis' bed and gave her a pill.

"What makes you so happy?" she said offhandedly, eyes sweeping past Charmaine as though no one sat on the far side of the bed. Then she went out, closing the door.

For a long time, Janis and Charmaine talked on. Too soon, visiting hours were over. "Don't forget me," Janis said as they parted. "Don't let the little ones forget me."

Outside, the Babsons told Charmaine for the first time that Janis was going to die. The tears that Charmaine had stifled all evening came freely, and she sobbed, "Why, why?"

Next morning, Janis herself learned the truth. A young intern and a nurse new to the floor came into her room. "And what's wrong with you, my pretty?" the doctor asked gaily. Before Janis could speak, the nurse, reading from her chartbook, said, "She has leukemia."

The intern flashed her a furious look, but the damage was done. Janis, who knew what the word meant, lay alone until afternoon, turning it over and over in her mind. When Rita came, she said, "I have leukemia, don't I?"

Rita stood ashen-faced. She had a wild impulse to flee. "What makes you think that?" she said finally. Then Janis told her what had happened.

"How would you feel if you did have leukemia?" Rita said quietly. "Would it frighten you?"

Janis shook her head. "If that's what I have, it must be God's will that I should have it. What is there to be afraid of? Anyhow, I might still get better."

In a little while, though, she came to grips with herself, making a silent transition from hope to acceptance. Triumphantly, she said, "You know, Mom, I've been praying so hard to get better, and I always wondered why I didn't. Now I know—because God didn't mean for me to get better. He wants me."

They sat together without speaking. Rita felt a great calm. All these months she had steeled herself to see Janis through this dread moment. Now the moment was here, and Janis was seeing *her* through it.

Later, in a very businesslike way, Janis asked about purgatory. "Do you think I'll have to stay there long? I've got quite a few scores to settle up, you know."

Rita Babson held her very close. "You've been in purgatory for over two years, darling. When dear God is ready for you, I'm sure He'll take you right to heaven."

On Saturday, May 6, Janis told her mother that she wanted to make a will. "People do that before they die, right?"

"Yes," Rita said after a pause.

Noting her mother's unhappiness, she said, "Please don't be sad, Mommy. That's the one thing that bothers me, that you and Daddy will be sad. You still have the other kids. And I'll be there whenever you need me, I promise."

So Janis prepared for her long last journey:

". . . My new bike is for Charmaine, and my paint set goes to Roddy."

None of this is true, Rita was thinking. It just isn't happening. It is a nightmare, and I can wake up if I really put my mind to it.

But, she went on stoically writing in her notebook as Janis dictated. Janis asked that her brace be given to some other child who might need it, that Freda be told where she was buried in case she wanted to visit the grave. "Give Daddy my prayer book and my piggy bank, and I want you to have my bath salts. And, Mommy, please don't forget about the Eye Bank."

Rita walked quickly to the hospital chapel to pray.

On the morning of May 12, Rita brought Janis a new picture of Ste. Thérèse. Janis gazed at it tenderly. "She's smiling," she said. "She's expecting me."

Soon Janis was drifting in and out of coma. An oxygen tent had been placed over her head to ease her breathing, and the nurses were instructed to give her morphine as often as necessary. It had little effect on the pain, now, though.

Across the hall someone was playing a radio, and a nurse stopped to ask if Janis wanted it turned down. Rita was about to say yes when Janis shook her head feebly. "I love it," she whispered, and tried wiggling her toes in time to the music. With a last trace of her impish grin, she said, "If these darn sheets weren't so tight, I could really beat it out."

Rudy stayed on through the night, while Rita went home to sleep. When Rita returned the next morning, a nurse, who had plainly been crying, stopped her in the corridor. "Please tell her how nice she looks," the nurse said. "She wanted us to—get her ready."

They had bathed her and combed her hair, although each touch and movement were agonizing to the child. Then Janis had insisted on wearing her new pink nightgown with the tiny white flowers. They had had to slit it up the back to get it on.

"Oh, you look lovely!" Rita said when she walked in.

Janis smiled. She was clear-eyed but very weak. "I'm ready any time now," she said. "But I'd like you and Daddy to stay with me."

She had remembered that it was Karen's birthday, and asked if it was a nice day. Rita told her it was. "I'm glad," she said.

She drifted off, awoke, slept again. Once she asked Rita if she could be weighed after she died. "I want to know if I'm going to heaven the way I used to be—nice and thin."

"Your body is only a dress, darling," Rita said. "Anyhow, how could I tell you?"

Janis laughed aloud. "Of course! I'm getting dumb in my old age." She closed her eyes. "But you will dress me nicely, won't you? And put a ribbon in my hair?"

In the late afternoon, as though struggling up out of a bad dream, she opened her eyes and spoke very clearly. "Daddy! Have you made the arrangements with the Eye Bank!"

Stricken, Rudy exchanged a look of raw pain with Rita. He admitted that he had not.

"You promised me! I want you to do it now. Please."

The Babsons had talked a great deal about Janis' persistent request. They never doubted that it was more than mere whim—or that they'd be haunted with guilt if they failed her. Yet did such a little girl really understand?

Now, in their exchange of glances, they thought they knew. She

222

did understand. This was the gift she wanted most of all to bestow.

Rudy went to one of the nurses. "Miss Chapman," he began uncertainly, "Janis—she wants to give her eyes to the Eye Bank when she's gone. I don't know how to—I . . ." He shook his head. "I promised her, but I don't know what to do."

"I'll phone Dr. English," Miss Chapman said. "We'll arrange it, Corporal Babson. Tell Janis not to worry."

In an hour, an intern came with a form for Rudy to fill out and sign, and the business was done. Janis smiled at her father. "Thank you," she breathed.

By 9 p.m., Janis was so weak that she made no more effort than to open her eyes from time to time to look from Rita to Rudy. Content that they were close by, she would sigh and slip off again.

Then, quite suddenly, she struggled to sit up. Her eyes were wide and staring straight ahead, as though she couldn't see enough of what stretched before her.

"Oh, is this heaven?" she called out. "Mommy! Daddy! Come quick!"

They bent to her, held her, amazed at the sudden strength in the wasted little arms pulling them into a last embrace. And then there was no strength at all.

It was 9:25 p.m. Hours later, Janis' precious eyes were en route to Eye Bank headquarters in Toronto.

All the St. Nicholas school was at the funeral. Elizabeth Hayes, sobbing, was held and comforted by Miss McPhee. Janis' closest friend, Tricia Kennedy, had moved away, and could not get to the service. Janis lay serene and lovely in her pale-blue party dress. The pert velvet ribbon her mother had tied in her hair would have delighted her.

"Janis was heartbroken to discontinue school, for she wanted so much to finish the grade with the rest of the class," said the Rev. Frederick Brossler, pastor of St. Augustine's Church. "Well, a happy and peaceful journey to you, Janis. You have graduated with highest honors."

The Babsons came home from the cemetery uplifted, somehow. Janis' life would always be unique and wonderful to them, of course. But they sensed something more, an answer to their grieving question—why?—although they did not yet know quite what it was. Her uncle Bob Quinn put it this way: "That child's ten years on this earth are not all there is to it. It can't be."

Soon afterward, in Chalk River, Ont., a local reporter was interviewing a newly arrived family for a meet-your-neighbor page. They were the Kennedys, formerly of Côte des Neiges Road. He asked if they had any human-interest stories to round out his copy.

"I do," Tricia piped up. And then she told how her best friend, Janis Babson, dying of leukemia, had pledged her eyes to the Eye Bank.

The reporter phoned columnist Tim Burke of *The Ottawa Journal* and Burke went to see the Babsons. The day after his story appeared in the *Journal*, 27 Ottawans signed pledges donating their eyes to the Eye Bank. It was a one-day record—and was almost immediately broken when, at a meeting of the local Kinsmen club, 50 members spontaneously bequeathed their eyes. Not long after, 175 Mounties and their families did the same.

The ripples continued to spread. Burke's story was picked up by the Canadian wire services. A few months later, a nun who had heard Janis' story wrote a touching memoir, entitled *Janis of City View.* Letters began descending on the stucco house on Côte des Neiges Road. Rita and Rudy devoted an hour or so each evening to answering them.

Finally, in Toronto, a retired druggist named Abe Silver read about Janis. He was so moved that he established the Janis Babson Memorial Endowment Fund at the Hebrew University in Jerusalem for prizes in leukemia research.

But most remarkable has been the continuing growth in Ottawans' pledges to the Eye Bank. From 1959, when unofficial records were first kept, until the day Janis died, a total of 644 had promised their eyes at death. In the two years following her death, there were 1,710 pledges, including all the Babson family. Week after week, Ottawans inspired by the grace and goodness of a little girl take the step which someday will bring sight to many hundreds of blind men and women.

Janis forgotten?

She remains, as she hoped she would, very much a part of the life she loved so deeply.

To
Some
Good
Purpose

My own prescription
is to live life
to some good purpose,
live it dangerously
if need be,
but with all one's strength
and common sense

WILDER PENFIELD

"Look, Man! Look!"

By Dr. Nelles Silverthorne

For a small country, Canada has produced a surprising number of world-renowned doctors. The stories of some of them—William Osler, Wilder Penfield, Frederick Banting and Charles Best, Wilfred Grenfell and Hans Selye—were told in the Reader's Digest book Canada: This Land, These People. *On these next 24 pages are stories of five other Canadian doctors, each outstanding in his own field and in his own way: a great pediatrician, an international leader in rehabilitation medicine, a lonely and beloved country doctor, a man who dedicated his life to the Indians of the West Coast, and an unassuming Albertan who demonstrates rare wisdom and insight as a general practitioner.*

They used to say of Dr. Alan Brown, Canada's pioneer pediatrician, that he could walk behind a patient leaving the admitting desk at Toronto's Hospital for Sick Children and tell you what the patient's trouble was. Those of us who studied under him believed it implicitly. His passion for detailed examination was plain enough—I can still hear him saying, "Look, man! Look!" But then he would make a diagnosis so dazzlingly intuitive that it smacked of black magic.

With a kind of built-in medical radar he'd be reacting to a focus of infection before the rest of us had our stethoscopes unpacked.

I was making rounds with him one Saturday when we came to a listless little lad with a low-grade fever. "Glandular fever," the resident physician had written on the chart. "Frequent throat rinses prescribed."

"Tonsils, without looking," Brown muttered to me. Then, "Open your mouth, sonny."

On Monday morning, returning from a weekend, the resident rushed to Brown's office: "Where's my patient? What about the rinses?"

"Rinses, my foot!" Brown snorted. "That boy never had glandular fever. I had his tonsils taken out and sent him home. Look, man! Look!"

Brown *was* the Hospital for Sick Children—or "Sick Kids," as everyone in Toronto calls it. All you heard there was "Dr. Brown says" or "Dr. Brown thinks." And with good reason. He had come in the days when pediatrics was scorned as a fad and stayed on as physician-in-charge for 33 years, never accepting a penny for his services. He ran things to suit himself—which is to say, in the best interests of the patients. "Sick Kids" became one of the great hospitals of its kind.

I was a brand-new medical graduate when I arrived at the Hospital for Sick Children to become his disciple and protégé. All the really significant things I learned about pediatrics I learned from this fiery little man who could make you feel like Hippocrates if you'd done your homework or blast you to dust for a slovenly diagnosis.

In theater clinic he was the consummate showman. Once he gently handed us a baby who the day before had fallen from a third-

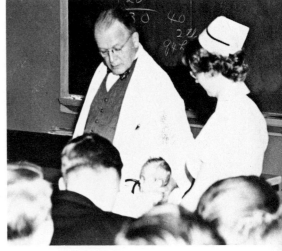

story window. "Now tell me what's wrong with him," he said.

One after another, we offered complicated diagnoses involving internal hemorrhages and fractured vertebrae. Dr. Brown shook his head wearily. "There's not a thing in the world wrong with this baby," he said, "and if you'd use your eyes instead of your preconceived notions you'd see it."

Far from expending all his caustic wit on students, he had a fair share left for parents and doting aunts. "Grandmothers," he was fond of saying, "are a baby's worst friends. Respiratory infections don't fly in the window, you know. They come from relatives who haven't got sense enough not to hang over a defenseless infant's crib and spray it with their germs."

In spite of his outspokenness, Brown maintained the most crowded waiting room in Toronto. He was a brilliant doctor and, when he picked up a sick child, the embodiment of gentleness. For all his explosiveness, he was an electrically inspiring teacher. Of 255 practicing pediatricians in Canada when he retired in late 1951, 186 were trained by Alan Brown. Of 11 chairs in pediatric medicine in Canadian universities, four were occupied by onetime Brown students.

It was as a lad in turn-of-the-century Toronto that Alan Brown decided to become a doctor. His mother, Canada's first woman medical student, had traded medicine for marriage, and as the oldest of her four children Alan picked up the torch. From the first he was single-minded about it. True, an uncommonly pretty girl named Constance

Alan Brown was always magnificently the same, always exuding a faint aroma of baby powder, always dapper with a perky bow tie and shoes shined to mirror brilliance. And always those clear blue eyes looked straight at you, ready to turn steely at stupidity. One morning at the University of Toronto he asked his class, "What is klim?" In the back row a doubtful voice began, "I think, sir, that it's the condition following—" "It's no condition!" snapped Brown. He whirled on Nelles Silverthorne, the author of this story. "What's klim, Silverthorne?" "It's—uh—milk spelled backward, sir," he gulped. The class broke into laughter, but the blue eyes softened. "You happen to be exactly right," he said, and turned back to the hushed class. "The point is, give your brains a chance to work instead of lapsing into a coma every time I ask a question."

Alan Brown introduced a bustling air of enlightenment at "Sick Kids" (right, the old building on Toronto's College Street). Frederick Banting went there as an intern and was a staff consultant at the time of his history-making discovery, with Drs. Charles H. Best and J. J. R. Macleod, that a substance called insulin offered new life to millions of diabetics. Drs. Frederick Tisdall and T. G. H. Drake sparked extensive nutritional studies and, with a whoop of joy at finding kindred spirits, Brown joined in. The three developed a vitamin-enriched precooked cereal that became famous as Pablum. All royalties went to the hospital's Pediatric Research Foundation.

Hobbs finally pierced the wall of medical texts around Brown. But the courtship was a trying one. Once the young doctor-to-be left her in a hospital waiting room and rushed off to a postmortem, after which he forgot all about her and went home. She became Mrs. Brown nevertheless, and the marriage was a 47-year success.

Most pre-World War I doctors approached childhood ills with a deadening sense of inevitability. A youngster admitted to a hospital with diphtheria, pneumonia or meningitis had barely one chance in two of coming out alive. What can you do, asked the doctors, when all you have to work with are aspirins and mustard plasters?

Brown stubbornly refused to share this view. He went to New York to study at Babies Hospital, then on to the great medical centers of Europe for more training. And in 1914, the first full-fledged pediatrician in all Toronto, bursting to put his skills to work, he presented himself at the Hospital for Sick Children—only to be turned down cold. There was no place at "Sick Kids," the hidebound staff told him, for the upstart notions of a "foreign-trained baby-feeder."

Alan Brown dug out figures on the infant mortality rate at "Sick Kids": an appalling 155 deaths for every 1,000 admissions. He went to John Ross Robertson, chairman of the hospital board of trustees. "Give me a place on the staff and a free hand," Brown said bluntly, "and I'll cut that rate in half."

Robertson, whose own daughter had died of scarlet fever not long before, agreed. Soon Brown was sweeping through the hospital like a gust of fresh air, ventilating the wards and clinics of musty practices. First to go was the time-honored technique for cutting feeding time in the nursery—one aide standing between two cribs with a bottle in each hand. "Pick 'em up!" Brown ordered. "There isn't any more important way you can spend that 20 minutes."

Among the other upstart notions introduced by the "foreign-trained baby-feeder": immunization against diphtheria; pasteurization of hospital milk; the use of ultraviolet light to cut down secondary infections; a pediatrics course for unskilled helpers in the nursery. Brown more than fulfilled his promise to Robertson and was soon named physician-in-chief.

230

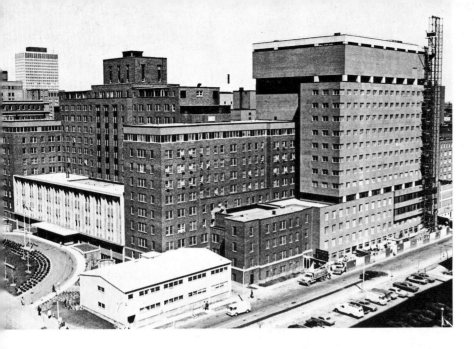

The new "Sick Kids," one of the world's great children's hospital, was Alan Brown's greatest achievement. There were many others. He was among the first to point an accusing finger at diet as a cause of dental cavities. A pamphlet prepared under his direction stripped the miasma of shame and superstition from mental illness in children. He badgered Toronto's welfare clinics until they all routinely administered diphtheria toxoid. Among the pithily phrased assertions he flung at modern mothers with their formula-fed infants was, "You're subletting your duty to a cow. Cow's milk is for calves. Now go and use what the good Lord gave you."

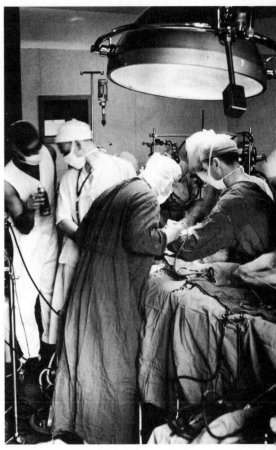

Years later, during a battle with dairymen over compulsory milk pasteurization, Brown marched up to Ontario's Premier Mitchell F. Hepburn during a formal dinner party and declared, "If you want to know why we need pasteurization, come to 'Sick Kids' tomorrow."

Hepburn came—and saw children with bovine tuberculosis, a grim by-product of raw milk. "I know you have political problems," Brown pressed, "but sometimes a situation calls for plain guts." Within the year, Ontario became the largest governmental body with compulsory pasteurization.

In the late 1940s Brown began talking about a new home for "Sick Kids," a building with the latest research facilities and equipment. Though hospital money is notoriously hard to come by, none of us was greatly surprised when he produced a scale model of an 11-story, 647-bed new "Sick Kids" and said, "There she is—be ready in '51."

It was to be his memorial and his most enduring achievement. He spent so much time at the site during the construction that his granddaughter, riding past one day, cried, "Mommy, look! There's Gramps' new house!" It became one of the great centers for pediatric research and treatment, its $13,900,000 price tag a tangible mark of the goodwill built up by "Sick Kids" staffs. Here was a lab where ophthalmologists would develop an artificial eye woven to natural muscle, so lifelike it fooled a class of medical students; here damaged hearts would be stopped, repaired and set to beating again. From all over the world, children would come to "Sick Kids" in search of the latest and best medical help.

For almost a year Brown strutted the gleaming corridors, showing off the new hospital as though it were his personal possession. Then, abruptly, he quit. "Go as hard as you can for as long as you can," he said to me on the bleak evening when he broke the news. "But when you can't give your best—quit!"

He maintained his private practice for a while. But one hot summer day in 1960, Dr. Brown made rounds for the last time. Next evening he suffered a cerebral vascular accident—how he would have scoffed if I used so unscientific a term as stroke!—and died as he would have wished to, quickly and with no fuss.

The Gift
for Inspiring Hope

By David MacDonald

When Canada was asked in 1965 to provide a rehabilitation center for the war-maimed of South Vietnam, Ottawa naturally sought aid from Dr. Gustave Gingras of Montreal, one of the world's top specialists in treating and training disabled people. And "Gus" Gingras just naturally gave it. When others need help, he feels, we should always say, "OK, sure thing."

A roly-poly little French Canadian with close-cropped hair and merry brown eyes, Gingras promptly flew to Saigon, where he was appalled to find that 60 percent of all wounded Vietnamese were permanently crippled. Despite massive American assistance, 35,000 amputees still had only makeshift artificial limbs—or none. Worse, to Gingras, was the despair he sensed in crowded children's hospitals. "I saw hundreds of kids, but none of them ever smiled."

Convinced that the proposed rehab center was desperately needed, he lost no time in recruiting staff for what seemed like an OK-sure-thing. But it wasn't. For 14 months, while Gingras fumed, neutrality-minded Canadian diplomats balked at putting the clinic into Vietnamese military hands, as Saigon insisted, and discussions bogged down.

Mon Dieu, children suffer through all this damn talk," Gingras angrily told foreign-aid officials in Ottawa. "Now it's time to *act!*" So he finally talked to newsmen. As he'd hoped, irate Canadians on reading of the delays raised such loud protests that the government quickly came to terms: it would build a $2,500,000 center at Qui Nhon, north of Saigon, as part of a new civilian-run rehab program.

For his further part, Gingras organized a team of 12 Canadian doctors, nurses, physiotherapists and prosthetists to work there, trained 20 Vietnamese therapists in Montreal, then flew back for the Qui Nhon center's formal opening in 1969. There, watching two small polio victims learning to walk again, he felt fully repaid. "This time," he fondly recalls, "the children were smiling."

As an expert in rehab medicine, a recipient of the prized Lasker Award for international service, Gus Gingras has spent more than a quarter-century helping people in many lands to overcome physical handicaps caused by war, disease, accidents or birth defects.

It's no small job: the world's disabled total more than 300,000,000, including five Canadians in every 100. But he tackles it with a contagious air of confidence. A Falstaffian figure at five-six and a round 200 pounds, Gingras is bouncy, ebullient, given to booming laughter. At his multimillion-dollar Rehabilitation Institute of Montreal, whether he's romping on its nursery floor with a lame child or joking among elderly arthritics, his natural *bonhomie* serves as good medicine. "I want my patients to be cheerful," he says. "That's the spirit they need to face their problems."

It also helps to have a Samaritan for a doctor. Once, on a visit to Bolivia, Gingras met a sad-faced Indian boy, who'd lost both arms, amputated after he'd touched a high-tension electric cable. "I think," he said through a translator, "we must get you some new ones." He wangled an airline ticket and the boy went to Montreal, where stump surgery readied him for gas-powered mechanical arms. For months, Gingras and his wife brought him home on weekends, took him to

A vital ingredient of Dr. Gustave Gingras' medicine for the disabled is his own hearty laugh and smiling *bonhomie.* Most patients, like the youngster opposite, have been Canadians. Others, among them Santos Ramirez, an armless Bolivian boy, have come long distances to be rehabilitated at Gingras' institute in Montreal. With Santos Ramirez in this 1954 picture are occupational therapist Doris Campbell and (standing) a famous visitor, Nurse Geneviève de Galard. She had recently left Indochina, having won world acclaim as "the angel of Dien Bien Phu," during a great battle in which she remained with besieged French soldiers whose positions were being overrun by the communist enemy.

movies, gave him presents—Gingras even gave him the overcoat off his own back. Now, nearly 20 years later, they still correspond regularly, his protégé happily supporting himself by working at a government agency in La Paz.

"The great thing about Dr. Gingras," says another former patient, "is his gift for inspiring hope." Crippled by polio in 1955, when he was a young college professor, Neil Compton spent weeks in a wheezing iron lung, then 18 months at the rehab institute. However hopeless he felt, Gingras wouldn't let him give up. Today, though still confined to a wheelchair, he is a full professor in the English department at Sir George Williams University in Montreal. When Gingras received an honorary degree there in 1967, the citation read by Neil Compton was a moving expression of the deep gratitude in many hearts. "To thousands of disabled people," he declared, "the work of Dr. Gingras has meant the difference between life and living death."

Yet he didn't plan it that way.

At college, Gustave Gingras played the title role in Molière's *Le Bourgeois Gentilhomme* and dreamed of a stage career, until his family deflected him into medicine. "He wasn't a very promising student," notes a former teacher. "It was only later that he developed his fantastic sense of responsibility to others."

Late in World War II, fresh from medical school, Gingras was posted to a Canadian Army hospital in England. He was struck by the outlook of soldiers who'd been permanently disabled. "Some were crushed by the loss of only one finger," he says. "But others wouldn't even let paralysis keep them down. All they wanted was help."

Moved by their plight, Gingras put off postwar plans to study neurosurgery and, at the urging of Montreal's famed Dr. Wilder Pen-

Some of the many accomplishments of rehabilitation medicine: at the Canadian center near Saigon, a Vietnamese goes for a fitting of his artificial leg; at his home in Montreal, after rehabilitation at the Ste-Anne-de-Bellevue military hospital, paraplegic veteran Charles Kelsey paints a fencepost....

field, took on rehabilitation work at a veterans' hospital in suburban Ste-Anne-de-Bellevue. "He had loads of optimism," Dr. Penfield remembers, "which was just what his patients would need—and he had the initiative, kindness and intelligence to go with it."

Small and still thin at 27, but with a moustache cultivated to make him seem older, Gingras was assigned to a ward filled with bedridden young paraplegics. He coaxed them through long, hard rehabilitation sessions until most could struggle out of bed, move around in wheelchairs or walk with the aid of braces and crutches. "*Voilà!*" he'd cry, beaming. "That's the first step back." Besides starting psychological counseling and job-training programs, he took his patients to hockey games, picnics—anything to transport them into the outside world.

"He made us feel," recalled George Petrie, crippled at 20 in an ammunition-dump explosion, "that we didn't have to spend the rest of our days in Ward 1B."

When Petrie spoke of going back to college, for example, Gingras helped arrange for his enrollment at McGill, drew up his lecture schedule, got other student vets to drive him back and forth. After earning a B.A., Petrie studied law, married and became a successful notary. In fact, most of Ward 1B's paraplegic veterans have long since made good on "civvy street," as lawyers, stockbrokers, watchmakers, draftsmen.

Then came Helen Regan, a young stenographer who'd broken her back in a fall and spent two years in bed, paralyzed from the waist down. In 1946, Gingras slashed government red tape to get her admitted as the first civilian rehab patient at Ste. Anne's Military Hospital. As therapy slowly revived both her body and morale so she could sit erect, he hired her to type his records. Now married to an engineer,

... veteran and civilian join an army RPTI (remedial physical training instructor) in a badminton game at Ste-Anne; and Neil Compton (above, with Gingras), although crippled by polio, teaches again at Sir George Williams University in Montreal. Gingras' work, said the citation when SGWU awarded him an honorary degree, has meant for disabled persons "the difference between life and living death."

she has been Gingras' personal secretary—a highly efficient one—ever since.

From then on, he felt mounting concern for all other handicapped civilians who languished for lack of adequate rehab facilities. So in 1950, backed by local Rotary Clubs, Gingras helped found the Rehabilitation Institute of Montreal in the converted poolroom of an old hotel. With outmoded equipment and only three aides, he soon achieved amazing results.

Then, as now, he took a warm personal interest in every case. "It should be compulsory for all medical students to attend his clinic," another physician wrote in *The Montreal Star*, "and learn that a doctor must always treat a *patient*, rather than a goofoofoo valve in an object all wrapped in white."

In 1953, as his reputation spread, the United Nations asked Gingras to make an on-the-spot survey and to plan a rehabilitation program for Venezuela. A year later, near Caracas, he opened the first South American center to offer a complete range of rehab services, and arranged for local doctors and nurses to get special training in Canada. He also talked the Venezuelan government into starting its own school of physiotherapy.

In 1959, when 10,000 Moroccans were paralyzed after consuming adulterated cooking oil, Gingras was the first Canadian doctor to fly to their aid. Put in charge of 180 medical and paramedical volunteers from 16 lands—the biggest rehabilitation team ever assembled by the League of Red Cross Societies—he faced a daunting task. Reported one U.S. news magazine: "Most of the victims can look forward to a lifetime as cripples."

But Gingras had higher hopes. Darting about by plane and jeep, often laboring around the clock, he set up emergency clinics in a garage, an army barracks, even a morgue. "Watching him work was like watching a comet," one colleague later observed. "All you saw was a fiery trail."

Under Gingras, doctors assessed all 10,000 cases, then therapists began reeducating muscles made useless by the poisoned oil. The results: in a year, 8,000 patients were returned to normal life. After 18 months, incredibly, only 272 were classed as incurable paralytics. To cap his mission, Gingras got the World Health Organization to build a rehab hospital in Morocco, as well as Africa's first physiotherapy school.

Since 1956, Gingras had been campaigning to build a modern new home for his Montreal institute, with 110 beds and facilities for 200 out-patients. Besides planning every detail, from the size of its limb-making prosthetics lab to the gay colors in children's playrooms, he led a Rotary Club drive for $3,500,000, lobbied for government grants, talked himself hoarse at fund-raising dinners. Every time builders quit work, for lack of money, Gingras went begging for more. "I used to be a pretty fair physician," he told one friend, "but now I'm just a medical con-man."

His new hospital, its staff now grown to 265, opened in 1962, just when the tranquilizing drug thalidomide was causing 5,000 babies to be born with cruel deformities.

Helen Regan, now Mrs. Andrew Lippay, was the first civilian paraplegic patient at Ste. Anne's Hospital near Montreal. Once rehabilitated, she became Dr. Gingras' secretary—and still is.

In Canada, which had 115 such cases, Gingras was asked to care for 43 of the infants, most of them born with pathetic little flipper-like limbs. His first task was to persuade grief-stricken parents to keep their babies, instead of hiding them away in institutions. "He made no promises," one young mother remembers. "But he gave us hope."

While the thalidomide children were gradually learning to toddle and play with the aid of mechanical prostheses, Gingras kept searching for better devices. In 1964 he read about a Russian invention which used myoelectricity—the tiny impulses emitted by contracting muscles—to control a motorized plastic hand. So he flew to Moscow and bid $30,000 for Canadian patent rights.

"But we haven't got the money," cautioned an aide.

"*Eh bien*," Gingras replied, "I'll scrounge for it." And he did.

Working from the Russian prosthesis for adults with below-elbow amputations, Canadian engineers evolved the world's first complete electromechanical arm for children. Fixed to a plastic vest, the three-pound limbs can be directed by "muscle electricity" picked up through skin electrodes, or (for thalidomide victims who have fingers on their shoulders) by simple switches. Either way, each motor-driven arm bends at the shoulder, elbow, wrist, hand, thumb and forefinger, all drawing power from waist battery packs.

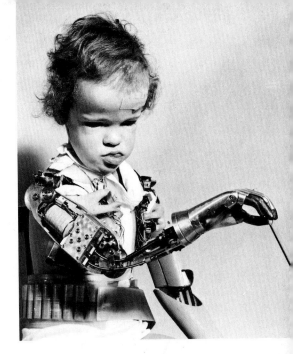

After only eight hours of instruction, a four-year-old thalidomide child named Bernadette was using her "Canadian Arms" to pick up balloons, drink from a cup and paint pictures. Today, Bernadette and the other deformed youngsters are faring well in regular public schools. Those without arms have gas-powered prosthetic hooks, to be replaced with the more efficient electromechanical devices, costing from $1,100 to $2,000, when they're older.

Meanwhile, thanks to Gingras, the Canadian Arm is a godsend to adult amputees as well. First to benefit was 20-year-old Pierre Provencher of Montreal, who lost both hands in an explosion. Fitted with lifelike electronic hands so deft that he can drive a car, shave himself and make delicate model planes, he now earns his living as a laboratory technician.

Gingras has never ceased to marvel at the strength of the human spirit. "The key to successful rehabilitation isn't the doctor's skill," he maintains, "but the patient's will. When a man loses a leg, or his sight or anything else, he's got to think of all his remaining assets—*oui*, count his blessings—and make the most of them."

A man of bubbling *joie de vivre*, Gingras leads a busy social life with his wife Rena, a former nurse. He has been elected to head the Canadian Medical Association; has served as president of Quebec's College of Physicians and Surgeons; is rehab chief for a veterans' hospital; professor of rehabilitation medicine at the University of Montreal; and director of its rehab school, which he founded. But at the center of everything is his own institute, where 22,000 Canadians so far have learned to cope with crippling disabilities. Up at 5:30 each day, Gingras usually arrives there by 6.

"It's Gus who makes this place go," says Dr. David Sherman, his close friend for many years, and the institute's director of research. "He's got the divine spark."

Gingras insists that disabled children should be educated in the usual way, not shunted aside into "special" schools. Children such as this victim of the drug thalidomide, equipped with electromechanical arms devised by Canadian engineers, prove him right. They do well in regular schools.

Little Man, Lonely Man

By Keith Munro

He was the loneliest man I ever knew, and one of the shyest. We became close friends and I think it was because we both stuttered.

When I first saw him I was impressed by the dark, glowing eyes and huge head atop a body not much over five feet tall. He took an $8\frac{1}{2}$ hat—or he would have if the stores where he lived had carried hats that big. They didn't, so he wore caps. They stretch.

That head was full of wisdom, some of it medical because he was a doctor. But most of it was psychological because he was a healer.

It was a backwoods community he served. Half his time was spent fighting the blizzards of winter and the mud, slush and floods of spring.

He had moved there in 1907 as a young medico fresh from college. He wasn't ambitious. He'd counted on making his living by serving the families of lumberjacks and the millworkers in the village. But he was the only doctor for miles around and he soon found that he couldn't refuse the sick and dying in the outlying settlements. So his practice spread until it covered some 400 square miles of farms and wilderness.

He was *le docteur* to more than 1,000 families, getting about by buggy, by sleigh, by horseback, by canoe.

There was the time a young bride tried suicide because her husband brought another woman home to their shack. The crazed wife shot herself but succeeded only in inflicting a bad head wound. Word got to Little Doc in the middle of the night. He piled on all the clothes he could, for it was far below zero, and struck out across the frozen lake.

That was nearly his finish, for down swept a raging blizzard and in no time he couldn't even see his horse's head. But he kept going and at dawn he arrived.

He found the patient half conscious. He cared for the wound, then went after the doltish husband with harsh words. Both operations were successful. Later Doc returned and delivered a healthy baby to a happy couple.

There was never any question of socialized medicine up where Little Doc labored. You could pay or you couldn't, and his service was the same either way. A confinement could cost as much as $5 with pre- and post-natal care thrown in. Sometimes he got paid.

Doc knew at least 500 families intimately. When John Robitaille, a young, vigorous lumberjack, came down with pneumonia Doc attended him carefully for a couple of days. Then he said to the young wife: "I'm sorry. He won't live till morning." Then Doc hurried down the road to where Jeanne Rushforte was having her first baby.

In the morning John Robitaille was dead. Doc knew he would be, for he had been in the sickroom when John's father had died, and he'd been there when *Grandpère* passed away. He knew how much strain the Robitaille heart would stand. Doc's father, who had worked his way through Edinburgh medical school, had taught him this. "Study your families. Learn what their weak points are," his father had counseled, and the son learned the lesson well.

Like so many old-time country doctors, Doc could diagnose disease by the smell. He could tell as soon as he entered the house, before he saw the patient, whether it was smallpox, or diphtheria, or scarlet fever. That was important because in those days there were no laboratories handy where smears could be sent for diagnosis.

In a day when vaccination was far from popular, Doc vaccinated school kids and adults by the hundreds. He took around with him a huge picture of one of those disease organisms that look so frightful through the microscope. "This is what's in you when you have smallpox," he would say. After the patient had had one look at the fearsome thing, Doc couldn't scratch his arm and rub in vaccine fast enough for him.

Nobody was better at delivering babies than he. Up in that country families with 15 children aren't unusual. In all, Doc presided at the birth of at least 2,000 citizens, and he never lost a mother.

His most important tenet was: "A doctor's business is to interfere with nature as little as possible." Fresh air, lots of water, rest and, if needed, a mild physic. That was his prescription for almost everything except fractured skulls. If a patient insisted on medicine he was given sugar-coated bread pills that Doc made himself. "One every four hours with several glasses of water" were his usual directions. Thus the patient got plenty of water at least. Doc never claimed anything for the pills, but the fame of their curative properties spread.

He had a dread of surgery, yet when surgery was needed his small hands were deft and sure. There was the time young Phil Guilmette mangled his hand in a thresher. The simple and safe thing would have been amputation at the wrist. But Doc hesitated. In this rough country a man with only one hand is a liability to himself and to his family, so he gave the boy chloroform and went to work.

When it was over Phil had a stub of a thumb and two stubby fingers—enough to guide an ax and do a hundred other things that a stump of wrist couldn't.

The kitchen table was Doc's workbench. One time, while doing a tonsillectomy on little Bill Martin, he ran out of catgut. He sent one of the men out to the stable to pluck some hairs from the tail of the old gray mare, boiled them and threaded them in his surgical needle. Bill Martin is as healthy today as though he'd been sewn up with the finest catgut.

Doc had been up there five or six years when he really won the hearts of his people. In the midst of a February blizzard, word came of an outbreak of diphtheria in an outlying region. Filling his pockets with antitoxin, Doc started out in his sleigh. It was night when he reached the stricken community, but there was no time for sleep. All night he labored. All the next day, all the next night, until every child and most of the adults had been immunized, and he and his stock of antitoxin were exhausted. After that he was their man.

Doc had been brought up a Methodist, but this community was 90 percent Roman Catholic. The priests were his close friends; they were almost the only persons there who had read the books on philosophy and psychology that he had read, and who spoke his language. More important, Doc soon discovered that the priests supplied something that he couldn't. He knew that many of our ills are of the spirit. That was when it was time to call the priest.

Doc and Father Sloan were especially close. More and more they appeared in the sickroom together. Came the day when this part-nership paid off—in how many lives saved, nobody will ever know.

It was toward the end of 1918, when the influenza epidemic struck and in a few short weeks killed more people than had four years of war. There was no way to avoid it or cure it. The people were in a panic.

The epidemic hit Little Doc's part of the country hard. Whole families were stricken, often so suddenly that there was no one to go for the doctor. For days Doc didn't have his clothes off. Still the epidemic gained on him. This was when Father Sloan and he joined forces for their crusade against death.

The priest's flock and Doc's practice covered about the same area. The padre would read from his pulpit Doc's instructions to flu sufferers: "Go to bed and stay there. Lay off whiskey and medicines. Keep windows and bowels open."

Mass over, the priest and the doctor would set out by buggy or car, drive over back roads and lumber trails, caring for the sick. When they came to a house with no smoke feathering the chimney, they went in. They knew the whole family was down. While Doc ministered to the stricken, the priest carried in wood, built fires, heated soup. This happened in a hundred lonely cabins before the tide of disease ebbed.

Father Sloan often talked about the fight Doc had to get his patients to breathe fresh air. In that harsh country the windows are sealed for the winter with storm sash and weather stripping. Doc opened windows but often found that as soon as he'd left the windows were closed again.

"Doc would get mad," the priest recalled. "He got so he'd hide the windows in the haymow. They got fresh air whether they wanted it or not. Doc just wouldn't let his people die."

He didn't either. In 1,500 cases of flu he lost only two patients—one girl and one boy.

Those weeks took grave toll of both doctor and priest. Father Sloan came down with pneumonia and Doc nursed him through it. Then Doc took sick. He went on answering emergency calls, though, despite a raging fever. Many of the patients he saw weren't half as sick as he was. But Doc was tough.

His people tried in many ways to lighten his load. They began sending a sleigh or a buggy to pick him up when they wanted his services.

But there were still the emergencies; bushmen still cut themselves with axes or trees fell on them. There were epidemics. And every year there was a huge crop of babies.

As the years wore on, Doc began to pay for his nights without sleep, for his bouts with snow and cold. He developed rheumatism and arthritis. He was pretty sure that diabetes had taken hold, although he hadn't enough interest or time to find out.

May 27, 1934, was a bitter day for Little Doc. He had taken a patient to the city hospital. It was an interesting case and he wanted to watch the operation. The head surgeon looked at the unshined shoes, the baggy pants that didn't match the shabby coat, and haughtily

refused him entrance to the operating room. Doc drove home, enveloped in despair. He remembered that he was but two days away from his 51st birthday. His younger brother was a famous gynecologist, his five sisters had all married successful men. His father, 50 years a doctor, had died full of honors and had left a large estate. But he himself had made only $1,500 in the past year.

He thought bitterly of how his wife, the only person on earth who understood his lonely, introverted soul, had died of a brain tumor. Her last words to him had been: "Look after our boy." Well, the boy was in school, and at least Doc had taken out enough insurance so that the boy's education was assured. But he himself was a failure.

Thirty-six hours later, when his birthday dawned clear and crisp, the world was beating on his door. Honors and gifts were showered on him. His name was in headlines in every newspaper in the world. All because a few hours earlier he had gone to a lonely, unpainted farmhouse and delivered a woman of five baby daughters whom she and her husband named Yvonne, Marie, Annette, Emilie and Cécile. Together the five weighed only a little over ten pounds. Nobody gave them a chance for life. But Little Doc stayed there, stubbornly fighting for those flickering lives until he won. The Dionne case made medical history.

The shy little man with the big head and the great heart was Dr. Allan Roy Dafoe.

Darby of Bella Bella

By Hugh W. McKervill

Darby of Bella Bella was already a legend when my wife, Marilyn, and I joined him at his small hospital in the wildly beautiful coastal country of British Columbia. Long before I was born, he had taken his bride and a brand-new medical degree into this isolated spot. There he stayed for nearly half a century, ministering to the bodily ills and spiritual hungers of the Indians and the few white fishermen and lighthouse keepers who wrested a livelihood from the North Pacific and its long, lonely beaches.

Bella Bella was my first ministry, and Dr. Darby greeted us at the dock of the little settlement, 300 miles north of Vancouver. As we walked along the boardwalk that joined the cedar-posted homes, copper-skinned children trotted beside us vying for attention. He had a word or a pat on the head for each one: "You need a haircut again, Johnny. Arthur, it's time you had a tetanus booster. Come down to the hospital this afternoon and bring your brother."

For Dr. George Darby (here with Mrs. Darby) no West Coast logging camp or trapper's cabin was too remote to visit if there was illness. Admiring the way Darby threaded his boat through a perilously narrow channel, a friend once said: "You seem to know these reefs pretty well." "Guess so," Darby replied. "I've hit most of them, one time or another."

"How do you keep them all straight?" I asked.

"Oh, it's not hard when you've brought them all into the world, and all of their parents and some of their grandparents, too."

For 45 years Dr. Darby was pastor, counselor, judge, doctor, father and friend to the people scattered along all the hundreds of miles of craggy coastline between Vancouver Island and the Alaska panhandle. He had been their carpenter, plumber, wharfmaster, postman and chief of water supply. And most of all he had been God's messenger. "I am here to do what I can," he told me, "because God cares about all people. And he who would be great must be the servant of all."

George Darby drew no clear distinction between body and soul, between his practices as doctor and Christian minister. The healing process, he firmly believed, was speeded by devotions; so operations at Bella Bella's United Church hospital (above, biggest building) were begun with prayer and the sick were treated with Scriptures as well as with pills. In an all-out assault on tuberculosis, a scourge among the Indians, he built a separate TB wing on the hospital. Then, in cooperation with others, he prevailed on the legislature of British Columbia to establish a specialized center at Nanaimo on Vancouver Island. In seven years, Indian deaths from the dread disease dropped from 203 to 16.

George Darby was a third-year medical student at the University of Toronto when he first saw the brooding land and those hardy, needful people whose rugged lot was to be tempered by his lifelong devotion. He had been sent by the Methodist Church to man, for a few months, the little hospital at Rivers Inlet, 45 miles southeast of Bella Bella. The church's Bella Bella mission maintained the hospital during those chaotic weeks each summer when the silver salmon battled their way upstream to spawn, and when otherwise reasonable men battled nature and one another, in a frenzied struggle to reap enough of the ocean's bounty to see them through the rest of the year.

All things yielded to the salmon run. Families were often neglected and accidents frequent. A man breaks his arm and continues to fish with one hand, bone poking through the skin above the other; he is willing to risk permanent disability rather than lose a day having it set. A woman thrashes and moans in the agony of a breech birth. "She ought to be in the hospital at Ocean Falls right now," Darby bitterly tells the suffering woman's mother. "But the boats are all out for the fishing," is the reply.

Young Darby was appalled to see men in so stark a struggle for survival that life's higher meaning and life itself were held more cheaply than a netful of salmon. He ached to help them. Two years later, having graduated and completed his internship, he returned to

Bella Bella for good, this time bringing with him Edna, his bride of scarcely two months.

The first years were filled with uncommon difficulties. The hospital was a bare frame building with an operating room and beds for nine patients. Instruments were sterilized in an old coffee urn; the stove, sole source of heat and cookery, regularly belched soot over patients and staff. When the sewer line clogged, it was Darby who probed its length until the congestion was finally located. When the cow frightened the lad hired to tend her, it was Darby who had to calm the recalcitrant animal and, more often than not, milk her.

His working day had 18 hours, and his most difficult task at first was to win the trust of a people long conditioned by bitter contacts with white traders to trust no outsider. Not long after his arrival, Darby was called to the home of a 16-year-old boy, accidentally shot in the stomach while hunting, and found the villagers already gathered in a grim death watch. The medicine man, dancing around the inert form on the floor in a clatter of shells and buttons and the swishing of a dirty feather headdress, mumbled patronizingly that there was nothing to be done: clearly evil spirits had entered the boy's body and would soon carry him off.

Darby knelt to examine the lad. So long had the boy lain there with no attention that his abdomen was distended with infection.

Darby got to his feet and said, "I must take this boy to the hospital." There was no response. Desperate, he sought the eyes of the haggard mother, and furtively, barely perceptibly, she nodded. Darby swept the boy up and strode out. He heard the medicine man howling behind him, elbowed past people who had recovered from their astonishment and now pranced threateningly at his side. And he prayed for God's assistance, for if the boy died in the hospital he might as well pack up and go back to Toronto.

"Bolt the door!" he shouted to the matron as he marched into the operating room.

Soon a great crowd surged and shouted outside the frame building, the medicine man whipping them into a frenzy. The day passed, then the night, and still they pressed in on the hospital, and it was plain that their anger would not be contained much longer. And then, soon after dawn the second day, all unexpectedly, the door was thrown open and the white doctor was ushering them inside. And there was the boy, so far from dead that he was grinning broadly and finishing off the hearty breakfast Edna was feeding him. Once Darby had drained the infection and extracted the bullet, the patient's youthful resilience had done the rest. Now the doctor tossed the misshapen slug to the boy's father. "There is your evil spirit," he said. "You may come back in a week and take your son home."

It was a critical turning point. The first direct clash in the classic battle between science and superstition had been won by the white doctor.

Before he was 30, Darby had been ordained a minister and appointed justice of the peace. Now he was charged with official responsibility for the spiritual, medical and social well-being of the people up and down the many miles of rugged country. A knock at his door

Sea and mountains were ever present in Darby's work. Every Sunday he visited shut-ins, bringing the word of God along with his medicines. He would examine the patient, then pull out a tattered New Testament. The patient's family gathered close while he read. Then he translated the holy words into Chinook, the universally understood trader's jargon of the coast Indians. Everything, it seemed, was Darby's job. When a line snagged as the steamer pulled away from the Bella Bella wharf and wrenched the whole rotting structure into the bay, Darby turned out to be the only man in the village able to compute the number and length of needed pilings, so he supervised the arduous reconstruction.

might take him to a family quarrel, a pair of inflamed tonsils, or a dead wolf for which a bounty was due the hunter. When he held court for petty crimes, which all but vanished during his years at Bella Bella, plaintiff and defendant usually wound up shaking hands, with God as a witness. "We'd better have a prayer before we go home," Darby would say. Then, in the typically chatty manner in which he communed with the Lord, he would pray:

"Our Heavenly Father, we thank Thee for Thy guidance and ask Thy forgiveness for Tom, who just wasn't thinking when he did this foolish thing. And, oh, yes, Lord, please help John to forgive him, too, since Tom has promised to return the money."

The passing years brought significant changes to Bella Bella. Under Darby's direction, a new hospital was built, complete with X-ray equipment and radiophone, so that the boats and canneries could call immediately in case of need. The medical staff had grown from a single matron to seven general-duty nurses, and at last the doctor found time to indulge his bent for research and preventive medicine. When three members of a family were stricken with a mysterious food poisoning, he painstakingly traced their diet until he came to a preparation of partly fermented salmon eggs, which he felt sure contained a deadly botulism organism. He sent the stuff to the provincial laboratory, where his analysis was confirmed. Furthermore, the data he provided revealed, for the first time, the rate at which the deadly organism de-

Dr. Darby had a great memory for the names and faces of his Indian people. "It's not hard," he said, "when you've brought them all into the world."

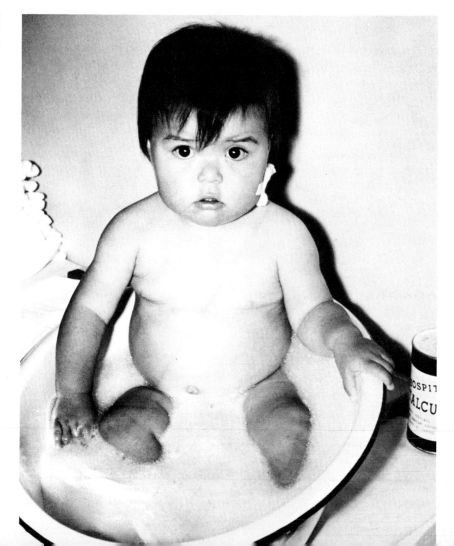

velops, and it contributed a vital link in studies of a critical illness that had appeared in many primitive parts of the world.

But if there were rewards, there was also a heart-wrenching penalty for Darby's dedication. For the time came when his daughter and three sons outgrew the little school at Bella Bella, geared to the needs of the native children, and it was clear that Edna would have to take them to Vancouver 300 miles away, for the rest of their education. There was no question of Darby himself leaving. "I never thought for a moment that he would," Edna has said, "and I never asked him to. He was desperately needed in Bella Bella then. It was his life."

And so, for most of the next 20 years, Darby gave up the intimacy of family life for all but the summer months.

When World War II broke out, two of Darby's sons volunteered. On a summer day in 1943, with the doctor in the operating room preparing for surgery, the matron brought him a telegram. Jim Darby, his oldest boy, had been lost over the English Channel. Darby's eyes misted over for a moment, but his hands remained steady. He completed the operation, left specific instructions for the care of the patient, then went to tell Edna. He seemed suddenly weary, older.

By the time Marilyn and I came to take over the ministerial duties, a second doctor had been appointed to assist Darby the year round. And in 1959, he finally let Edna persuade him that the time had come to let younger men continue his work at Bella Bella. One day, not long after, as the Darbys brought the hospital launch into the inlet at Wadhams for their final rounds, the entire landing seemed to erupt in a colorful mass of people and boats. They had come from the villages and fish camps along 300 miles of coastline, 3,000-strong—Indians, Japanese, Irish, Norwegians, Americans and Canadians—and they meant to honor George Darby for his half-century of selflessness.

The banquet table ran for 50 yards. The gifts, ranging from a six-foot totem pole to great buckets of fresh fish, would require three boats to take them to Bella Bella. And when the great assemblage sang out, "For they are jolly good fellows," neither George nor Edna could restrain their tears. Then Darby rose to speak. "I hope no one will ever say of me that I stuck it out here. It was a privilege and I thank you."

But it was not in Darby's nature to retire. He was delighted when the Church appointed him coordinator of its hospitals in the West.

It was during an inspection trip in 1962 that Darby first noticed symptoms of abdominal cancer in himself. Typically, he was furious; he had too much to do to leave yet, and he spent the next weeks tying up loose ends, making certain his children were well settled and that Edna's future was cared for. Then he slipped away to that God he had served so long and valiantly.

His ashes were brought to Bella Bella, where I read the funeral service to a packed church. Then, in great stillness, the ashes were carried to the place where the Indians had built a stone memorial for him. It was autumn, a time when the weather on the Pacific Coast is often wild. But on this day the sun shone bright; and as one man looked into the clear, still sky, he said to me, "I guess the Doc is still looking after things."

George Darby (here with fellow United Church clergymen) spent 45 years battling nearly impossible odds. Word of his brilliance as a surgeon had filtered outside and he had been offered positions at important hospitals in Vancouver and Edmonton at five times his $1,800-a-year salary. He never gave them serious thought. "This is what I was meant to do," he said. "This is my place."

Dr. Dave, GP

By Percy Wray

When Dr. David Lander first came to southern Alberta to practice medicine, he was an enigma. A painfully shy young man, with tousled black hair and a Polish accent, he always had his nose in a medical book. He seemed more reserved than the outgoing country doctors we'd known. But that was only a first impression, more than 30 years ago.

I was the local insurance agent and notary, and I became volunteer ambulance driver in Turner Valley. The village and its twin, Black Diamond, two miles away, make up our community of 2,000 in the foothills of the Rockies. In those Hungry Thirties I was also secretary-treasurer of the community, with the responsibility of doling out "relief" to the needy and listening to their pleas for more. After hours, I took to dropping into Dr. Dave's office, on the ground floor of the Black Diamond Hotel.

One day I told him about the ulcer that had nagged me off and on for months. "Comes and goes," I said, "and diet doesn't help."

He leaned forward, brown eyes keen as a detective's.

"Just when do you get the pains?"

I thought a minute. "Well . . . seems like every time I'm on this relief job."

Dr. Dave smiled. And after further discussion he said, "Don't you see? You're shouldering all the worries and complaints of these poor people, and your body is rebelling. Try to accept this: You didn't cause the Depression, you are doing your best for them, and you can do no more."

I took his advice and, with proper diet, the pains vanished. I'd learned that Dr. Dave was one of those warmhearted practitioners who treat not only bodies but souls. People in our community who once thought him cool soon came to revere him.

Dr. Dave is perhaps the best possible kind of doctor for today's troubled world—a general practitioner, fully versed in modern diagnosis and treatment, but also equipped with a rare understanding of human emotions. "You can't practice good medicine without looking into the heart, too," he says. There he often finds emotional stress that breeds physical sickness. He attributes at least 30 percent of our common ills to secret frustration, shame or loneliness. Yet these emotional causes often go unrecognized.

Dr. Dave believes that his kind of "psychiatrically oriented GP" could handle 85 percent of the cases in medicine today. Unfortunately, his species is dying out. Of the more than 300,000 physicians in Canada and the United States, fewer than one-quarter are GPs—the kind of family doctor who knows the community inside out, the patient's job, family, home and skeletons-in-the-closet.

Here are some cases:

The 16-year-old daughter of a poor family couldn't eat or sleep. Finally, under Dr. Dave's fatherly probing, she explained that she was in love with a rich boy but felt ashamed to let him visit her home.

A 19-year-old young man, about to return to his seminary after Christmas holidays, developed a bad case of nervous tension: he trembled and perspired heavily. The eldest of a devout Roman Catholic

Time for tea and a chat with a patient. "That's good medicine too," says Dr. Lander.

family, he was studying theology because his parents wanted a priest in the family, but he yearned guiltily for the secular world.

A man suffering from eczema admitted that on a recent business trip he'd strayed, for the first time in his life, into an affair with another woman. ("The Lord may forgive us our sins, but our nervous systems never do," says Dr. Dave. "If we don't rid ourselves of the emotional stress by word or action, our bodies try to do it for us. And if our eyes don't cry, then some other organ, like the skin, will.")

Once a patient perceives the emotional basis of his ailment, and takes a dose of Dr. Dave's common sense, he usually begins to feel better. To the guilt-ridden husband Dr. Dave said, "What's done is done. The important thing is: what kind of husband will you be from now on?" To the teen-age girl: "If this boy just worries about the size of your house, the sooner you find out the better!" To the troubled student: "Many good Catholics were never cut out to be priests. It's no disgrace." And he helped obtain through the bishop the boy's release from the seminary.

Dr. Dave kibitzes at a cribbage game in the hospital recreation room, then joins a patient at shuffleboard. He says of the shortage of general practitioners: "The trouble is, medical students and interns have had little opportunity to observe the GP at work. So, quite naturally, they have chosen the specialist as their idol. Yet general practice can be the most satisfying in medicine, because every human being is an enigma, a jigsaw puzzle, and only the GP knows how *all* the parts fit together."

Simple as it seems, this brand of medicine is so rare that patients seek out our doctor from Calgary and Edmonton, 30 and 200 miles away. His fame has so spread that organizations all over Canada bid for his speeches which he sprinkles with such lines as:

"It's not so much what you eat as what's eating you."

"The worst diet for an ulcer is to come home to a dish of cold shoulder and hot tongue."

"Illness can be due to a germ, a bullet or a mother-in-law."

Dr. Dave believes that more doctors should try to develop what he calls "a third ear." When a patient comes in with a problem, the doctor first explores carefully for organic disease. If physical tests are negative, he says, "I can't yet find what accounts for your symptoms, but we'll keep looking." Then he schedules an all-important first interview, at least an hour long—late in the day so the patient won't feel uneasy over a lineup in the waiting room outside. His first task is to establish trust and rapport.

He leans forward in his tiny office, gray suit neat, graying hair rumpled, eyes knowing and kind behind their spectacles. "You can talk absolutely freely," he says. "I guarantee your privacy. And you should also know that I'm equipped with emotional shock absorbers." Slowly at first, then frequently in a torrent, to his murmurs of understanding, patients unfold their profoundly personal problems.

"People are like houses," Dr. Dave says. "You look at a street struck by a storm: one house stands untouched; another is crumpled; a third has lost the roof or a door. We, too, react differently to storms. But if we know our weaknesses, we can strengthen them. I try to help people shore up their defenses."

Dr. Dave has known his share of storms. Winnipeg in the mid-1920s was not particularly kind to the 12-year-old son of a poor Jewish laborer, newly arrived from Poland. The sensitive boy was always at the bottom of the social and economic ladder. As a teen-ager, determined to get an education, he took a job in a tannery at $6 a week, and hated it. Later at the University of Alberta medical school he was, a classmate remembers, "one of the backbenchers, serious, rather shy, not particularly brilliant, but dogged." After graduation in 1936, he worked a year in the provincial mental hospital, which whetted his interest in psychiatry. Then he came to our community.

A bachelor, Dr. Dave has given us his whole life. Ordinarily he is with his patients night and day, seven days a week. By 8 a.m., every day, he is in the office for a quiet half-hour with his medical journals. Then, pushing his Chrysler to the edge of the speed limit, he drives to Turner Valley's 24-bed hospital and charges up the steps, his coat off and trailing before he is in the door. The hospital is relaxed and cheerful. Patients ring for the nurse when *they're* awake. Children, recuperating and restless, can help serve meals or make beds. The self-serve kitchenette is open 24 hours a day.

"We do things a big hospital can't," Dr. Dave tells you. "I can say to a nurse, 'That patient is depressed so please see that she has her hair done and her makeup on before I come on rounds.' That's medicine too, you know; good medicine."

As he makes his rounds, Dr. Dave consults the nurses—"my eyes and ears," as he calls them. Which patients have been in low spirits, cheerful, active? Who has had visitors, and how did each react to them? When one out-of-town patient was receiving no visitors, Dr. Dave found a former high-school classmate in town and got him to make daily visits. When a Sarcee Indian child confined with an infectious disease pined for her family, the doctor let her father pitch a teepee on hospital grounds and talk through the window every day. He pays particular attention to terminal cases. "If you can't cure, you should at least comfort," he says. "Even a dying patient should be visited daily and be treated just as though he were going to go on living."

By 1:30 he is driving back, perhaps pausing at a variety shop for a coffee or a dozen chocolate bars to restock his candy box for young patients. Then on to his modest office.

No matter how trivial the complaint may seem, he is always alert and courteous. To the aged, in particular, he shows respect. "One must never deflate them. Old age is deflating enough." One elderly patient who lived seven miles from town invariably arrived an hour early for her periodic checkups. "I think she's using our waiting room as a social center," his nurse said. "I think you're right," agreed Dr. Dave. "And let's keep her coming. It's her way of keeping in touch with life."

Dr. Dave, like all other members of the College of Family Physicians of Canada, takes 100 hours of refresher studies every two years. As a group, GPs were never more expert, and the need for them was never so great. But today they comprise less than half of Canada's physicians, since the career of the specialist seems to offer more prestige than that of the "family doctor."

Any intern lucky enough to follow in the steps of a man like Dr. Dave will learn that the GP's rewards are highly personal, but beyond price. Take the special way Dr. Dave took care of George Godkin, a Turner Valley painting contractor. When George's home was gutted by fire, he staggered out with second- and third-degree burns covering 65 percent of his body from head to knee. For two months he was kept alive with transfusions, penicillin and 24-hour nursing. Through one critical period, Dr. Dave himself slept near the patient.

Then George left the hospital to face a second crisis: he was scarred beyond recognition, not yet ready for plastic surgery, too weak and grotesque to get a job. As he hobbled into coffee shops, squeamish customers walked out. At home, tension became unbearable as his wife tried to feed the family of six on a welfare payment.

Finally, after the bitterest quarrel of the marriage, Godkin announced, "I'm leaving. You'll be better off without me!" He thumbed a ride to Black Diamond and trudged toward the Calgary highway. Dr. Dave spotted him as he passed the office and instantly sized up the situation. Before Godkin had walked another 100 yards, the doctor's car was beside him. "Get in, George," said Dr. Dave. "Tell me all about it."

George did. Dr. Dave persuaded the family to try again. The community raised more than $4,000 to help pay bills. Urged by letters of explanation from Dr. Dave, doctors at Rochester's Mayo Clinic gave George an acceptable new face. Soon he was back at his old job.

And Dr. Dave, thank heaven, continued happily at his.

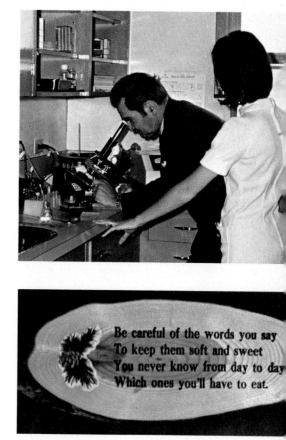

Dr. Lander discusses a pathological specimen with a laboratory technician. Typical of the plaques in his office is this admonition about the danger of having to eat words.

Miracle
of the Big Honkers

By Manly Miner

For my father, Jack Miner, life really began on a February afternoon in 1904.

There he was—a 38-year-old, the deadliest game-bird hunter in southwestern Ontario—down on his knees fondling seven live Canada geese! While I watched with the bursting excitement of a seven-year-old, Father carefully freed the wing-clipped geese in a muddy pond beside our farmhouse near Kingsville, Ont.

Then he rose, wiry-strong and straight as a rifle barrel, his blue eyes alive with the new idea.

Jack Miner and his son Manly, the author of this story, prepare to liberate a banded Canada goose at the Jack Miner Bird Sanctuary. This photograph, the last of father and son together, was made at Christmas 1943, not long before Jack Miner's death from a heart attack. He was 70. The sanctuary near Kingsville, Ont., the first of its kind in North America, brought Miner world acclaim.

"Now we'll see if others will join them," he said. "I've been their enemy. I wonder if they'll have me for a friend?"

At that moment the Jack Miner Bird Sanctuary was born. Tired of wanton killing and worried about the future of wildlife, Father was launching the first great experiment in North American conservation to draw widespread public acclaim: a haven for migrating ducks and Canada geese.

At first it was a dismal failure. No birds came that year or any of the next three years. Skeptical neighbors jeered and honked at him

253

whenever Father went to town. Then one glorious April day in 1908, 11 great Canada geese with their distinctive black necks and white chinbands skimmed in cautiously from a V-formation to join our decoys. "They've come! They've come!" roared Father. "I'm going downtown and see who'll do the honking *now*!"

Over the years thereafter, he personally gave refuge to millions of ducks and geese. He "sold" millions of people on conservation. He pioneered in bird banding, through which he documented the North American flight paths of migratory birds—epic 6,000-mile-a-year journeys. His banding records helped the passage of the Migratory Bird Convention Act, coordinating the efforts of Canada and the United States in protecting wildlife. Officials from Ottawa and Washington came to study his techniques. He even became a missionary of sorts: the biblical texts he eventually stamped on each bird band and changed daily stirred minor religious revivals in several corners of the continent.

A simple outdoorsman, unable to read or write until his 30s, Father achieved success that exceeded his fondest dreams. Countries as far afield as Russia copied his sanctuary. King George VI awarded him the Order of the British Empire; presidents and prime ministers sought his friendship.

His wind-burned face, like a gnarled-oak carving under the familiar battered hat, peered out from the newspapers. Lecture audiences all over the continent chuckled at his wit, nodded thoughtfully at his wisdom and went away to practice his teachings.

I quit school in 1910, at 13, to devote my life to his work, and began learning lessons never taught in classrooms. Everything Father taught and believed in was based on firsthand observation. Nature gave him his rules for living. "Understanding birds is easy," he'd tell my two brothers and me. "They're true to nature. But how do you understand people?"

One key to the human heart, he felt, was in wild creatures: "If I can get a child to love a bird, that child will love his fellow man." The other key was religion. Every human needs a faith, whether or not he admits to it, Father believed.

As a child in Dover Center, Ohio, one of ten children born to English immigrant parents, he watched the spring and autumn skies, tense with excitement, as the migratory flocks soared high overhead. At six, instead of starting school, he started a trapline. At ten, still dodging lessons, he was selling fur pelts. His mother finally coaxed him into a classroom for three months. But that year, 1878, the Miners moved to Canada, and Jack was lost to formal education forever. There was land to clear, vegetables to plant, a log house to build. He hewed railroad ties from dawn to dusk, carved ax handles from hickory saplings, and turned out up to 15,000 clay bricks a day in the family brickyard.

At every opportunity he took to the woods, his schoolroom and also his first church. "No intelligent man can live in the great outdoors," he often said in later life, "without being forced to believe there is an overruling Power." He lay belly-down for hours, mesmerized by the glitter of speckled trout in a stream. Once he crawled curiously into a bear den and almost knocked heads with an equally

Wild whistling swans—they make a soft musical note—stop off at the Jack Miner Sanctuary en route from breeding grounds in Alaska and northwest Canada to winter in the southern Atlantic states.

startled bear. He could mimic a timber wolf's howl. He mastered bird calls. He could tell from the seeds in a dead bird's crop exactly where it had been feeding. After hours in the bush, he would come home famished, and tired enough to "sleep a hole right down through the bed," his mind cleansed of all care.

He had an uncanny instinct for direction—rescuing 13 people lost in the bush over the years. This skill, combined with his marksmanship, made him a formidable hunter. He and his brother Ted became expert market hunters, selling a wheelbarrowful of game birds twice a week to "rich folks" as far away as Detroit.

He might have blithely gone through life as a relentless hunter had it not been for a tragic accident in 1898. Tracking moose with his brother and a friend, he suddenly heard the friend shouting hysterically "I've shot Ted!" Father washed the blood from his dead brother's face, carried the 200-pound body 13 miles to a stream, paddled 12 more miles through a blizzard to the nearest railway, and took his brother home for the last time.

Afterward, he thought about the fragile thing called life. Maybe it was time for him to give something to the world. He began to teach

Sunday school and, through it, taught himself to read and write. The new Jack Miner took a more critical look at hunting. The automatic rifle was replacing the muzzle loader. Farmland was leveling the forests. Hunters were steadily depleting the waterfowl. He began to realize that game birds *could* be wiped out. Yet what could he do about it?

The turning point came early one March morning as he was waiting, shotgun in hand, for a flight of geese he'd spotted the night before. He called a perfect "A-honk"; the leader returned it and led his flight toward the blind. Suddenly, just out of range, they wheeled away with rapid-fire danger cries.

Father went home brooding. "They remembered me from somewhere," he told himself. "They were saying, 'That's our deadly enemy. Everybody get, for your lives!'"

Father was now grappling with a new idea. He studied wild geese "until I felt like flying," came to admire their cunning. But if they were to survive, he knew they'd need human friends.

He graded a mudhole into a small pond, and bought seven honkers from a neighbor who had illegally trapped them. Not long after the first wild ones arrived in 1908, Father, to keep eager hunters from

Seated before the family fireplace, Mrs. Jack Miner chooses texts from the Bible to be stamped by her husband on the aluminum used for banding birds at the sanctuary. Bands bearing biblical quotations as well as Miner's name and address (opposite page) were found on birds thousands of miles from Kingsville, proving the great migrations that men had previously only guessed at.

taking easy game, banned all hunting around his "sanctuary"; it was betraying the birds' trust. The following year, 32 Canada geese came; the year after that, *350!* There had been one or two previous attempts at sanctuaries in North America, but none of this magnitude to attract the wily, suspicious Canada goose.

Success was mildly embarrassing. We'd begun feeding the geese with corn from our pockets, then from pails, then from sacks. Now we served their meals by scoop shovel from a wagon. There was another chore, too. In 1909 Father scratched "Box 48, Kingsville, Ont." on an aluminum band, wrapped it to the leg of a black duck. A month later a hunter in Anderson, S.C., shot her and returned the tag. Before this, naturalists could only guess that birds flew thousands of miles in migration. Here was proof. In subsequent years, from thousands of such bandings, Father was able to build maps pinpointing the flight paths of North America's ducks and geese.

All of this took time and money. Our family brickyard barely supported the Miners, much less hundreds of hungry birds. The year I left school to help with the work, Father began 30 years of lecturing (as often as five times a day, to audiences everywhere from Alaska to New York's Carnegie Hall). From the beginning he was a smash hit.

Father never prepared a speech. He'd start often by leading the audience in a favorite hymn. Then he'd tell fascinating yarns about wildlife and his work. But he also talked about humanity, reinforcing his points with "Minerisms": "Get all the education you can; then add the learning" and "Today is the tomorrow you worried about yesterday." He'd cite Canada geese as models to mankind: "They conduct themselves with dignity, never fight unless it's absolutely necessary to protect their family—and then their wrath is terrible. The gander takes only one mate in a lifetime, and I've never known one to make application for divorce."

Often emotional and sometimes ungrammatical, he was a "star"—a role that amazed and delighted him. Not only was he earning money to support his sanctuary but he was converting all manner of men to conservation. Henry Ford, Sr., was so impressed that he visited the sanctuary and paid to have a half-hour movie produced about it to be shown at Father's lectures. Richard B. Mellon, onetime head of the Aluminum Company of America, quietly looked over our work and announced that henceforth he would donate all the aluminum we needed for banding. (Mellon's researchers devised a soft, long-wearing alloy which came to us, free, starting in 1925.)

The geese, meanwhile, quickly learned that the sanctuary meant safety. Year after year, with some inexplicable instinct, they homed in on our little patches of water to rest and replenish their strength. "Anybody who says 'silly as a goose' is talking through his hat," Father said. Often he moved audiences to tears with stories of the birds' loyalty and courage. One of our neighbors once injured a gander and followed him five miles over rough country—right to the sanctuary's "hospital" gate. Father claimed that, "if a cat has nine lives, the Canada goose has at least 18—nine on each side of the border."

One day a neighbor broke a gander's wing with a shot. Father

tied the severed arteries on the ironing board that was his "operating table," amputated the damaged wing tip and released the bird in our park. He let out a feeble cry. Another gander, wheeling overhead, picked him out immediately from the honking hundreds. From that day, "David and Jonathan" were inseparable. When the flock migrated, healthy Jonathan tried vainly to get his crippled friend airborne, then settled down philosophically to live with him and us. Seven years later, a great horned owl attacked the hospital. Jonathan held it off until it blinded and killed him. Father, enraged, trapped and killed the owl the next night. He believed, and naturalists criticized him bitterly for it, that man had the right to destroy predators.

But through Father's urging, for survival of the species, areas around James Bay were closed to goose hunting; artificial baiting to lure waterfowl was abolished; governments began to meet regularly with conservationists to exchange ideas; trained game wardens replaced political appointees. He was world-famous now. Publications clamored for his articles, which he'd dictate to me (once he had 13 in print in one month). When George VI visited Windsor, Ont., in 1939, Father, arriving at the parade route as honorary chairman of the welcoming committee, got an ovation from 250,000 spectators. But his greatest thrill in life never ceased to be the sight of a northbound V in the spring sky.

Although he traveled for weeks at a time, we were never really apart. In later years, my brothers Jasper and Ted traveled with him, operating the movie projector and attending to details which left him free to study the wildlife of the area. I was his secretary, booking agent and bookkeeper. When Father was at home the place rang with his spirit and vitality. He liked to say that he was "as well preserved as a wildcat." (I once saw him wrestle a piano onto a wheelbarrow and move it 300 feet.) Every November of his life—in every kind of weather—he'd camp up north under canvas. He greeted all visitors impartially in an old plaid jacket and rubber boots. He invariably held prayers at breakfast, thanking God for the new day and asking His blessing on each of us, visitors included, by name. One American diplomat said, when I put him on his train to New York, "Your father's prayer this morning meant more to me than even the birds."

In 1944, Father died of a heart attack at age 70. We buried him on the sanctuary grounds. In the 1930s my parents had turned over the sanctuary to the Jack Miner Migratory Bird Foundation, a philanthropic trust to perpetuate his work. So Father lives on. Three years after his death, Canada set aside the week in which Jack Miner's birthday—April 10—occurred as National Wildlife Week. Now thousands of people come to the sanctuary every year to see, in the migratory seasons, one of the greatest free shows on earth. Just before dusk the honking Vs come in, wave after wave, off Lake Erie, for their evening feast. Cameras click and whir as total strangers smile and chat with each other, and make room for the children to watch.

Father would have loved all this, for this is his dream come true. The big honkers are preserved for generations to come. And the people sense, for a little while at least, the brotherhood of man as they share this continuing miracle of the birds.

The Good Life
of Gleason Green

By Mary Coburn

I first met Gleason Green on his lobster boat, the trim white *Bonney Queen.* She was carrying 25 passengers from New Brunswick's Grand Manan Island, in the Bay of Fundy, on a day's outing to Machias Seal Island. Happiness spread out in waves over the group. A newcomer to such trips, I put it down to the sparkle of the day and the spirit of adventure.

Then Gleason came from the galley where he'd been making fish chowder for the crowd. Heads turned toward him, voices called bantering greetings. A ten-year-old boy at the wheel cried, "I'm right on course!"—and added hopefully, "Aren't I?" Gleason briefly checked the horizon and replied, "Wal, now, you're doin' pretty good," and gave the wheel a correction. All of us on deck looked out at the open sea and smiled. In Gleason's kindly, capable hands moment followed moment that day as smoothly and effortlessly as a flock of gulls lighting one by one on a strip of sand.

When we returned to Grand Manan, everyone paid Gleason $2.50 for the trip—everyone, that is, but the six children aboard. "No," I heard Gleason say firmly to the father of two boys. "Never charge for children—that's a rule on my boat. Fun belongs to children."

On the pier, I turned and looked at Gleason, who was already swabbing down the *Bonney Queen's* deck. This blue-eyed man, then in his early 60s, short and spare, sparse as to hair, large as to ears, was not only the top lobsterman on Grand Manan; for 30 years his fame as a boatbuilder had spread up and down the Atlantic seaboard. He combined business shrewdness with the generosity and bigness of heart I saw that day.

Gleason Green was born and raised in Grand Harbour, one of the seven fishing villages that line the east shore of beautiful Grand Manan Island, just off the New Brunswick and Maine coasts.

For a Grand Mananer, to work hard is a necessity; to have a respect for the forces of nature, a matter of self-preservation; and to give, as natural as to breathe. Gleason Green had all these qualities, but what he did with them, entirely unaided, was the product of genius. Oldest of nine brothers and three sisters, Gleason began his fishing career at an age when most boys are setting off for school, by helping his father handline halibut, mackerel and cod. "Haven't had more than three days of schooling," he confessed with a twinkle, "and the teacher was absent all three days."

Not that he scorned education. He sent all but one of his eight children to school on the mainland. "And I've had a lot of pleasure

". . . on an island small and remote, but the light is strong and gives comfort . . ."

259

Loyalists from the American Revolution started Grand Manan Island's fishing industry. Like Gleason Green (at right; and below, demonstrating a trap-hauler), most of the 2,700 islanders still seine their beautiful heart-shaped weirs and haul in lobster pots from the Bay of Fundy's icy waters. Below, with 200 lobster traps aboard, one of Green's boats heads out, "ready to set."

doin' it," he said to me in his soft rhythmical drawl. "You take a smart, lively youngster and give him an education and you've got somethin'. It's like takin' a good sound piece of lumber. You chip it off here, smooth it thar, shape it and you've got what's the most important thing about a boat—a good keel. You know she'll sail a true course, rough weather or smooth."

All but two of his children returned to live on the island; from morning till night I saw them and their children flow in and out of the neat white frame house where Gleason and his wife, Lulu, lived.

If he had little formal schooling, he did not stop learning. His shrewd, inquiring mind never asked *can* I do this; it asked *how* can I do it. He began building boats in the 1930s and some 3,000 of his craft have sailed the seas. Up and down the coast his boats are known for their soundness and trim lines. He built many in his own boat shed; then, as his business grew, he began to use boatbuilding shops in Nova Scotia. But, he said, "I always deliver the boat to the owner myself. Then I'm sure it's workin' right."

He became an expert on marine engines; every engine in his boats was personally installed by him. The Chrysler Corporation, intrigued by the number of orders and blueprints for engines and parts reaching them from one man on remote Grand Manan, became curious and asked him to visit Detroit. There he was lavishly entertained for a week by officials entranced by his simple honesty and astute business sense.

One night when a group of us were sitting in front of the fire, I asked Gleason how he got his start in life. He thought a moment. "Wal, now, it just come along," he replied. "I'll say this, I come up the hard way." He smiled. "Did I ever tell you how I got my first boat?"

He'd been saving his money for it, "snigglin' a few cents here, a dollar there," for four years. Just after his 16th birthday, he saw an advertisement for a boat for sale in Nova Scotia, or "Novie," as the Grand Mananers call it. Gleason counted his money. He thought he could make it with another good lobster catch. He wrote the boatbuilder: "I'm comin' for her." The answer came: the boat would be waiting.

The day before he was to go, he hired a boat and hauled in 1,800

pounds of lobsters between two in the afternoon and ten that night. The next morning he sold his catch to a Nova Scotian for $1.01 a pound—Grand Manan lobsters being the most sought after on the Atlantic seaboard. The Nova Scotian also agreed to take him, and the 500-pound engine he'd bought for his new boat, to Novie.

In Novie, Gleason set out with beating heart to find his boat. When he walked into the shed and announced his name, the owner looked at him in astonishment. He'd sold the boat to another man, he said unhappily. "But you promised you'd hold her!" cried Gleason. The boatbuilder explained: he'd had another offer and had turned it down, saying he was saving the boat for a man named Gleason Green from Grand Manan. The would-be buyer said that he knew Gleason and that he was just a 16-year-old boy, daydreaming. "He'll never come for it," he told the boatbuilder. And the boat was sold. "I was only a kid," said Gleason to me, "and about half cryin'."

The boatbuilder considered him silently, then went into a huddle with the men in the shop. He came back, grinning. "We're going to build you a boat. It'll take seven days; you'll stay with me."

At the end of a week Gleason loaded his engine into the boat, asked what course to take, and sailed her home, an eight-hour journey. She was the first 40-foot boat ever owned by a Grand Mananer, and when the men of the island saw her coming into harbor they crowded down to the pier to welcome the boy who'd had the guts to get her and sail her home. He called her *The Teaser*.

Gleason never let a dollar slip away for lack of trying. One day years later, as he was leaning over the side of his boat, his false teeth fell into the water. Quick as a flash he seized a draw bucket, threw it into the sea and followed it with a heavy piece of line to mark the spot where the teeth had gone down. Then he borrowed a diving suit and returned to look for his teeth. Down he went, 50 feet into the sea, and landed right beside the pail; two feet away was the rope. And, in between, "my false teeth grinnin' up at me."

When an off-islander remarked, "If they'd been my teeth I'd have let them lie there," Green looked at him sharply. "Then you come by $30 a whole lot easier 'n I do," he said.

During the Great Depression of the '30s, Gleason and Lu were hard put to care for their brood of eight children. One day a boat-

Gleason Green's guests lunch during a sunny summer trip off Grand Manan. Lobsters are the island's biggest money crop. Competition is keen and the lobster pounds, some holding as much as 100 tons, must be stocked against the summer months when demand is high and lobstering forbidden. When fathometers were first used in small craft, a friend on the mainland lent one to Gleason. With this new gadget, which was scorned by his fellow lobstermen, he was soon hauling up more lobsters than any other man on the island. One lobsterman took to following him—and setting his own pots in the same place. "He was welcome to the lobsters," Gleason said, "but what got me was he'd sit his pots on top of mine, snarlin' up my lines." One day Gleason put his lobster pots down—in the wrong places. After the man had "laid his'n right side o' mine and sailed off," Gleason said, beginning to grin, "I come back, hauled mine in and moved 'em over where I should a put 'em down first." The other lobsterman could never understand how Gleason went on getting such a rich haul when his own was so poor. "Now," concluded Gleason, "if I'd tried tellin' him what to do, he'd never have learned that baitin' someone else's hook don't do you a mite o' good."

builder sent word to Gleason that he'd like to see him. It was during Prohibition in the United States and rumrunning was big business. The man offered Gleason $3,000 if he would deliver 1,500 hogsheads of liquor. Everything would be ready for him: men would be at the dock with chains and winches. "And if you're worried about the police," the rumrunner finished, "I'll have them up for a card game while you're unloading."

Gleason said he didn't think he was interested. "Three thousand dollars meant an awful lot to me then," he said years later, "but I didn't want no part of it. I looked at it this way: first time, I'd make a lot of money; second time, it'd be easier to take it; and the next time, I'd be slidin' down real fast. Pretty soon I'd go wild and end down at the bottom. When I told Lu about it that night, she said to me, 'Gleason, you done just right.'"

His success in later years made no change in his life. He represented his beloved Grand Manan at county fairs on the mainland, broadcast its opportunities over the radio, hauled lobsters, fought for improvements in the local Fisherman's Cooperative—of which he was the principal founder—and took part in island politics.

Businessmen, educators, writers, scientists, summering on Grand Manan, saw at first only a modest lobsterman whose boat was available to take them places. Before long they were seeking him out, asking him to go fishing with them, talking to him as friend to friend. He soaked up information from them and grew younger with each trip. They soaked up his faith in good, his freedom from fear.

After several fishing trips on Gleason Green's boat, a psychiatrist said to me, "That man has learned the joy of being himself. And it's catching, thank God, when you're with him."

Gleason told me once: "When I look back on everything that's happened to me, there ain't anything I'd like changed, except maybe I knew more. I don't know as anybody anywhere could have had a better life than Lu and me. And we ain't through yet. There's an awful lot I still want to do."

I feel about Gleason the way the seamen do when they pass powerful Gannett Light in the Bay of Fundy: the island on which the lighthouse stands is small and remote, but the light it sheds is strong and gives comfort in good weather and bad. How many lives it has affected no one knows.

Gleason Green started the '70s with a new boat, the Bonney Maid, *"40 feet long and 14 feet wide, with a frame of oak and planked all in cedar that I cut myself in Maine." Like the* Bonney Queen *and other Gleason Green boats (*Bonney Boy *and* Bonney Bride*), she carries the name of Alexander Bonney, the first white child born on Grand Manan.*

Green visited Expo 67 in Montreal—"just being a tourist for a change"—then returned to the familiar old routine: lobster fishing in the fall, "layin' by" and building traps in the winter, running boat trips in the summer. Still fit and active, he made no particular concession to being in his 70s.

Nor any special plans, for that matter. "I'll live each day as it comes," he said.

Mr. Commonwealth

By George Ronald

In the sunlit courtyard of London's stately Marlborough House, reporters surrounded Arnold Smith, the secretary-general of the Commonwealth. "What *do* countries like Sierra Leone, Pakistan and Canada have in common?" asked one.

"The answer is simple," said Smith. "We need to learn to share a planet. Belonging to the Commonwealth can help."

That was in 1965, on the day Smith accepted the newly created job, which he has called "the weirdest in the world." Five years later, as this lighthearted Canadian career diplomat started his second five-year term, he served a stronger, more cooperative Commonwealth that *was* learning to share.

Smith sees in diplomacy a special opportunity—"and therefore a responsibility"—to participate in the evolution of a world community. Always in pursuit of this evolution, Arnold Smith is responsible equally to more than 30 countries as dissimilar as Cyprus and Ceylon, huge India and tiny Barbados—and of course Britain, which unwittingly started the whole thing by going empire-building centuries ago.

The Queen is the Commonwealth's "reigning" but not "ruling" symbol. As nations are freed of British colonial status they may elect to join the Commonwealth or not (like Burma and the Sudan); once members, they may leave at any time (as Ireland did in 1948) or be forced to withdraw (as in the case of South Africa in 1961).

The Commonwealth, says Smith, is in no sense a rival to the United Nations but rather a useful supplement, more flexible and more intimate than the world body. The UN's regional and continental decentralization, as for economic commissions and development banks, is desirable but not enough: "The dangers of regional isolationism are very real. We should not put all our eggs in one basket."

As secretary-general, Smith neither seeks nor accepts the instructions of individual governments. Nor must he initiate action that might be interpreted as a violation of any country's sovereign rights. "This job," says Smith, "has virtually no power, but there are interesting opportunities for influence. It uses more of one's total personality than normal diplomatic jobs."

Not long ago the Commonwealth was conceived of as "one fleet, one flag, one throne"—a slogan that appeared in the Ontario public school textbooks Arnold Smith used as a boy. Up to 1947, when India and Pakistan joined the original member states (Australia, Britain, Canada, New Zealand and South Africa), the Commonwealth was white, wealthy and well-fed. Now its nearly 900,000,000 people

One of Arnold Smith's teachers remembers a boy who was "a persistent, pertinacious perfectionist—his goal was 100 percent and he generally managed 95 to 99." A British journalist sees a Commonwealth secretary-general who "dislikes self-importance in others and wouldn't tolerate it in himself." Says Smith: "There's a good bit of this occupational disease I call diploma-titis. If you take it seriously when people call you 'Excellency,' you've had it."

Arnold Smith has served two stints in Egypt—early in World War II (he managed time out for a Dead Sea swim) and in 1958-61, this time as Canadian ambassador to the United Arab Republic. In 1955-56 he was a truce commissioner in Cambodia, one of a team that included G. Parthasarthy (left), who later became Indian ambassador to the United Nations, and Zygfryd Wolniak, who became Polish ambassador to Canada and later Poland's deputy minister of foreign affairs.

—one-quarter of the world's population—are more colored than white, more poor than prosperous, more hungry than well-fed. "Naturally we have stresses," says Smith. "What would you expect?"

But, he adds, "Commonwealth countries share many memories, hopes, traditions. There are similarities in the organization and ethics of professions, in legal systems and administrative techniques. There are shared ideals: the rule of law, a free press, free elections. The practice has been suspended in some instances, but the ideals still matter."

When he took on the job in 1965 the prospects for the Commonwealth were bleak. "A few weeks after I moved in," says Smith, "the Malays and Singapore got a divorce. A few weeks later India and Pakistan went to war. Then the white colonial government of Rhodesia illegally declared unilateral independence from Britain and some African countries threatened to quit the Commonwealth."

Smith was flying to Nairobi, Kenya, when the crisis erupted. Undismayed by the news, he went on to Tanzania, Zambia and Malawi, delivering the same simple message: to pull the Commonwealth apart would help nobody, least of all the black majority in Rhodesia. "Over and over I argued that in a crisis you must *use* your channels of communications and influence, not destroy them in angry posturing."

Smith made his point. Ghana and Tanzania did break diplomatic relations with Britain for not taking a tougher line on Rhodesia but they did *not* withdraw from the Commonwealth. For Smith, that crisis is not over. "The international community can't afford not to deal properly with Rhodesia," he says. "It is intolerable that 250,000 racists should grab power over more than 4,850,000 Africans in defiance of all authority. Sooner or later, a majority rule is inevitable."

Despite such racking problems as Rhodesia and the Nigerian civil war (which the Commonwealth and the Organization of African Unity failed to solve although both came close), people know the Commonwealth works. "I was impressed," said Smith after independence ceremonies in Guyana (British Guiana) in 1966, "by the way the Guyanese saw the Commonwealth—not merely as a means of continuing the old relationship with Mama Britain in a new free form but for what it is: curious and ambiguous perhaps, but a series of valuable latticework relationships, actual or potential, with all sorts of other coun-

As Canadian ambassador in Moscow in 1961-63, Smith witnessed the fascinating ferment of Russia's de-Stalinization. Speaking fluent Russian (his wife does too), he gained Nikita Khrushchev's confidence and helped part the Iron Curtain a bit by arranging a string of cultural exchanges. Left: Smith and his daughter Alexandra in Moscow's Red Square with members of the Red Army Choir, before the choir left for a Canadian tour. Below: he dances at a Uzbek party during a visit to Tashkent.

tries." As Julius Nyerere, president of Tanzania, put it: "The Commonwealth is stronger than treaties, less selfish than alliances, less restrictive than any other association."

One of the ablest diplomats Canada ever produced, Arnold Cantwell Smith came to the tricky Commonwealth assignment well prepared. He studied at Upper Canada College, the Lycée Champollion in Grenoble and the University of Toronto, and went to Oxford as a Rhodes scholar in 1935. When he finished law at Oxford in 1938, Smith married Alberta-born Evelyn Stewart whom he'd met on a blind date in Toronto. First he found temporary work with the League of Nations secretariat. Then he worked in Estonia editing an English-language newspaper, *The Baltic Times,* and later serving as British Legation attaché in Tallinn. "I got into diplomacy," he says, "more or less by accident and as an acting Englishman."

When Russia invaded Estonia, Smith went to Cairo to the Middle East political warfare division of the British Ministry of State. In 1943 he accepted a lesser post in the new Canadian legation in Russia, jumping at the chance of transferring to his own country's service.

Working up the diplomatic ladder, in 1958 he was appointed ambassador in Cairo. Egyptians found the new Canadian envoy engagingly informal. On one occasion, he descended from an aircraft at Cairo airport, briefcase in hand, with three hula-hoops hung around his neck—gifts for his three children.

Smith's next ambassadorial posting was in Moscow. There, in early September 1962, he was secretly informed—"I still can't say how" —that Khrushchev was planning a showdown with the United States over Berlin. Though Smith informed the West, his warning got little attention until the plan became clear in October and aerial reconnaissance showed Russian missiles in Cuba. "Khrushchev wanted nuclear weapons there as a lever to get the West out of Berlin," says Smith. When faced with President Kennedy's quarantine of Cuba, Khrushchev told Smith, Russia—outmatched in the area—had to back down or respond with global war.

Back in Ottawa in 1963, Smith settled into a stint as Canada's assistant undersecretary of state for external affairs. Lester Pearson, then the prime minister, persuaded him to be a candidate for the new $30,000-a-year Commonwealth post, which he won on the first ballot.

The secretary-general's job is not all conference and crisis. It includes such formal affairs as Commonwealth fashion shows, this one attended by Princess Margaret. In London, Smith's rank entitles him to a chauffeur-driven Daimler (license CSG-1—for 1st Commonwealth Secretary-General) and a ten-room flat in Carlton Gardens, not far from his office in Marlborough House. In diplomatic assignments in many parts of the world, Smith has earned a reputation for informality. One hot day in Egypt, as he and a party of archeologists went ashore from a Nile steamer to view the temples at Abu Simbel, a squad of soldiers presented arms. It dawned on Smith—wearing sandals, slacks and a loud sport shirt—that this was a guard of honor for him; someone had phoned ahead. He slipped back aboard, put on a tie and jacket, disembarked again and formally acknowledged the guard's second salute.

He eventually put together a multinational staff of 180 men and women working with a $1,600,000 budget (30 percent from Britain, 19 from Canada, 11 from India, 10 from Australia).

A highly successful Commonwealth initiative has been the Colombo Plan for developing countries in South and Southeast Asia, now expanded to include non-Commonwealth recipients and donors. Canadian engineers, for example, helped build the great Warsak dam in Pakistan. Australia has sent more than 1,000 experts in agriculture, education and communications to Malaysia, India and other countries. India has trained thousands of people in many professional disciplines from other Colombo countries and set up a technical training institute for such studies in Malaysia. A Special Commonwealth African Assistance Plan (SCAAP), loosely patterned after the Colombo Plan, has been set up for Africa. A Caribbean Meteorological Service is supported by Commonwealth nations in that area.

Another creative scheme is third-party technical aid. Here the richer Commonwealth countries finance technical experts from less affluent member nations for projects in other developing countries. "Let's say a statistician is needed for a job in Swaziland," Smith explains. "Under this plan he might be found in Jamaica or Pakistan and be paid by Canada. We blur the awkward distinction between 'donor' and 'recipient.'"

Commonwealth cooperation is particularly helpful to younger members. Soon after Botswana became independent in 1966, diamonds were discovered and outsiders flocked to this remote country. Having suddenly to negotiate on royalties and tax arrangements with multi-billion-dollar international corporations, Botswana's President Seretse Khama appealed to the secretariat for help. Smith sent Canadian and Ghanaian experts who helped Botswana get a far better deal with the diamond syndicates than she could have negotiated on her own.

In arranging such cooperation, the secretary-general has no patience with bureaucratic timidity. "What irritates me most," says Smith, "is the civil servant who thinks he has done his duty if he can find sophisticated reasons for saying 'no' to any new idea. They think that saying 'yes' means sticking your neck out. But your neck is *always* out. That's what makes life exhilarating.

"I once complained to my wife that I sometimes feel like Sisyphus, trying to roll a heavy boulder uphill. She commented tartly: 'Pushing boulders uphill is what we are here for.'"

Deeply concerned about man's search for truth, Smith is what he calls a practicing Christian. "Individuals and nations alike," he says, "find their souls by finding God, by recognizing the real values in life and doing something about them."

From his mother—who had taught Greek and Hebrew at Ohio Wesleyan University Smith learned the value of daily Bible reading. As soon as he awakens, he reads for 10-15 minutes from his mother's Bible—a well-worn volume stuffed with notes and clippings like a time-tested recipe book. "There's a tremendous amount of hardheaded insight into political science in the Bible," he says. It is the volume he most often recommends. "By the way," he'll remark, "if you want a *really* good book on that . . ."

Smith, who logs some 100,000 miles a year on his job, sets himself a hard pace. Fortunately, he combines a gift for absolute concentration with the ability to switch off completely. The family's 70-acre farm in France's Aquitaine, 80 miles east of Bordeaux, is where he unwinds best. There he reads his fill of light fiction or, singing Gilbert and Sullivan arias at the top of his voice, chugs around on a small tractor. He roams the countryside, using flawless French and appropriate gestures as he bargains for antiques at village markets. The farm produces "a good red wine" that the Smiths hope one day to bottle and label for their friends. Meanwhile, they have planted good Canadian corn and have shared with the *Aquitains* the delights of hot buttered popcorn. *"Mon Dieu,"* said one old man at the first demonstration, *"du maïs explosif!"*

In London, the Smiths' relaxations are theater, ballet and art, including scouting the galleries. They have an international collection of bronzes, carvings and paintings. Typical of their cosmopolitan library is Capt. Frederick Marryat's *The Settlers in Canada,* published in 1844 in Leipzig and bought by the Smiths in Moscow a century later.

Their Carlton Gardens flat is ideally situated for quiet diplomacy—in easy walking distance of Whitehall, Buckingham Palace, St. James's Palace, the British foreign secretary's residence and a number of major embassies and high commissions.

Smith recognizes the occasional need for diplomatic corner-cutting, as when Michael Okpara, former premier of Eastern Nigeria (Biafra), flew to London at the height of the Nigerian civil war. Okpara could not officially enter Britain but it was imperative that he see

With his top aides, Secretary-General Smith prepares for a Commonwealth heads-of-government meeting. "We coordinate views on dates, venue and agenda," says Smith. "We prepare background papers and fill inkpots." From left: T. E. Gooneratne of Ceylon, a deputy secretary-general; Dr. H. W. Springer of Barbados, assistant secretary-general, and A. L. Adu of Ghana, a deputy secretary-general. Although the great gatherings of government leaders, every 18 months or so, get most of the headlines, the important work of Commonwealth mutual assistance goes on every day. Intra-Commonwealth grants, loans, public investments and technical-aid spending total some $750,000,000 a year—with benefits beyond calculation in mere dollars. Scholarships enable Ghanaian dentists to study in New Zealand, Pakistanis to specialize in chemistry in Canada, Malaysian agriculturists to take advanced training in India. Hundreds of university teachers go on exchange assignments to other countries.

Arnold Smith travels about 100,000 miles a year, to Commonwealth countries in many parts of the world. Top: with General Yakubu Gowon at the opening of an education conference in Lagos. Above: with Mrs. Smith outside the Ming Court Hotel in Singapore after a 1971 meeting of prime ministers and presidents. Singapore officials chose this license number for the car assigned to Smith on grounds that he was dealing with 31 Commonwealth Heads of Government.

the secretary-general. Smith drove to Heathrow Airport and hurried into an Immigration room *outside the Customs area.* There, technically not in Britain, the two men conferred.

To Smith the Commonwealth secretariat seemed the ideal instrument for mediation of the Nigerian conflict and he never worked harder in his life. In April 1968, after scores of preliminary conversations—among them the airport meeting with Okpara—he brought together Chief Anthony Enahoro, federal information commissioner, and Chief Justice Sir Louis Mbanefo, representing Biafra. Nine days of meetings—in Smith's apartment, because it was felt Marlborough House would be too formal—ended with a decision to hold full-dress negotiations in Kampala. There, one side proposed Smith be chairman; the other demanded a head of state. Smith got them to negotiate without a chairman—and did the job unofficially himself. When the two sides clashed and Mbanefo tried to walk out, Smith quietly persuaded Uganda's President Obote to call the leaders to his office and urge them to continue. The talks went on for another week. Suddenly, on instructions from Colonel Ojukwu, the Biafrans really walked out.

"It was the most irresponsible act I've ever seen in my diplomatic experience," Smith said later. "Here was a real opportunity for a compromise, a good deal for the Ibos because Tony Enahoro was ready to accept it if Sir Louis would. But Ojukwu's plan was to use the talks only for political warfare and propaganda and then to blame Lagos for the break. It was a tragic decision Ojukwu made for his people."

Smith maintained contact with both sides and encouraged new negotiations (such as those in 1968 at Niamey and Addis Ababa under the aegis of the OAU). He tried again at the Commonwealth conference in London in January 1969. Nigeria, a Commonwealth member, was represented; Biafra was not—but Smith had suggested that a Biafran team of ministers be ready for talks *outside* the conference.

"Biafra agreed that they would meet the Nigerian delegation at my flat," says Smith. "Nigeria was ready. But the day before the conference was to open, Ojukwu changed his mind and ordered his delegation out of England. He was playing for all or nothing, not for a compromise."

Arnold Smith knows better than any other man the immensity of the Commonwealth's troubles. "Anybody in a job like mine, responsible to a large group of mostly poor countries, finds that his main problems are with the rich and powerful," he says. "I feel no complacency about the future. But if we can help deal with the problems of white and non-white and of rich and poor, the Commonwealth will make a tremendous contribution to the future of mankind. If we can't, the Commonwealth might disintegrate. So might the world. We can't go on living on a planet that's two-thirds slum—not with safety."

But Smith remains optimistic. He believes that man is essentially good, that all the great problems *can* be solved, that peace *is* attainable. "I think mankind will make it," he says, "because I think mankind basically will have enough sense." Then, in the straightforward language of his simple faith. "I believe that ultimately things are in the hands of God. He knows where He's going. He knows where we're going too."

268

Marlborough House

Secretary-General Arnold Smith (above, with Prince Charles) works at Commonwealth headquarters in Marlborough House, one of the world's most splendidly ornate office buildings. The great red-brick house on London's Pall Mall (top, seen from the garden) was built by Sir Christopher Wren in 1711 for John Churchill, first Duke of Marlborough. It became the traditional home of the Queen Mother or the heir to the throne: Edward VII lived here as Prince of Wales and it was Queen Mary's home until her death in 1953. Now it contains the Commonwealth secretariat offices, a reference library on Commonwealth subjects, a press center, a television studio and accommodation for Commonwealth conferences (top right). Magnificent staircases are embellished with Louis Laguerre's superb wall-paintings of Marlborough's famous battles—Blenheim, Ramillies and Malplaquet. On the grounds are a royal cat-and-dog cemetery and a revolving summerhouse where old Queen Mary could always face the sun.

The Joyous Feast of Family

By Isabel Stevenson, M.D.

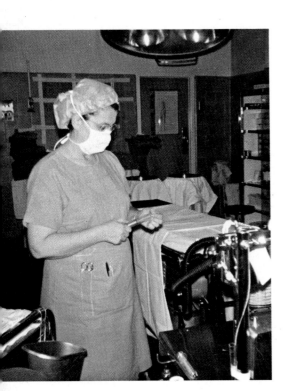

Dr. Isabel Stevenson sets up for anesthesia in a surgical room at the Calgary General. "Whatever I have done for my adopted children," she says, "they've done far more for me."

It was a moment to cherish—later. I'd gone to a restaurant with my two small daughters, Mary and Margaret, and their infant brother Jeffrey. At the next table, a young woman fell to admiring Jeff. "Have you any babies?" asked Margaret, age four.

"No," she replied. "I'm not married."

"That's all right," piped up Mary, a chirpy moppet of seven. "Neither is my mommy."

Blush as I might, it was true. I *am* an unwed mother, with three children who have filled my heart with maternal joys that spinsters aren't supposed to know. What saves me from society's frowns—but not always—is the fact that my family is adopted.

This, in itself, is rare enough. Adoption by a single parent is a fairly recent trend in Calgary, where I work as an anesthetist. But in addition, there's a decidedly one-world cast to my brood. Since I first adopted a baby in 1961, I've felt no reason to reject homeless children simply because their color doesn't match my own.

And so Mary is part Chinese, a bright blonde with almond-shaped eyes.

Margaret, darkly adorable, is part Prairie Indian.

And Jeff happens to be a fair-haired Caucasian. His arrival was duly noted by a female acquaintance who probably boycotts Brotherhood Week. "How nice," she purred, "that your name will be carried on by a *white* child."

Most of my friends and relatives are now happy for me and my family because *we're* happy. But we could all do without those patronizing people who, seeing me kiss my girls good night, exclaim, "You're just like a *real* mother!" After all, childbearing is merely a biologic act; most women can manage it in nine months. To be a "real" mother, natural or adoptive, takes years of patient, loving care.

Since our family is so clearly different from most, it would be foolish to pretend otherwise. Rather than trying to hide the truth like something shameful, I've already told all three how they came to me and why our coloring isn't quite the same. For them, however others may feel, adoption and mixed race must become accepted facts of life.

And so an incident at Mary's school made me just as proud as any "real" mother could ever be. In a classroom discussion on family relationships, one boy stated that children without parents were sent to orphanages. "No they aren't," insisted Mary, her head held high. "They get adopted, like me."

For me, the dual role of breadwinner-homemaker is always demanding, often discouraging. Yet nothing has ever rewarded me so well, in the priceless coin of contentment.

Some might envy the life I led before. At 34, as a staff specialist at the Calgary General Hospital, I had my own home, car and summer cottage, plus enough money to indulge most of my whims. I was more than slightly self-centered and, with such independence, I wasn't in any frantic rush to get married.

Then, in December 1960, I saw a cartoon Christmas card on our hospital bulletin board. It pictured a little old lady at a festive table, carving a turkey for her life's companion—a cat. Even while smiling, I felt a stab of pain: all *I* had at home was a pampered dog. "In 30 years," I reflected, "that old girl could be *you.*"

That Christmas seemed to emphasize how much I'd received during my lifetime—largely through the sheer luck of being born into a well-fixed family—and how little I'd given to others. As a doctor, I also knew that less fortunate accidents of birth resulted in thousands of unwanted babies.

Perhaps if I opened my home, and my *heart* . . .

A few days later, at the Alberta public welfare bureau in Calgary, I offered to take in a homeless child, explaining that I had a full-time housekeeper to help care for it. A social worker turned me down flat, saying. "You're single." (Technically, anyone over 21 could adopt a youngster in Alberta, as in many Canadian provinces, but very few one-parent adoptions had yet been arranged.)

Then I wrote to a med-school classmate in another city, asking him to help arrange a private adoption. He tried to dissuade me—"Why tie yourself down if you don't have to?"—but he did mention one possibility: an unwed teen-ager, soon to give birth, was planning to release her baby for adoption. "The girl's white," he added. "But the father's Chinese."

"Never mind that," I replied. "See what you can do."

Not long after, my classmate phoned to say that the baby was about to be born. "I still think you're asking for trouble," he said. "But you'll have to decide right now. Boy or girl, is it yes or no?" I hesitated for a second. "Either way, it's yes." Then, a silent prayer: *Dear God, don't let me fail this child.*

Within the week, I drove 200 miles to pick up a tiny, helpless infant. Back home that night, pacing the floor with her, I found that she had colic, diaper rash and the lungs of an infant Ethel Merman. Though I'd studied pediatrics, all I remembered was what went *wrong* with babies. After a week of sleepless nights, I phoned another doctor and poured out my worries. He just laughed. "Give her a quarter grain of phenobarb—then take some yourself."

By then, I'd begun facing mixed reaction to Mary's adoption. While our hospital's nurses were so pleased that they held a surprise shower for me, some of my friends voiced strong disapproval, which hurt deeply. "What will people *think*?" asked one, thereby revealing what *she* thought. Out of genuine concern for me, even my own parents were upset by Mary's multiracial background. Happily, as time went on, they both grew very fond of her. When I later mentioned that

Mary, Margaret and Jeff, photographed at Easter 1969. More pictures from their family album are on the next two pages.

271

Mary, July 20, 1961

Mary's first birthday
Jan. 26, 1962

Winter 1965

Mary and Margaret
Christmas 1963

Fall 1965

Margaret
Spring 1966

Mary, Margaret and Jeffrey
Aug. 1967

Margaret and friend
Spring 1967

Margaret's birthday, 1967

C'mon, let's pose! 1967

Winter fun, 1968

Combined birthday party
for Jeff and Mary, 1969

Halloween 1969

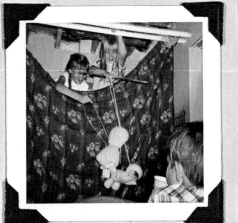

Christmas 1969

"The Play", Summer 1970
Admission 1¢

Fall 1970

I might adopt a sister for Mary, my father's response was an unrestrained, "Wonderful!"

Equally heartening was the fact that official positions also softened—largely because Alberta's first single-parent adoptions had worked out well. In 1963, when Mary began showing the temperamental signs of being a "lonely only," I again called at the provincial welfare office to ask about getting another baby.

Expecting a further refusal, I was almost floored by the supervisor's reply. "Fine," she said. "What kind?" The welfare workers had no trouble "selling" me on Margaret, a month-old darling of white and Indian parentage, with jet black hair, gray eyes and glowing pink skin.

Shortly after Margaret's arrival, my mother suddenly died, our housekeeper left to raise a family of her own, and we all moved in with my ailing father, who hadn't long to live. It was an unsettling period for little Mary. Like the firstborn in many an ordinary family, she resented the new baby as a rival for my affections. Once, after she'd dumped Margaret's food on the floor to get attention, I spanked her. She didn't even whimper. But when I caught her expression—smiling!—I began to weep. "Oh, Mommy," she cried, throwing her arms around me, "you *do* love me!"

As they grew older, an unexpected addition to our family helped draw my girls together. In the spring of 1967, at a public meeting where social workers outlined the need for more adoptive parents, I found myself thinking of all the couples who were raising four or five kids on much less than my income, and doing a fine job of it.

The upshot was that I soon brought home five-week-old Jeffrey, a blue-eyed cherub who'd been with foster parents. "They are glad I am getting a home of my very own," read a note pinned to his blanket. "Please take good care of me." While I was tucking Jeff into his crib, Mary and Margaret fled from the house. Moments later they came scampering back up to the nursery, hand in hand, with half a dozen playmates in tow. "There he is!" they exclaimed, faces shining with shared pride. "Our baby brother!"

In their innocence, most neighboring youngsters seem totally color-blind to the varied hues of our family. Not so, alas, with some adults. On hearing of my latest adoption, one woman asked me, "What mixture is this one?"

"None. He's just sort of white."

"Ah," she said approvingly, "a *real* Canadian."

Much as I'd prefer to ignore such attitudes, I'm aware that my girls' racial backgrounds make them vulnerable to the views of others. Since I can't rid the whole world of racial prejudice, I hope to arm them with the best defense against it: a quiet confidence in their own innate worth. To achieve this, I've exposed both girls to various facets of Indian and Chinese culture that they can admire.

Most vital of all is the attitude of my children toward themselves. One evening, when she was four, Mary suddenly asked why she didn't have a father like her friends.

"Because I adopted you," I replied as calmly as possible. "And I'm not married." Then I explained that her natural parents had been

too young to provide all that they had hoped for her. Because they loved her so much—*not because she wasn't wanted*—they had given her to me to care for. Mary stared at her plate and abruptly changed the subject. "I don't like onions for supper," she said. But she had taken it all in, because later I heard her repeating my explanation to Margaret, when *she* began to wonder.

Whatever I have done for my adopted children, they've done far more for me. The desire to enrich their lives has broadened my own horizons. I find myself giving more, not only of money but of myself, to church and charitable agencies that serve others. Formerly rather retiring, I've grown quite assertive. I once soundly lectured two older boys for taunting a young Negro about her color; racial bigotry is a personal affront now, because it can affect *my* kids.

But most of all, I've found a long-lacked sense of fulfillment. I felt it as never before one Christmas Day, when we all sat down to dinner. As I began carving the turkey, I couldn't help recalling the old lady and her cat. Jeff was gurgling beside me in his high chair while the girls chattered happily together, each child so different, yet each so precious in his own way. Glancing around the table at their radiant faces, I was overwhelmed with gratitude for what these children have given me—a chance to share in the joyous feast of family.

275

Maverick
from the Miramichi

By Irwin Ross

When Beaverbrook acquired the London *Daily Express* in 1916, its circulation was 229,000. It now sells well over 4,000,000 and blankets Britain with simultaneous publication in London, Manchester and Glasgow.

He sat in the mild October sun on the terrace of his country home outside London, an old man bundled in a huge coat, a black fedora crushed on his head, one hand resting on the telephone at his side. "Vines," he called out, "get me my 'pending' folder." The secretary—one of four—came on the run. "Vines," he shouted two minutes later, "get me Mr. Baker." The deputy editor of the London *Daily Express* was soon on the line. The old man uttered a gruff "Hello" and asked, "What's the news?" He listened intently, interjecting occasional comments. "You have a photographer out there, I hope.... What else is going on?... Between England and France?... Now, would you take a leader?" Then Beaverbrook rapidly outlined an editorial for the next day's paper—too fast for anyone to take notes, but I was well aware that at the other end of the line a tape recorder was preserving his words. (All of Beaverbrook's chief executives had tape recorders, to keep up with him.)

Even as an old man, Lord Beaverbrook was as hard-driving and irrepressible as ever, after a fabulous half-century career of newspapering, politicking and generally setting Britain on its ear. The last of the old-fashioned press lords, he put his personal stamp on three huge London newspapers—the morning *Daily Express*, the *Evening Standard* and the *Sunday Express*.

To Beaverbrook, journalism always meant causes and battles—which he gloried in. I once asked him about his feud with Stanley Baldwin, the Conservative Party leader in the '20s and '30s. "Vines," Beaverbrook boomed, "what was that remark Baldwin made about me being a prostitute?" The secretary reported that Baldwin had accused him of seeking "power without responsibility—the prerogative of the harlot throughout the ages." Beaverbrook threw back his head and roared with laughter.

He flipped the pages of a fat scrapbook dealing with the 1945 elections. "Wonderful! Wonderful!" he exclaimed, pointing to attacks he had sustained. *The Times* had taken him to task in an editorial, "The Bad Wolf." The *Cooperative News* tagged him "Minister of Chaos"; another article proclaimed, "Beaverbrook in Blunderland." Most of the assaults were dutifully reported in the Beaverbrook press, except once in June 1945, when the *Daily Express* ran the statement: "To make space for Mr. Churchill's broadcast speech, reports of attacks on Lord Beaverbrook last night have been held over."

Zesty, full of enthusiasm, at times Beaverbrook was a little in awe of his own durability. "People wonder why this tree is still standing," he once said. "*I* wonder why."

The answer, he speculated, may have had to do with "the emotion and passion" which infused all his works. "I am the victim of the Furies," he once wrote. "On the rockbound coast of New Brunswick the waves break incessantly. Every now and then comes a particularly dangerous wave smashing viciously against the rock. It is called The Rage. That's me."

The Rage administered his vast enterprises from an overstuffed chair in the study of his country home, Cherkley, in Surrey, an hour from downtown London. He had two telephones within reach, a dictating machine, a button board to summon his secretaries, pads of note paper, stacks of correspondence, newspapers, books. He scanned letters and memos, tossing discards to the floor; by noon he was ankle-deep in paper. At regular intervals he telephoned the editors and business managers of his three papers. His first question was always "What's the news?" and he often had an item or two to contribute to it from his vast network of government contacts.

As inspiration seized him, Beaverbrook snatched up the microphone of his dictating machine, and fired away with ideas, criticisms, exhortations. Every day, recording discs were dispatched by courier to the *Express* office in Fleet Street. "Too much space given to car-

Max , Lord Beaverbrook.

"The Beaver's" own employes were at liberty to criticize him in his own paper—and his cartoonists freely availed themselves of the privilege. David Low's caricatures of him—moon-faced, with wide, smirking mouth—were famous.

This was the Presbyterian manse at Newcastle, N.B., where Max Aitken lived as a child. It is now a library. Young Max is second from the left in the group that posed for the photo at top. In the center of the trio on the right is Dr. F.B. Yorston, his schoolmaster.

toons," a communiqué might admonish. Or, "First edition of the *Daily Express* has no Indonesian pictures. Why?" He expected a prompt reply by phone or teletype. Business conferences went on while he was getting his hair clipped, breakfasting in bed or taking his bath. When he used to go riding, a mounted secretary would accompany him, taking notes on a pad.

The years 1940-41 were Beaverbrook's heroic phase. In May 1940, it became apparent that Britain was woefully unprepared to defend itself in the air. One of Churchill's first acts as prime minister was to make Beaverbrook minister of aircraft production, giving him complete control.

Beaverbrook was no production genius. He was, however, probably the most energetic and ruthless man in Britain. Convinced that the six months ahead would determine the country's fate, he was prepared to use any stratagem, any procedures, to obtain the vital weapons. He worked seven days a week, 18 hours a day, and imbued his colleagues with missionary fervor. At scores of aircraft factories he addressed the production-line workers, overwhelming them with eloquent appeals, telling them that the nation's fate depended on them.

He stepped on bureaucratic toes—taking factory space wherever he could find it, seizing equipment under the control of other ministries. A typical maneuver involved a shortage of a certain steel alloy. The Beaver could get nowhere with the Ministry of Supply, the normal procurement channel, so he authorized an associate to obtain the alloy through a friend in the United States. When the shipment arrived in Liverpool, the harbor had been severely damaged in an air raid and 100 ships were waiting to be unloaded. Again through unofficial channels, Beaverbrook arranged for his cargo to be unloaded out of turn—without the knowledge of the Ministry of Supply.

These tactics created considerable resentment, but what counted in the end was that Beaverbrook produced the planes without which the Battle of Britain could not have been won. In May, when he took over, the metropolitan air force had fewer than 800 serviceable Hurricanes and Spitfires; in September, despite severe combat losses, the figure was 1,228 serviceable craft. Churchill put it well:"Lord Beaverbrook is at his very best when things are at their very worst."

Until Beaverbrook received a peerage in 1917, his name was William Maxwell Aitken. Max, as he was known, was born in 1879 in Maple, Ont., one of ten children of a Presbyterian minister who moved to New Brunswick the following year. There he grew up in the Miramichi Valley. After high school Max briefly studied law, then sold insurance and ran a bowling alley in Calgary; he was in the meat business for a while in Edmonton. In his early 20s, back east in Halifax, he went to work as a bond salesman, and immediately demonstrated a flair for corporate facts and figures as well as great persuasiveness with customers. He made ten percent of what he sold, and by the time he was 22 he had run up sales of $1,500,000.

Before long he was promoting industrial mergers—in steel, electric power, cement and other industries. He would arrange the mergers, then sell the securities of the new firms to the public. At 31, he had amassed a fortune of $5,000,000 and earned a reputation as a financial buccaneer.

With his wife he went to England in August 1910 on a visit. At the behest of his friend and fellow New Brunswicker Bonar Law, one of the powers in the Conservative Party, he stood for parliament in the election of December 1910. The young Canadian won an upset victory, became a celebrity overnight and immediately plunged into the thick of party politics.

In 1916, Aitken had a major hand in the maneuvers that led to the installation of Lloyd George as prime minister. For his efforts he was elevated to the House of Lords as the first Baron Beaverbrook—a distinction he was later to regret, for it removed him from the true center of power. Also in 1916 he bought control of the *Daily Express,* a struggling paper for which he paid $87,500. His motive was purely political, to promote the future of Bonar Law and push his own campaign for preferential treatment in Britain for Empire products, and tariffs against the rest of the world.

To convert the multitude, he had first to seek a wide audience; and to reach a wide audience, he needed a highly readable product. Ironically, when he finally attained an audience of millions he found that many people enjoyed his papers who would not buy his opinions. Beaverbrook set out to learn the craft of journalism himself and, over the years, the distinct style of his papers took shape: simple, crisp writing, echoing the staccato beat of Beaverbrook's own speech, emphasis on the human element, plus dramatic eyewitness reporting. Arthur Christiansen, for 25 years editor of the *Daily Express,* said the aim was to present the news "in such a way that it would be interesting both to the permanent secretary of the Foreign Office and to the charwoman who brushed his office floor in the morning. My approach was based on the idea that when you looked at the front page you said 'Good heavens!', when you looked at the middle page you said 'Holy smoke!' and by the time you got to the back page—well, I'd have to utter a profanity to show how exciting it was."

Stumping Britain in 1931, Lord Beaverbrook pours out his ideas on "Empire Free Trade," demanding high tariff walls around the Empire and special consideration for British farmers. No advertiser could expect favored treatment from Beaverbrook's newspapers. The *Evening Standard*'s witty and corrosive film critic, Milton Shulman, earned the enmity of the film companies and in 1953 they all withdrew their advertising from the Beaverbrook press. Movie advertising was worth $700,000 a year but Beaverbrook refused to budge. Shulman stayed in his job and after four months the boycott began to crack.

Newly appointed minister of aircraft production, Lord Beaverbrook manages a smile as he leaves a cabinet meeting in London in May 1940. Especially in his later years, he devoted much time to benefactions in his beloved New Brunswick, spending $20,000,000 on schools, skating rinks and other gifts such as the Beaverbrook Art Gallery (right). He and Sir Winston Churchill helped rule Britain in both world wars.

The ideas that Beaverbrook tried to sell did not change substantially with the years. No journalist more eloquently hymned the glories of the British Empire or mourned its dismemberment with greater anguish. After 1951, when he opposed the government's Empire policy, the figure of the Crusader atop the front page of the *Express* was in chains. In the 1920s and early '30s he campaigned strenuously for "Empire Free Trade," battling the orthodox Conservative leadership and even putting up his own parliamentary candidates. (Beaverbrook lost.) He ardently opposed British entry into the Common Market.

He was always a maverick in Conservative politics, opposing the official line on such subjects as freedom for Ireland (which he favored) and the enforced abdication of King Edward VIII (which he opposed). His papers ridiculed the hereditary peerage, extolled economic freedom for the individual, glorified affluence for the multitude. Over the years, he unquestionably affected British attitudes on these issues.

He published a series of political chronicles of the great events in which he was both eyewitness and participant, starting with World War I. Each volume sparkles with the brilliant insight of a man who was one of the chief architects of modern British history.

He and Churchill were the last survivors of the governments that ruled Britain in the two world wars. "It must be nearly time for an accounting," Beaverbrook mused as an old man. "I must have my late night final before long."

He was in a sprightly mood at a huge stag party given by his fellow Canadian press titan, Lord Thomson of Fleet, to mark Beaverbrook's 85th birthday in May 1964. "I don't feel much different than I did when I was 84," he said that night.

But he hinted that it was time for him to embark on a new project. "This is my final word," he said. "It is time for me to become an apprentice once more. I am not certain in which direction, but somewhere, sometime, soon."

He died two weeks later.

No Sense At All
in Stopping

By Irwin Ross

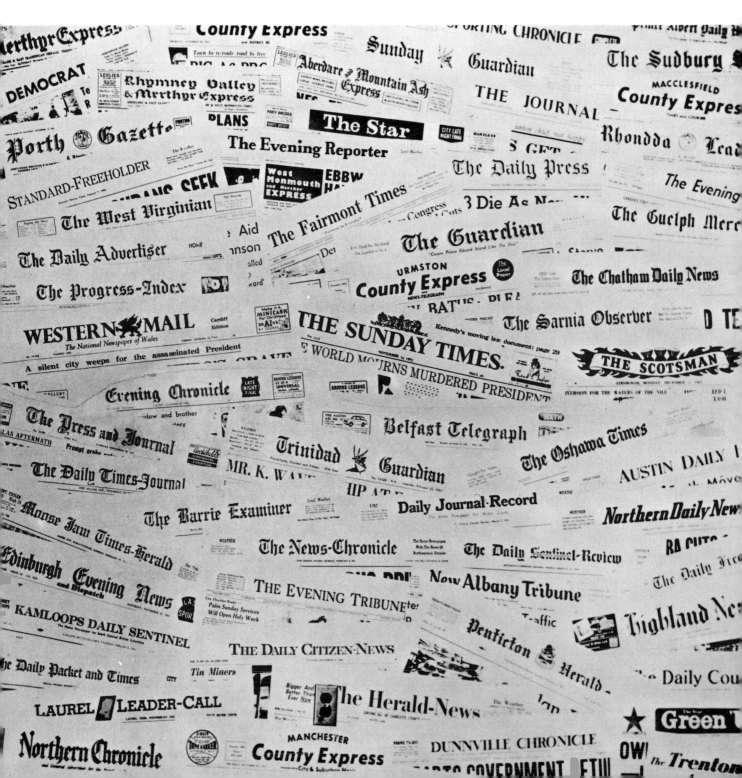

For Roy Herbert Thomson the road to success was paved with failure. When he was 25, he failed miserably as a farmer in Saskatchewan. Four years later, his auto-supply business in Toronto went to the wall. He was still teetering on the brink of insolvency when he was 40. And in 1953 he lost a bid for a seat in the House of Commons as the Conservative member for York Centre.

Yet he became one of the world's biggest press magnates, with a considerable fortune. Though London-based, Lord Thomson of Fleet owns more than 40 Canadian newspapers, more newspapers in the United States than any American, and more newspapers around the globe than any other man in history. In addition, he has accumulated a large list of magazines and trade journals, book-publishing houses, radio and television corporations, travel companies and an airline.*

The late-blooming millionaire with the ruddy cheeks, thick spectacles and well-upholstered waistline is in his late 70s. He stoops a little with the years but is still bustling and energetic. He has gone through life extending his hand and saying, "My name's Thomson. Call me Roy." He clearly likes people, and people invariably like him —which has been one of the secrets of his success. Another has been a monumental drive to succeed. And he had courage: he ran risks, continually mortgaged the present to grasp at the future. Thomson's explanation is simple:

"The dominating factor in my life is that I wanted to make money. There are lots of less worthy ambitions."

Thomson has wanted to do other things as well, though he usually does not talk about them. It was not an obsession with money that led him a few years ago to donate $12,000,000 to set up a foundation to train budding journalists from underdeveloped countries. If profits were his primary goal, he would not have taken over the money-losing London *Times*, pledged his fortune and that of his family to its continuance. Nor would he say, in an unguarded moment, "When I go, I want to have the best Sunday paper and the best daily paper in Britain." The latter statement is unusual for Thomson; as a colleague once put it, "He hates to admit to any noble instincts."

Instead Thomson delights in talking about his money-drive. In 1958, after receiving a government license to run Scottish commercial television he found that his profits were enormous. "It's just like having a license to print your own money!" he told a reporter in Canada.

He was equally candid in his campaign to get into the British House of Lords. In a sharp departure from British custom, he voiced his aspiration directly to the prime minister (then Harold Macmillan). When Macmillan replied that he could not recommend a Canadian citizen, Thomson promptly took out British citizenship. In 1964, he was made a hereditary peer. "I believe that when you want something, you should go after it," he explains. On another occasion, he commented that his peerage "was the best way to prove to Canadians that I'm a success."

Thomson's every characteristic is more emphatic than in most

The weekly *Timmins Press* ("If It Will Help The North, We Are FOR It") came first. This issue of May 7, 1934, announced that Roy H. Thomson, president of the Northern Broadcasting Company, was the paper's new publisher. "The dominating factor in my life," Lord Thomson has said, "is that I wanted to make money." He makes it with *Guardians*, *Chronicles* and *Tribunes*, many an *Express* and *Times*, various *Sentinels*, *Heralds* and *Journals*, a *Reporter*, a *Democrat*, a *Citizen*, a *Standard-Freeholder*, a *West Virginian*, a *Scotsman*, a *Packet and Times*...

---

* As this book went to press, the Thomson "chain" included 46 newspapers in Canada, 50 in the United States and 90 in other countries. Thomson's Britannia Airways, with nine jets, was Britain's second largest independent airline.

mortals, and none more so than his frugality. He still rides the Underground to work, buys but one suit a year. One day, he was showing off a new overcoat to his son Kenneth. He had bought it at a sale, he said, marked down by £18 15s. (then about $50); he'd only had to queue for half an hour. "Can you think of an easier way to make £18 15s. in half an hour?" Thomson exclaimed.

When he travels by air, he almost always goes tourist class. "If you forced him to fly first class," Ken Thomson says, "he'd be miserable all the way over the Atlantic knowing he was wasting all that money."

Thomson has never forgotten how long it took him to get where he is. His father was a barber in Toronto, his mother a hotel chambermaid. They were always poor. Young Roy was a shy, withdrawn lad peering wistfully out at the world through thick lenses which he first wore when he was seven. His bad eyesight made athletics hazardous for him, and he spent most of his leisure time sprawled on the floor reading books (Horatio Alger's were great favorites) and poring over baseball statistics. Unlikely as it seemed, he began to tell people that he would be a millionaire by the time he was 30.

When he was 13, he enrolled in a business school where he learned typing, shorthand and the rudiments of bookkeeping. At 14, his schooling ended, and he got his first job—as a clerk in a coal yard. At 19, he became a salesman—a providential change, for he gradually overcame his shyness as he impressed customers with the virtues of his company's rope, twine and fishing tackle. In 1916, he felt sufficiently well-established to marry Edna Irvine, whom he had been determinedly courting for some time. On their honeymoon in New York, he diligently read every newspaper sold in the hotel. He had no professional curiosity about newspapers at the time; he was just passionately interested in reading them.

After several restless, unsuccessful ventures, Thomson in 1925 gladly accepted an Ottawa franchise to sell radios, which were then enjoying their first sales boom. Three years later, he shifted his base of operations to northern Ontario, where, he knew, there was a vast untapped market for radios. But since most of his customers could get nothing but static, he decided to open a radio station in North Bay.

With a promissory note for $500, he bought an ancient transmitter, then persuaded a local movie house to give him space backstage for a studio in return for free advertising. He hired an announcer, and on March 4, 1931, the station went on the air, the first in northern Ontario. Before long, it was making money, and Thomson found it easier to sell radios. The station clearly met a need. Also, Thomson was an inspired salesman of commercials. He proceeded to set up other stations in the gold-mining towns of Timmins and Kirkland Lake.

In 1934, Thomson's tiny empire acquired its first newspaper, the weekly *Timmins Press*. The purchase came about in an odd way. Thomson had a difference of opinion with the paper's publisher, who threatened editorial reprisals against Thomson's radio station. To settle the matter, Thomson offered to buy the paper. The owner agreed—for $6,000. Since his cash reserves were still meager, Thomson offered $200 down and promissory notes to cover the balance. The owner was aghast at the terms, but Thomson, always the soul of reasonableness

Announcement

THE TIMMINS PRESS last week was placed under new management, with Mr. Roy H. Thomson, president of the Northern Broadcasting Company, becoming the publisher as from May 1.

Immediately after taking over the newspaper and commercial printing business here, Mr. Thomson made the following announcement to our readers and to the business men of Timmins and Northern Ontario:

"The Timmins Press will continue to be published each Monday from the present office, 3 Spruce street north, in Timmins. It will be my endeavor to so direct it as to merit your confidence in it having only the best interests of this section of Northern Ontario at heart.

"In politics, The Press will be independent. I believe a newspaper should represent all shades of political opinion and that its readers are entitled to ALL the news, presented in an impartial manner and not colored to suit the political views of its management. I also believe that those in public office should be given credit when credit is due, and criticized when their actions call for criticism—and this irrespective of party, creed or belief.

"I believe The Press should present to its readers primarily a comprehensive word picture of the ebb and flow of life in their community. It is my opinion that in the past the Porcupine Camp has been neglected insofar as news coverage is concerned. Although the leading events of the community have been reported, numerous other events worthy of and deserving space have been left unchronicled. In accord with general newspaper practice, items published in The Press, other than editorials, will be news which we will endeavor to present in a fair, unbiased, impartial manner. The opinions of the management will be set forth in the 'Editorial' columns.

"I pledge the support of this newspaper to all movements of a constructive nature sponsored by individuals or organizations. And I ask your support in making this paper, your paper, properly representative of this great and rich section of Northern Ontario.

"I express the sincere hope that our efforts to give the Town of Timmins and Northern Ontario a progressive, modern newspaper will meet with the approval of the public. Perhaps at no time in the past has the newspaper played so important a part in the life of the community, and for society generally, as it does today. Old ideas are fading into the background with new conceptions of things political, economical and moral being pushed to the front by Progress. It is only with the greatest effort that citizens are able to keep themselves informed on even the most important developments in the world, and in their own country.

"The responsibility of a newspaper to the community is large. I assure you we realize this responsibility, and will do our best to discharge our duties in connection therewith."

(Signed)
ROY H. THOMSON.

MR. ROY H. THOMSON

Thomson's announcement to readers of *The Timmins Press* when he acquired the weekly in 1934 said in part: "I believe a newspaper should represent all shades of political opinion and that its readers are entitled to ALL the news, presented in an impartial manner and not colored to suit the political views of its management. I also believe that those in public office should be given credit when credit is due, and criticized when their actions call for criticism—and this irrespective of party, creed or belief."

Optimistic about his chances of election to Parliament in 1953, Thomson beams as he discusses campaign strategy with Frank Quartermaine (left), his manager, and A. A. "Lex" Mackenzie, member of the Ontario Legislature for York North. Thomson was defeated.

in such deals, pointed out that if he went broke the paper would revert to the publisher. The deal went through.

Despite sparse equipment, Thomson soon decided to go after more readers by expanding—first to twice-weekly, then to daily publication. His gamble paid off. The *Press* flourished, even though it was sometimes so short of editorial matter that it had to print the same story twice in the same issue.

In 1937, Thomson moved to Toronto, running his newspaper and radio stations by remote control and casting about for new properties. Throughout the 1940s and 1950s, at every publishers' gathering, he would startle people by asking, "Want to sell?" By 1952, Thomson owned more than 20 newspapers in Canada and the United States. He had also acquired a reputation as an uncouth fellow, one who bustled onto the scene with a wad of cash in his hand, trying to buy up everything in sight. In fact, he rarely had much cash of his own. His basic financial technique was to "pyramid"—mortgage present assets to buy new properties, which in turn would provide additional assets to raise further loans.

While reluctant to spend money on himself, Thomson is quite happy to pour huge sums into his newspapers for better plant and equipment. He is dogmatic in his view that in journalism excellence pays off. "It's the same thing as honesty being the best policy," he says. "If you make a paper better, it will show a profit." Then, as now, he insisted that his editors have a completely free hand: in

Canada, he has Liberal and Conservative editors; in Britain, he has Conservatives, Laborites, Liberals. "I give an editor only two instructions," he says. "Tell the truth, and represent the people in your community. We'll take care of the financial end."

His business managers are under close scrutiny. Though local management is in control, he moves his own executives in to show how costs can be cut, circulation and advertising revenue raised. Every paper has a monthly and a yearly budget, covering raw materials, overhead, salaries. Operating results are regularly compared with budgetary projections, thus managerial deficiencies are easily spotted.

Lord Thomson rides the London Underground—and reads another man's newspaper, the *Daily Express* of his fellow Canadian, Lord Beaverbrook.

In 1951, Thomson's wife died after a protracted illness. It was a severe blow and it took him a long time to recover. Restless and temporarily bored with wheeling and dealing, he took a brief fling at politics, running unsuccessfully for the Canadian Parliament. Then, at 59, an age when many men are beginning to think of retirement, he embarked on a whole new series of ventures.

Thomson had long wanted to expand into the United Kingdom, but had found nobody willing to sell to him. Suddenly, in 1953, he was asked if he wanted to buy the *Scotsman*, the most renowned paper in Scotland. Thomson leaped at the chance. The *Scotsman* company, which also owned the deficit-ridden evening *Dispatch*, was operating comfortably in the black within a year of Thomson taking over.

From there he invaded England. Purchasing the Kemsley newspapers in 1959, a chain which included three national papers—the *Sunday Times*, *The Empire News* and the *Sunday Graphic*—plus a flock of provincial papers—he started to set Fleet Street, the traditional seat of British newspaper publishing, on its ear.

He closed down the sensationalist—and money-losing—*Empire News* and *Sunday Graphic*, and began building up the *Sunday Times*. He expanded the size of the paper and its editorial staff, added the first weekly color supplement in Britain and a separate business-news section—all of which involved an investment of millions. As a consequence, the *Sunday Times* has increased its circulation from 900,000 to 1,500,000 and become hugely profitable.

Meantime, Thomson kept expanding in all directions—buying newspapers, magazines, book-publishing firms, and starting television stations in the Caribbean, Australia and Africa. He has mostly lost money in the underdeveloped world, but he says, "I think we have a duty to perform in Africa if we in the West want to have them with us."

Mainly, however, Thomson has diversified because few things give him greater joy than making a deal. And some of his deals are works of pure art. When he bought two of his travel companies and the nonscheduled airline, for example, he proposed a minimum price, plus a sliding-scale payment based on the profits of the companies for the first three years under the new ownership. Since the old managements were to run the companies, they had an obvious incentive to maximize profits. In three years, Thomson paid nearly $5,600,000 for the companies—but the profits for the period covered the sale price, and in the end the deal cost him nothing.

Thomson shows no intention of resting on his laurels. In 1967 came his two biggest coups: acquisition of Britain's elite daily paper, *The Times;* and purchase of the Brush-Moore chain of papers in the United States—12 dailies and six weeklies (price: $72,000,000). One Canadian purchase, the prestigious Peterborough *Examiner*, was acquired in a transfer of shares reputedly worth $3,500,000.

Money, for its own sake, has long since ceased to interest Roy Thomson. But he says that, for a businessman, money is the only scale against which to measure success.

Asked at what point he will stop, he says, "No sense at all in stopping—as long as I can grow and build."

The Indomitable
Nurse Bennett

By H. Gordon Green

Trusted and resourceful, with a snap and force—and a laugh—that belied her age, Nurse Myra Bennett became a legend on Newfoundland's remote and rugged northwest coast.

Take the day when the villagers of Bellburns found a fisherman, more dead than alive, on the gravel road that traces the shoreline up the treacherous Strait of Belle Isle. Their first thought was to get him the five miles to Daniel's Harbour where, if he had a chance at all, Nurse Bennett would know what to do. Forewarned by telephone, she was waiting to take command—hot blankets and rum at the ready. Two hours after coming under her crisp care, the still spent fisherman was at least fit enough to be moved the 60 miles south to the nearest hospital.

For the fisherman who'd been wrecked on the craggy shore after five days battling a violent storm, Myra Bennett had meant the difference between life and death. For Nurse Bennett, he was one more entry in her medical log of an unrelenting struggle that stretched more than half a century.

Life, for Myra, was a continual challenge. She nursed thousands and saved hundreds of lives. She raised three children and clad them—and herself—in homemade clothes. Her spare time was used for such "jobs" as baking, putting up preserves, drying fish on the rocks in summer for winter food, writing about midwifery for a nursing journal or instructing the outports in hygiene and health. A staunch advocate of breast-feeding, for example, she insisted it is essential in a place where diet is so limited.

So renowned was her stand on this subject that, when she went into a St. John's drugstore for a dozen bottle nipples, the clerk asked sarcastically why *she* would want them.

"Why, to feed my lamb," was her tart reply.

Her knack for improvisation was needed from the start of her career. As a midwife in London's slums before World War I, she would often have to start a delivery by hanging an apron over the window to keep street urchins from watching. During the war, when most of Britain's young doctors were in France and those left at home were overworked, a nurse-*cum*-midwife was apt to be called upon to take care of almost any medical emergency. So Myra broadened her skills, developing an ability to keep cool when others gave way to panic. When the war was over and everything again seemed routine, she read an account in a nursing magazine of a homesteader's wife in northern Saskatchewan who had died alone, in agony, waiting for her husband to bring the nearest doctor. She realized then that she wanted to go where her skills were *really* needed.

At this same time, the wife of Newfoundland's governor, Sir Charles Alexander Harris, was in Britain looking for nurses. Lady Harris asked if she could meet the nurse who wanted to go to Canada.

"We need nurses just as badly in Newfoundland," she said, "and we have a boat leaving soon for St. John's. Would you go?" She would.

In May 1921, she arrived in the little fishing hamlet of Daniel's Harbour—which remained her Newfoundland home—where she became the only medical help along 200 miles of storm-swept coast. "I never did any more of doctor's work than I had to," she said. But

In Britain in 1915, newly graduated Nurse Myra Grimsley: already she had learned to keep calm in crisis. A thousand crises and more than 50 years later, at a picket fence bordering a field of dandelions in Daniel's Harbour, Nfld., the Myra Bennett who had become a legend. She was made an M.B.E. (Member of the Order of the British Empire) for her work, and Newfoundland's Association of Registered Nurses made her a life member "for her half-century of noble and notable service in the field of nursing."

the nearest doctor then was over a day's voyage to the south in what is now a part of the city of Corner Brook. The nearest medical help to the north was the Grenfell Mission at St. Anthony, a two-day journey by sea, or five days overland by dog team.

Everything she'd learned was quickly put to use. She delivered babies, set broken limbs, performed kitchen-table operations by lamplight and sutured and dressed wounds of every description. She brought some 3,000 babies into the world—among them her own grandson, Noel, whose premature arrival interrupted the Bennetts' Christmas dinner in 1956. She even delivered one mother on the eve of a journey to Corner Brook for her own confinement.

"One of my hardest jobs was simply to educate mothers," she said. "They didn't like being told such things as that you can't cure mastitis by applying a weaselskin to the breast."

All kinds of such superstitions had to be overcome. Tuberculosis was common, and people scoffed when she insisted that the disease is contagious.

One old man was so far gone with tuberculosis that he could no longer work outside, but to make himself useful he would look after the young children around the house. When Myra first saw him he was sitting in a rocking chair, an infant grandson on his knee, and chewing food as best he could with what remained of his teeth before transferring it to the mouth of the youngster. She remonstrated with him, but too late. Three months later, the grandfather lay dying in one room and the youngster in another. "It was a lonely battle those first few years," said Myra. "And sometimes I felt that I wasn't making any progress at all."

Nurse Grimsley poses with the Newfoundland governor, Sir Charles Alexander Harris (wearing cap), on his visit to Daniel's Harbour in 1921. The others are J. D. Henry (left), an oil prospector, and Captain Hamilton, aide to the governor. Nurse Grimsley's salary was $1,000 a year, out of which she had to pay her board.

In 1922 in another of her quick and sure decisions, she accepted a proposal of marriage made one Sunday when she and Angus Bennett were walking home from vespers. She knew her prospective husband and his family well. She had attended his mother when her tenth child was born, and had spent a lot of time in the Bennett home. "I extracted a tooth for Angus' mother today," she wrote in her diary that September, "and she sent me up a large sea gull."

"I ate it baked," she said, "it was delicious."

Perhaps the most grueling of the Bennetts' adventures began the bitter February night a lumberman came pounding on their door to say that Angus' younger brother, Alex, was badly hurt. Angus threw the harness on Doll, the mare, and Myra (who was pregnant) was ready as soon as the horse. It was four miles to the lumber camp through snow so high that Angus had to walk ahead of the horse with the lantern to make sure of the way.

At the sawmill Alex lay prostrate in the snow with his right foot almost completely severed; only a thin strip of flesh in the front held it to the rest of the leg. It would be an amputation case, Myra concluded, and did what she could to give temporary relief and prevent further loss of blood. She bandaged the leg together and somehow got Alex back home and into their kitchen.

Waiting for them was Alex's mother who by this time was hysterical. Myra, with characteristic coolness, locked her in a bedroom. Next she sent for a neighbor. "Here's a roll of lint," she said to the

nervous woman. "Make me some bags to hold snow. I'm going to pack his leg!"

Alex was in terrible pain and Myra was tempted to give him an anesthetic, but he was in too much shock to risk it. She cleaned the stump of the leg and the mutilated ankle joint, picked out the pieces of splintered bone and the top half of the ball joint. "I knew that we would have to get the doctor from Bonne Bay," she said, "but I didn't want that foot flopping around till he got to us, so the neighbor and myself began stitching the foot back onto the leg."

In the morning, her wire to Bonne Bay brought back an unexpected answer. "Can do more for him *here*. Sounds like amputation case."

So at 10 a.m., Myra, Angus and his injured brother began the demanding 60 miles over snow and ice to the doctor. Old Doll sank at every step and Myra and Angus walked beside the sled to lighten the load. After a few miles, afraid the mare would play out completely, Angus left the trail they had been breaking over the ocean ice to try the drift ice along the shore. It was a long and treacherous job to pick a path through the huge tilted ice pans. Just as the mare looked as if she would drop from exhaustion, eight men from Parson's Pond, alerted by the telegraph operator, arrived to help. They unhitched the horse and towed the sled to their village.

Next morning, at 20° below zero, the trio set out again. Three days and two nights after they had left Daniel's Harbour they reached Bonne Bay and the doctor had a first look at the patient. The foot which Myra had sewn on was surprisingly pink. "I'm not so sure we'll have to amputate after all," the doctor said. "You've done a wonderful job."

A few days later he told Myra, "It'll heal." Alex Bennett had his foot. There was no ankle joint in it, but he still walked on it.

Many years later, long after the North got doctors, good hospitals and roads, many of Myra's people were reluctant to take their ills to the new government clinics. One hardy old liveyere—as permanent residents of Newfoundland are called—cheerfully summed up the feeling in the outports: "If Nurse Bennett told me there was nothin' she could do for me I wouldn't bother no doctor nowheres. I'd just fetch me straight to the undertaker!"

Daniel's Harbour as it was when Myra Grimsley went there in 1921, before her marriage. Houses are hidden behind the fishing stores which line the water's edge. Angus Bennett, here preparing to haul wood with a dog team, played a major role in his wife's work. A resourceful man who'd gone to sea as a 15-year-old, he sailed for her, took charge of her dog team, harnessed the horse, built their house and became her right-hand man when the kitchen served as an operating theater. Later, when there were three boisterous children, Angus would stay to keep house while Myra went down the coast on some extended errand of mercy. Even in her 80s, Myra continued nursing—and pulling teeth. When someone needed to have a tooth "hauled," Angus was called from his general store to hold the patient while she wielded the forceps. The 50-cent fee went to the church on a hill nearby. "When they come to me," she said, "how can I refuse them?"

Bound to Be Known as Joey

By Jeannine Locke

The Hon. Joseph Roberts Smallwood, premier of Newfoundland and the northern territory of Labrador, was bound to be known as Joey. Barely five feet five and spry, with an impish grin, jutting nose and blue eyes beaming through horn-rimmed spectacles, he has the look and irreverent style of a cartoon cricket. His agile wit, low threshold of indignation and rolling, off-the-cuff eloquence have made him a national institution. For instance, who but our Joey would turn up to greet the Queen, as he did on her visit to St. John's in June 1959, with such genuine devotion for the monarchy and a conspicuous split in the seat of his striped trousers? Who but our Joey would say happily, in summing up his career, "My judgment has invariably proved sound"?

But it's not simply as a character that Joey Smallwood is appreciated. When he retires, he can be sure of not just fading away; his role as elder statesman touting "the great Canadian family" is already secure. It was Smallwood who, in 1949, almost single-handedly hauled Newfoundland into union with Canada. "A shotgun marriage," many Newfoundlanders grumbled at the time. And mainland Canadians weren't much impressed with their tenth province—a centuries-old British property not much bigger than Ireland, noted mainly for fog, codfish and a mite of a man named Smallwood who, judged by newspaper pictures, didn't own a decent suit. No one save Smallwood himself would have predicted that Newfoundland would contribute to Canadian history one of its most exhilarating chapters.

In 20 years the little province could point to: a population increase from 300,000 to more than 500,000; a quintupled budget; almost quadrupled personal income; a 2,500-mile network of new roads connecting, for the first time, more than 600 communities; resettlement of 150 isolated, uneconomic outports; more than 1,000 new schools and double the number of teachers; a 20-year rural-electrification program almost completed in six; decreases of 90 percent in deaths from tuberculosis and diphtheria and the highest birthrate in Canada. "When Joey became premier," said Albert Perlin, a St. John's historian and newspaper proprietor who at first opposed Smallwood's dream of Confederation, "Newfoundland was a place the world scoffed at—the slum of the Empire. He put it on the map. Joey's responsible for dragging us into the second half of the twentieth century."

Newfoundland's Operation Bootstrap was conducted by Smallwood in typically epic style. Luring new industries to offset the island's risky reliance on fishing and logging, he became a globe-hopping en-

Newfoundland Premier Joey Smallwood sports a Trudeau button at the 1968 Liberal convention which chose Pierre Elliott Trudeau as party leader. Twenty years earlier, during the regime of Louis St. Laurent, Smallwood had played a leading role in bringing Newfoundland into the Canadian Confederation. Opposite page: Smallwood samples Newfoundland public opinion.

trepreneur. One of his projects, the harnessing of Churchill Falls in the fastness of Labrador, was as boldly conceived and launched as any British imperial adventure at the peak of Victorian power; and it was to the last of the great Victorians, Sir Winston Churchill, that Smallwood took his design for developing the world's largest single source of industrial power.

In August 1952, the go-getting Newfoundland premier told Britain's prime minister about Labrador's untapped iron-ore deposits and vast timber growth—and about the falls, 245 feet high, half again as high as Niagara, that would generate the power to exploit "the continent's last remaining storehouse of undeveloped natural wealth." He had in mind "a great consortium of companies and capital in Britain" that would explore and develop Labrador's resources in return for mineral, timber and hydro rights. He even suggested that British enterprise and know-how might find in Labrador the means to rebuild some of Britain's lost power in the world.

"I like the feel of it," Churchill growled. "It is a fine imperial concept." He promised to have others look into the matter. Several days later Joey was invited to lunch at the stately head office of the London House of Rothschild, the same banking firm which financed the building of the Suez Canal and Wellington's victory at Waterloo. Out of that luncheon came the British Newfoundland Corporation, a syndicate of companies, mainly British and Canadian, which the

Rothschilds put together. Smallwood's idea subsequently attracted some 20,000 shareholders, more than 90 percent of them Canadian.

But the fate of Churchill Falls was still undecided. One formidable problem was to find a power market big enough to make the one-billion-dollar project practical. In 1963, negotiations began with publicly owned Hydro-Québec, which was to build the world's longest high-voltage transmission lines (735 miles to Montreal), take half the power for its own uses and resell the rest to New York's Consolidated Edison Co. But in October 1966, Quebec agreed to buy almost all Churchill Falls' output. Then Canadian engineers began a ten-year construction job, as big as Grand Coulee and Egypt's Aswan High Dam combined.

In economic development, Newfoundland still has to catch up to its nearest maritime neighbors, but Joey can point to an almost miraculous improvement in the quality of life in his province. While he neither expects nor cares to be remembered for building roads or even for taming Churchill Falls, he is proud of four new arts and cultural centers in St. John's, Corner Brook, Grand Falls and Gander (two of them converted Expo 67 pavilions, quickly snaffled by Smallwood): "I happen to believe what Christ said, that man does not live by bread alone."

And one of the first acts of his government after Confederation was to elevate Memorial College, in St. John's, to the status of a university. Started in 1925, it had an enrollment of 298 in 1949. By 1970, Memorial had 7,000 students, $40,000,000 worth of new buildings, and a faculty drawn from almost all over the world.

To find a university president, Smallwood advertised the position in the North American and British press, dispatched his minister of education across Canada and the United States to interview promising prospects and went shopping himself in England. Having in mind Memorial's projected medical school, he settled on Lord Taylor of Harlow, the British physician-author. Lord Taylor declined, in writing, and got back from Smallwood the crisp reply: "I don't like your letter. You probably think we're a benighted place. Would you and Lady Taylor come out as the government's guests, without commitment?" They came—and stayed.

Smallwood's greatest pride is that Memorial is open to all Newfoundlanders with the capacity and desire for higher education. In 1966, when most mainland colleges were raising fees, Smallwood announced that his government would start paying the tuition of all Memorial students and provide salaries for seniors whose parents were residents of the province. Later, a means test was imposed, as unpopular with students as the tax boost was with their parents. But Smallwood could still claim: "We have the only university in the Western Hemisphere that gives free tuition to students requiring it and salaries to needy third-, fourth- and fifth-year students."

Born in the outport of Gambo, the eldest in a lumber surveyor's family of 13, Smallwood was a mover and a shaker even as a child. Starting as a printer's devil on a St. John's newspaper, he quickly graduated to reporting, then quit to see the world, bouncing from papers in Halifax and Boston to New York and London. He returned

Joey Smallwood, a radio storyteller ("The Barrelman") in the late '30s and early '40s, became a latter-day Father of Confederation when, in Ottawa in 1949, he signed the document which made Newfoundland part of Canada. Seated with him in the picture opposite are Prime Minister Louis St. Laurent (extreme left), Sir Albert Walsh (who became lieutenant-governor of Newfoundland) and F. Gordon Bradley. Smallwood chanced to meet Richard M. Nixon, then a private citizen, in Helsinki in 1965. A few days later, in Moscow (above), they tried unofficially—and unsuccessfully—to see Nikita Khrushchev.

to Newfoundland in the mid-1920s—just in time for the great Depression which not only stunned the island's codfish economy but toppled its almost 80-year-old system of self-government. By 1934 Newfoundland had reverted from dominion to colonial status, under the rule of a British governor and an appointed commission, and one out of every three citizens was on the dole.

Smallwood married Clara Oates, from Carbonear, fathered a daughter and two sons and launched into labor organizing. For four years he tramped on foot across the largely untracked island, cruised its 6,000 miles of ragged coastline in a small boat and succeeded in reviving unions of fishermen, pulp-and-paper and railway workers. In the process he developed the bantam-rooster fighting style and oratorical flourishes that are now as famous in Toronto as in Tickle Cove.

Hired in the late '30s to perform on radio for 15 minutes daily, Smallwood told inspirational stories of Newfoundland life and became the island's most popular voice. On the side, he produced two volumes

Behind Smallwood in his office in the Confederation Building at St. John's are statuettes of Sir John A. Macdonald and Georges-Etienne Cartier. At home, Smallwood reads to his son Bill's children: Douglas and Tanya, Billy and Robert . . . and Clara Smallwood looks on happily as granddaughter dances with her admiring grandpa.

of *The Book of Newfoundland,* a bulky collection of essays, many of them his own, on the island's stormy history. A decade later, he used his intimate knowledge of the island and his mastery of radio—"one of the things," he says, "that God invented with Newfoundland in mind"—to sway the outports for Confederation.

The Newfoundland National Convention in 1948 voted against even including union with Canada on the ballot in a referendum that would decide the island's constitutional future. Smallwood appealed to his radio audience for support and within days he had 50,000 signatures to a petition asking the British government to add Confederation to the convention's two choices—restoration of dominion status or continuation of colonial rule. When Westminster agreed, Smallwood launched his campaign. By aircraft, small boat, on foot and via radio, he reached the most remote outports with his message of salvation through union with Canada.

His efforts swung the tide—on a second referendum, Confederation won by 7,000 votes. At midnight, March 31, 1949, Newfoundland became Canada's tenth province.

Nothing so exhilarates Smallwood as a fight against stiff odds. Early in 1959 he took on the combined forces of the federal government and the labor movement, which he had once served. What started his war with the mainland was a general strike in the Newfoundland pulp-and-paper industry, which the International Woodworkers of America had called against his will. When a collision between strike leaders and local police triggered a bloody riot, Smallwood demanded RCMP reinforcements from Ottawa. The federal government refused to be involved, whereupon Smallwood settled the strike himself by evicting the IWA from the island and replacing it by a less militant union of his own.

Infuriatingly dictatorial at worst, Smallwood can be utterly charming at best. At the 1967 Confederation of Tomorrow Conference in Toronto, provincial leaders were called to consider the crisis in relations between French- and English-speaking Canadians. When the conference threatened to bog down in constitutional arguments and bad feeling between Canada's founding peoples, Smallwood reduced the issue of bilingualism to plain, human terms. Turning on his colleagues, he asked with a grin: "Who but a narrow, intolerant bigot would deny the right of all Canadians to educate their children in their own language?"

That question set the climate thawing around the table. At the end of the conference, Quebec's Premier Daniel Johnson could remark: "We have all traveled quite a distance."

In the years since Smallwood brought Newfoundland into union with Canada, the tiny premier, his island province and its mainland partner have also come a long way. Newfoundlanders, no longer isolated from one another or the mainstream of Canadian life, have become a very different and more independent breed.

If Newfoundland no longer needs a father-figure, the premier will have been responsible. Memorial University, the apple of his eye, has generated the most articulate opposition to his "one-man rule." And that's an irony which is surely appreciated by Joey Smallwood himself.

The "Unadoptables"

By Janice Tyrwhitt

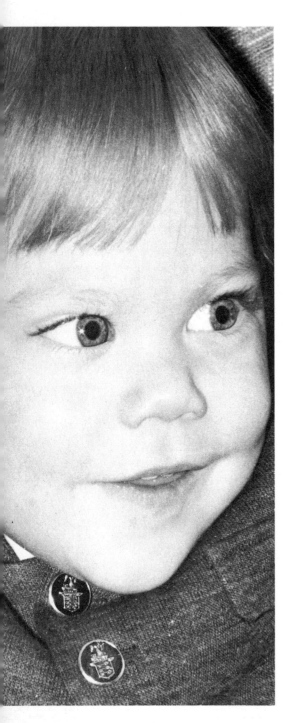

For three years after his mother and father had broken up their shaky marriage and abandoned him, eight-year-old Keith had been in the care of a children's aid society in a northern Ontario town. Keith's mental slowness demanded more patience than most people could give, and though he badly needed a home of his own, few couples in the mining town where he lived wanted an extra child—and no one wanted Keith.

Luckily for him, his social worker turned to Laurie Charleson, the tender-hearted woman who masterminded a remarkable scheme to find homes for children *nobody* seemed to want. Her official title was adoption consultant for the Province of Ontario, but in the 53 children's aid societies under her guidance she was known as the miracle worker who, time and again, found parents for "unadoptable" youngsters.

The only person who scoffs at this legend is Miss Charleson herself, now retired. "There's no such thing as an unadoptable child," she says. "If a child in our care stays homeless, it's our own fault."

When she heard about Keith—in the mid-'60s—Laurie swung into action through her Adoption Resource Exchange. First she ran Keith's picture in *Today's Child*, a daily column in the Toronto *Telegram*, with this description: "Keith is an engaging youngster with hazel eyes, light-brown hair and a fair complexion, splashed with a few freckles. Because he has no parents, he is an insecure little fellow and urgently needs a warm, affectionate home. His favorite sports are baseball and skating, and he would like to live on a farm."

Then she put him on Toronto television channel CFTO, where 60,000 viewers watched him chatting happily with an announcer. Within a few days, four families asked for the boy no one had wanted before, and soon he was adopted by a farm couple with grown children. They all encouraged his interest in animals and soon he was busy raising a calf of his own. No longer condemned to a shadowy second-hand existence, Keith was at last growing up with the kind of love and security Laurie Charleson considers every child's birthright.

An unusual case? Not in Ontario. Keith is but one of several thousand supposedly "hard-to-adopt" children—part Negro or Indian, physically handicapped, emotionally disturbed or just too old to fit neatly into a new family—who owe their chance of normal happiness to Laurie Charleson and those who carry on her work.

Though she seemed to work miracles, Laurie never looked like a fairy godmother. Tall and rangy, she still limps a little from a childhood attack of polio. Her voice is husky, her wide smile authentically magic.

Her talent for slashing red tape and tradition made Laurie Charleson one of the most controversial—and successful—adoption workers in North America. The methods she used to find a home for Keith violated professional custom and shocked cautious social workers. But by using press and television regularly, day after day, Laurie proved that this kind of direct appeal really works. Within one six-month period, she ran pictures of 26 Negro children in *Today's Child*; 20 were adopted—the majority by white couples. Only Laurie wasn't

surprised. "I've learned a lot from adopting parents," she said. "The community is always ahead of the social worker, and we've got to catch up—fast."

She devised a unique series of conferences at which social workers from all parts of the province could swap information about couples in search of children—and children in need of parents. Although vast in area, Ontario has only 7,000,000 population, and adoption workers had seldom looked farther for homes than the next county. Now, as she described each child at the conferences, workers from *all* the districts reached into their notes or their memories to suggest couples who might welcome the youngster.

At one meeting, an alert worker from a small town realized that two girls being discussed were sisters of two boys who had just been

Laurie Charleson proved homes *can* be found for "hopeless" children. Her approach to the problem of adoption: face it, *share* it, use all the mass media help you can get—and let human nature do the rest.

299

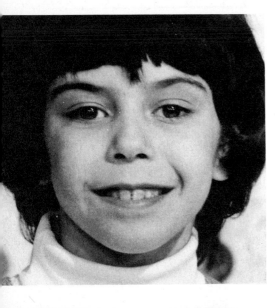

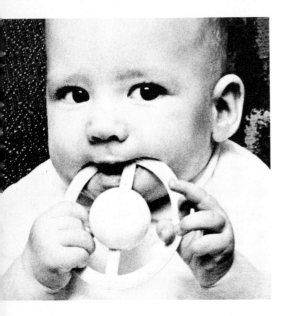

sent from a city agency to a family in her county. "The boys are getting on so well that the family might take the girls, too," she suggested. The family did.

When Laurie proposed the first conference, in the late 1950s, agencies protested that they couldn't afford to send workers across the province. "You can't afford *not* to," she snapped back. "You'll save money if you find a home for just one child." As a direct result of each meeting more than 100 youngsters were finding homes.

"Laurie's changed our whole philosophy of adoption," the director of the Children's Aid Society in Barrie, Ont., said at the time. "She's taken a principle used in every other phase of human relations and applied it for the first time to adoption: when you've got a problem, *share* it."

Her system of pooling information worked so well that it was studied by the Child Welfare League of America. It organized an Adoption Resource Exchange of North America, the first continental adoption plan designed to cut across national borders as well as state and provincial boundaries. "Laurie Charleson's leadership makes Ontario's exchange one of the most successful," said Joseph H. Reid, director of the league. "I wish there were more people like her."

In 1966, more than half the 12,000 Ontario children who needed homes were adopted, a percentage that astonished workers in other parts of North America, where they were happy if they could place a third of such youngsters.

What impressed social workers in big cities, where the only "easy-to-place" youngsters were blue-eyed baby girls, was the fact that Ontario couples adopted so many boys and older children. Of 6,543 Ontario children adopted in 1966, 51 percent were boys, 62 percent were more than a year old, 30 percent were more than four years old, and a heartening proportion had mixed racial backgrounds or physical problems. In Metropolitan Toronto alone, more than 75 children of mixed race were adopted during the same period.

"Ontario's bold use of the mass media is really ahead of what we're doing in the United States," said Mrs. Patricia G. Morisey, director of the child and family welfare division of the Federation of Protestant Welfare Agencies in New York. "Laurie Charleson has had an impact on the whole field of adoption."

Her impact had never been more needed. As recently as the mid-'50s there had been six couples waiting to adopt each child. Suddenly, and alarmingly, the situation had changed. While the rate of illegitimate births had risen sharply, the low birthrate of the Depression years and medical advances in treating sterility combined to reduce the number of young couples applying to adoption agencies. Suddenly, in Toronto and other major Ontario cities, and in some states such as California and Florida, there were more children who needed homes than parents who wanted to adopt. In some communities, even an "ordinary" six-month-old boy was labeled "hard-to-place." The reason: too *old*!

But Laurie faced the problem with unquenchable zeal. "Plenty of people want a ready-made family," she said. "Let's keep brothers and sisters together." In 1967 a middle-aged couple, who had already brought up seven children of their own, took in six youngsters orphaned by an automobile accident. The eldest was a girl of 16 who had done a fine job of mothering the little ones, but the youngest, a boy of seven, was so miserable that he refused to unpack his private treasures. Wisely, his new parents waited. After six weeks he announced, casually, "Well, I guess I'll get out my baseball bat."

Under Laurie Charleson's guidance, amazing home-finding stories became almost routine to Ontario social workers. When half-Chinese twins, tiny girls who needed open-heart surgery, were pictured in *Today's Child*, a dozen couples offered to adopt them. A two-year-old Indian boy with diabetes found a home with a small-town doctor and his wife, a registered nurse who knew exactly how to look after him.

"We've got to go more than halfway to meet people who want our 'special' kids—or any of our kids," Laurie insisted. Agencies used to close their doors to couples more than 40 years old; today in Ontario, it's not uncommon for babies to be given to parents in their 50s. Some agencies used to keep couples waiting up to two years, and insist that they wait another two years before applying for a second child. Now, when a couple first comes to an agency, a skilled worker may encourage them to plan a big family.

Laurie has no patience with the old notion that only well-to-do couples can afford extra children. A couple who adopted four brothers and sisters made less than $3,000 a year, and they were already raising five older children. But they managed a comfortable living in a farming community where few of their neighbors were better off.

While streamlining procedures, Laurie did not scrap precautions to safeguard the children and the adopting parents. During the probation period of six months that follows an Ontario CAS placement (sometimes longer for older children), fewer than one percent of adoptions break down. Once final, none has *ever* been broken. "Laurie's faith in human nature has paid off," says Mrs. Victoria Leach, her successor as adoption coordinator for the Province of Ontario. "Time and again we find that people who adopt an older, colored or handicapped child give—and get—just as much love as those with normal youngsters. Maybe more."

What convinced Laurie Charleson that there's a home for every child was her experience as adoption specialist for the York County Children's Aid Society in the early 1950s. Shocked by the plight of 20 older children apparently in permanent foster care, she persuaded priests and ministers to appeal from the pulpit and soon rounded up 60 couples ready to adopt a school-age child. In 1956, when she joined the Ontario Department of Welfare, Deputy Minister James S. Band suggested she use the same kind of offbeat appeal and *advertise* for homes for hard-to-place youngsters.

Within three years, her ads brought more than 4,000 replies, a third from U.S. citizens who picked up papers across the border. Social workers were especially skeptical when Laurie tried news photos of real children. "When we first ran *Today's Child* in June 1964, only three of the 53 children's aid societies agreed to take part in the scheme," said Helen Allen, the *Telegram* staff writer assigned to the column. "By fall, every one was in it."

TODAY'S CHILD
BY HELEN ALLEN
Toronto Telegram Syndicate

George has just had his fifth birthday. He's a slim, good-looking boy with brown hair, blue eyes, fair skin and the shy smile you see. His background is Canadian for several generations.

George's ambition is to be a farmer. He now is living in a farm-foster-home and he loves the life. He is ready to help with whatever chores a small boy can do and he is friends with all the animals, especially the horses. He likes small creatures, too — kittens, goldfish and even insects.

A healthy, active lad, George enjoys the outdoors, especially in winter. He is keen on skating, hockey and tobogganing. Puzzles, cars and trucks are his favorite toys.

George will be a fine son for a family where the parents enjoy spending time with their children, and where he will be the youngest with no others close to him in age. To inquire about adopting George please write to Today's Child, Department of Social and Family Services, Parliament Buildings, Toronto 182. For general adoption information, ask your Children's Aid Society.

Homes for many "unadoptable" children have been found with the help of the Toronto *Telegram* feature, *Today's Child*. Children's aid societies, lukewarm about showing real children, joined in enthusiastically after seeing the results the ads brought.

When they fell for a photograph of five brothers and sisters in *Today's Child*, William and Jeanne La Plante ended up by more than doubling their family overnight. The La Plantes, a Toronto couple, had a nine-year-old son, Jon, and a five-year-old adopted daughter, Lynne, when they learned that, out of 19 interested couples, they had been chosen as parents for five round-faced, dark-eyed youngsters aged three, four, six, seven and eight. In October 1965 they drove 500 miles to the isolated northern Ontario town where the children were in foster homes.

The idea was to spend the weekend getting acquainted, but the children spoke only French, the La Plantes only English. Finally, Bill's Polaroid camera broke the ice. After they all attended Mass on Sunday morning, the parish priest was so delighted by the sight that he slipped them $20 to take the children out to dinner.

In November the La Plantes flew their instant family to Toronto and plunged into the busiest six months of their lives. They bought groceries by the case and shoes by the dozen. They traded their car for a station wagon, built a third bathroom and hired a girl to help with washing, ironing and mending.

In those first few months the La Plantes often had misgivings. Lynne resented sharing a room with two newcomers, Denise and Michelle, and Jon's schoolwork slipped. Once he burst out, "Either those kids go or I go!" Later, when his mother found him with an arm round Michelle and her brother Danny, he grinned and whispered, "Let's keep them."

Agencies in other provinces and American states began to pick up Laurie Charleson's techniques. Winford Oliphant, director of children's agency services for New York State, asked her help. The Province of Nova Scotia consulted her before setting up another adoption resource exchange.

Drawing on Ontario's experience, the U.S. Child Welfare League's new national exchange links exchanges in 22 states and aims at elimination of out-of-date laws that impede adoption across state and national borders.

It's estimated that 25 children out of every thousand in the United States, and 28 out of every thousand in Canada, are now adopted, and no one really knows how many more youngsters North American families are willing to take in. One hopeful sign is the success of plans such as Minnesota's campaign for Parents to Adopt Minority Youngsters, Montreal's Open Door Society, Toronto's Committee for the Adoption of Colored Youngsters, and the Indian Adoption Project sponsored by the Child Welfare League of America. Their results hint that child-welfare societies and community agencies, working together, can accomplish far more than anyone would have thought possible a generation ago.

Orphanages are bleak institutions in which hundreds of children once grew up lonely and frightened. Today, the Province of Ontario no longer has—or needs—any. All have been closed or turned into centers for medical treatment or short-term care. Thanks to the way shown by Laurie Charleson they may eventually become obsolete elsewhere in the world too.

The Stunning Birds
of Fen Lansdowne

By David MacDonald

Detailed examination of the tiny feathers on an unmounted bird skin are typical of Fenwick Lansdowne's painstaking striving for perfection. His finished work—like this study—is rated superior to Audubon's.

When Fenwick Lansdowne set out to become a professional painter, he'd never had an art lesson. Crippled by polio, he couldn't get around without crutches or wield a brush in his right hand. Furthermore, contrary to the contemporary craze for pop, op and otherwise abstract art, the young Canadian painted nothing but birds—Great Gray Owls, Pileated Woodpeckers, Ruddy Ducks—that *looked* like birds. It could well account for failure, if he weren't such a solid success.

For today, in his 30s, Fen Lansdowne is ranked among the best wildlife artists of all time—a *rara avis* in his own right.

To the delight of friends in Victoria, who bought his early efforts for $10 or less, Lansdowne's stunning bird studies now command $2,500 or more in New York, London and Toronto. Since 1966, two lavish books of his watercolors have sold more than 60,000 copies, grossing more than $1,000,000. Such wide demand is due to the fact that Lansdowne portrays birds with pinfeather precision, plus a poetic sense of beauty that far transcends mere plumage. "What's so amazing," one critic has noted, "is that he can transform an ornithological subject into a true work of art."

In Lansdowne's hands, as in nature, the Common Tern soars to heights of uncommon grace, while the stark, dark Raven evokes a haunting mood of wilderness. With one pair of Swifts in an endless white sky, he catches the very spirit of life on the wing—purely, wondrously *free*. He is often compared with John James Audubon, the father of avian art. "Audubon may have been a greater student of birds," said Olin Sewall Pettingill, Jr., director of the Cornell Laboratory of Ornithology, "but Lansdowne's painting is far superior."

To Lansdowne, success is "pleasant"—but no reason to get ruffled. A quiet man, slight, fine-featured, totally unassuming, he's never been diverted by fortune—good *or* bad. "I used to paint birds and still do," he says with great calm. "That's all I've ever wanted."

A perfectionist who steadily keeps improving, Lansdowne works in a pleasant cottage-studio, taking about a week to turn field sketches into finished form. With the aid of unmounted bird skins, and a stop-action memory for the characteristic postures of every species he's ever seen, he first outlines his subject—using his left hand—on pastel paper. After completing the head in gouache, an opaque water paint, he then moves forward from the tail, defining each tiny feather in living color. "To me," he says, "there's something almost mystical about birds—perhaps because they can fly and we humans can't."

For Fen Lansdowne, becoming a painter took plenty of pluck. Born in Hong Kong, where his father, Jim, worked for a British firm, he was paralyzed by polio at ten months. In 1940, as war raged across China, the family fled to Canada. Jim returned to his job, only to spend four years in Japanese prison camps, and Edith Lansdowne placed their son in a solarium for crippled children near Victoria. A gifted artist, she sold watercolors, drove a milk truck and scrimped to meet medical bills.

Lansdowne's books, collections of his paintings with texts by John Livingston, have had spectacular success. In its first three years, *Birds of the Northern Forest* rang up 46,000 sales in Canada, the United States and abroad, despite its $20 price. Then *Birds of the Eastern Forest* (two volumes) began soaring and Lansdowne planned five more books, covering the Prairies, the Rockies, the Arctic.

J.F. LANSDOWNE
·1969·

Gold Finch

J.F. LANSDOWNE
·1969·

Robin

American Redstart

J. F. LANSDOWNE
1968

After a year at the solarium, Fen was confined to a wheelchair until he was eight, when spinal fusions helped him to walk on crutches. Unable to join school pals at play, he developed a passion for bird watching. He also revealed a precocious talent for art. "Fen drew ships, soldiers, pirates," his mother recalls—"yet no *birds*."

But one day, at 13, he suddenly began sketching two Red-Breasted Mergansers. "After that," he smiles, "almost everything I painted had feathers." Within a year he made his first sale. The price: $1.50.

While in high school, Lansdowne spent three summers as a lab assistant at the British Columbia Museum, studying the anatomy of

One of Lansdowne's early paintings, done for $15, sold later for $600. But the years between were lean: the artist could not afford a trip to Toronto for his first exhibition in 1956.

birds by dissecting them. Then, in 1956, color slides of his meticulous portraits were seen by John Livingston, director of the Canadian Audubon Society. "They were absolutely gorgeous," he says, "—*too* good for anyone but a trained, mature artist." When they proved to be the work of a self-taught teen-ager, Livingston arranged a one-man exhibition at Toronto's Royal Ontario Museum. It brought instant acclaim, a $1,500 magazine commission and a contract with a major art dealer.

By the time he was 21, Lansdowne's fame had spread far. During one show at New York's Audubon House, expert ornithologists raved about his uncanny realism. In London, viewers snapped up all 40 paintings—23 in the first *hour*. In barely a year, the price of Lansdowne works rose from $100 to $500. Since then, their value has again quintupled.

When he isn't off on field trips, sketching from the gull-clouded coast of California to nightingale nesting grounds in England's lush New Forest, Lansdowne lives at his Victoria studio. Though a celebrity in his hometown, he confines himself to a very few intimates—none artists or birdy types—and confides in still fewer. Before a trip to Ottawa in 1967, for example, Lansdowne told hardly anyone the reason: an invitation to dine with Queen Elizabeth and Prince Philip, who have two of his bird studies at home in Buckingham Palace. As a close friend notes, "Fen just doesn't like to talk about himself."

God's Greatest Nuisance

By John R. Chafe

In awarding the Rev. Dr. James J. Tompkins an honorary degree in 1941, Harvard University praised him as "a Nova Scotian priest through whose leadership and teaching an agricultural people learned to become masters of their own economic destiny."

A somewhat different description was given by a nun who once worked with him. "Father Jimmy," she remarked, "was God's greatest nuisance."

Both were correct. Dr. Tompkins won international renown as a pioneer of the Antigonish Movement, a remarkable self-help program that began among the impoverished fishermen, farmers and coal miners of eastern Nova Scotia during the Depression and has since spread to many of the world's underdeveloped countries.

But the way Father Jimmy brought the program about was by making a pest of himself. A frail little man with a small voice and a sharp tongue, he spent his life teaching, preaching, coaxing and cussing at his parishioners to pull themselves up by their own boot-straps. One of them summed him up this way: "Father Jimmy wouldn't even let out the cat for you. But he'd stay up half the night nagging *you* to do it."

He believed absolutely that the Lord helps those who help themselves. "If the government gives a man a $10 dole," he used to say, "he needs another as soon as it's gone. And he hasn't learned a damn thing, except how to stick out his mitt."

Nothing moved him as much as poverty, or angered him more than ignorance. One, he felt, was rooted in the other. Only when men knew and understood what kept them poor could they begin to cope with it. "The little people together is a giant," he'd say. "You've got to give them ideas. Then they'll blow the roof off!"

His ideas finally took root in Canso, N.S., during the '20s. I was working there at a transatlantic cable station and I watched Father Jimmy's people really blow the roof off. After years of exploitation at the hands of feudal fish merchants, they banded together in co-operatives. Through consumer and marketing co-ops, they cut costs and won better prices. Through credit unions—co-op banks—they wiped out debts that had kept them in bondage to the fish traders. Within a few years their incomes more than doubled. What made this success so impressive was the timing. At the bottom of the Depression, when most of the world was in trouble, Canso never had it so good. As a result, people from many parts of the globe flocked to that remote outpost to talk with the priest who worked economic miracles.

Instead of the Commandments, Father Jimmy spoke of co-ops and credit unions. Rather than the wages of sin, he railed about the price of fish.

Barely five feet, four inches tall, with a large head and wispy white hair, Father Jimmy looked like a gnome. In a derby and a mink-lined overcoat—made for Andrew Carnegie and sent to Father Jimmy by the billionaire's widow—he'd scurry around all day, minding everyone's business at the top of his squeaky voice. No thundering spellbinder, Father Jimmy was less at home on a platform than up on a pickle barrel in a country store. There he'd sit for hours, with his cigar stub held on a pin, tossing out ideas. "Ideas have hands and feet," he used to say. "They'll do work for you."

The smallest in a family of six-footers, Jimmy Tompkins came from a farm on Cape Breton Island, taught in a one-room school in his teens and later studied in Rome for the priesthood. At the age of 31 he joined the staff of St. Francis Xavier University—St. FX—a small college in Antigonish, N.S., where he had taught for a short time before he entered the priesthood. He taught algebra and Greek, and soon became vice-president. He traveled widely, recruiting a strong faculty and raising money for new buildings.

One day he heard of a unique experiment at the University of Wisconsin, where professors of agriculture went out from their classrooms to teach the latest scientific techniques to farmers. The idea lit a fire in him. He looked into the Workers Educational Association of England, which provided practical schooling for laboring-class men and women; the Folk Schools in Denmark. "Adult education," he decided, "should be designed for the best brains we have, to wrestle with the worst problems we have."

Nova Scotia had bad ones. Because of a postwar recession,

Preaching self-help, Father Tompkins and the Antigonish Movement introduced Nova Scotia fishermen, farmers and coal miners to a better life through greater independence. A 1927 "revolution" by fishermen who worked boats like this one led to a government investigation and, soon after, practical education and cooperative action.

hundreds of farms lay idle. There was widespread unemployment and unrest in the coal towns of Cape Breton. In two years the value of the fishery had fallen from $15,000,000 to $9,000,000. The result was mass migration; in 1920 there were 100,000 Nova Scotians in the Greater Boston area alone.

Father Jimmy's chance came in 1923, when he was sent to Canso, where he at once came face to face with his twin hates—ignorance and poverty. He met men who hauled enough food from the sea in one day to feed a hundred people, but whose own children had rickets from lack of meat and milk. Even young faces bore the hard lines of defeat. Poverty was their lot, and they accepted it. Father Jimmy couldn't. Instead of preaching about the hereafter, he decided to do something about the here and now.

He kept needling the fishermen. "Why do you get only a cent and a half for cod when it's sold in Halifax for 30?" he'd ask. Or, "How come you sell your lobsters for seven cents when hotels charge a dollar? Some smart son-of-a-gun's making a lot out of your hard work, eh?"

When he'd upset enough fishermen with his questions, Father Jimmy herded them into small study groups. "Learn all you can, and share what you learn," he'd say. He brought in judges, engineers, politicians to address them. Slowly they began to see that debt was the reason they didn't get a fair share of the fruits of their labor.

For years, the fishermen had mortgaged homes, boats and gear to fish traders or merchants who acted as agents for U.S. and Canadian seafood firms. These debts made them mere sharecroppers of the sea. They were underpaid for their catches—often in credit, rather than in cash—and overcharged for supplies. They were caught in an economic vise.

Father Jimmy felt that the way out lay through cooperatives. And though he couldn't impose his solution on the fishermen, he could steer them toward it. So he got them together to shingle his rectory and build sidewalks—anything to advance the idea of group action. Mean-

Typical of the co-ops that resulted from Father Tompkins' pioneer work is the processing plant of the Cheticamp Fishermen's Cooperative Society Ltd. in Nova Scotia's Inverness County.

The Rev. Dr. Moses Coady headed the extension department set up at St. Francis Xavier University at Antigonish, N.S. The Antigonish Movement eventually spread—under the auspices of the United Nations, the Colombo Plan and various private and government agencies—to the pueblos of Latin America, the jungle villages of Asia, the emerging countries of Africa, the far Pacific. This open-air study session (right) is on the island of Truk, in the Caroline Islands.

while, he waited for some sign of group indignation. "When a man gets up on his hind legs," he said, "no one can walk on him."

That sign finally came on July 1, 1927, Canada's 60th birthday. At a patriotic rally in Canso, a fisherman jumped up and shouted, "What have *we* got to cheer about?"

Then all the pent-up grievances burst forth, against the merchants, the seafood companies, even against the government. I was chairman of that meeting, which newspapers called the "Revolution in Canso," and I saw Father Jimmy on the sidelines. His blue eyes were dancing. After almost five years of his pushing, his men were finally up on their hind legs.

That night they brought him their petition to the government at Ottawa, demanding an investigation of the fishing industry. It was worded with "whereases" and "therefores."

"You're not lawyers," Father Jimmy snorted. "You're fishermen. So *write* like fishermen." He crossed out the fancy phrases and wrote in a few "hells" and "damns" of his own. Then he got 40 other priests to write another petition and back it with telegrams. Newspapers took up the cry. Within three months the government ordered a Royal Commission investigation. The revolution in Canso was paying off.

The commission recommended just what Father Jimmy had wanted: practical education—and cooperative action. The government named his younger cousin and protégé, the Rev. Dr. Moses Coady, of St. FX, to organize the fishermen into marketing co-ops, which sold their catches for higher prices than they'd ever seen before. At the same time, nine years after Father Jimmy had first proposed it, St. FX set up an extension department, also led by Father Coady. This was the Antigonish Movement's start, and it spread like good news. Though the movement was spearheaded by Roman Catholics and endorsed by Pope Pius XI, it was militantly nonsectarian.

It still remained for Father Jimmy to provide the most striking example of what ordinary people could achieve together. In Little Dover, five miles from Canso, 65 fishing families lived in the most abject poverty. Because the soil was so scrubby that only one cow gave milk, Father Jimmy asked the Department of Agriculture to send in some goats. A government agent took one look at Little Dover and recommended, instead, that the people be moved out. But the people stayed, and Father Jimmy stayed with them. Under his guidance, after more than two years of studying and saving, 40 fishermen launched the Dover Lobster Cooperative Society with a total of $182.

Not satisfied with a mere marketing co-op, they built their own cannery. Father Jimmy lent $300 for equipment and borrowed $700 more. In the fall of 1932, when other packers were going out of business because of the Depression, the Dover men boldly went in. They tended their traps, sold their catches to the co-op, helped one another can the meat and ship it to the market. Many sales were recorded on shingles or cigarette packs for me, as treasurer, to enter in the books. Within two months the fishermen, after squaring all the co-op's debts, paid themselves a profitable half-cent a pound above the going rate for lobsters. Two years later the co-op's volume of business had reached $28,000.

In both Canso and Little Dover, Father Jimmy's fishermen built boats and docks, bought trucks, opened a gas station—all cooperatively—and started a co-op store. Also, since most of them owned so little property that banks wouldn't lend them a cent, they became bankers, starting one of Nova Scotia's first credit unions. As Father Jimmy explained it, a credit union was a form of brotherly love. "You simply take what extra money you have—the savings in your sock—and let your neighbor use it a while, only you don't demand his right arm for security."

At 64, Father Jimmy was made pastor of St. Joseph's Church in Reserve Mines, on his native Cape Breton Island. Reserve was the Canso of the coalfields, a drab colliery town where men grew old underground. The work was dangerous, the pay poor. Strikes were common, for the coal company was run by absentee owners and the miners' union was infested with Communists. By the time Father Jimmy arrived, the Antigonish Movement had spread so rapidly that Reserve already had a credit union and several study clubs. But he soon found new work.

Most families lived in ramshackle company houses. One study group made a survey and told Father Jimmy their discovery: their rents paid for the houses every 20 years. "Then you turn around and give the houses back to the coal company," Father Jimmy said. "If you're that rich, why don't you build your own homes?"

There were ten men in Canada's first co-op housing development at Reserve. With credit-union savings and loans from the Nova Scotia housing commission, they bought land and materials and hired a carpenter to guide them. But they did most of the work themselves between shifts at the coal face, digging foundations, pouring concrete, raising beams and painting walls.

It was a proud day in 1938 when the ten miners moved their families into bright new six-room homes of their own. In gratitude to the man who'd convinced them they could do it, they called the development Tompkinsville.

Father Jimmy's death in 1953—he was 82—brought tributes from many lands. But perhaps the most meaningful came from one of the coal miners who buried him on a hillside overlooking Tompkinsville. "By heaven," he said, "there was one hell of a man."

From its small beginnings, the Antigonish Movement became the strongest social force in the Maritimes. Here Father Tompkins visits a family outside their co-op house in Tompkinsville, a Cape Breton Island development named after him.

Index

Acknowledgments

The condensations reprinted in this book are used by permission of, and special arrangement with, the publishers holding the respective copyrights.

My Own Dear Land, by Robert Choquette, from *O Canada, Mon Pays, Mes Amours*, ©1969 Sélection du Reader's Digest Ltée, Montreal. **Our Wonderland of Mountain Parks**, by Paul Friggens, *Reader's Digest*, May '70 (The Grandeur and the Glory of Canada's Mountain Parks). **Where Tomorrow Is Now**, *Reader's Digest*, October '69 (In Canada's Great Tomorrow Country), condensed from *Time* (May 2, '69), ©1969 by Time Inc., New York. **The Changing, Changeless Lakes**, by Noel Mostert, *Reader's Digest*, October '68 (The Glorious Great Lakes), condensed from *Holiday*, (May '68), ©1968 by Curtis Pub. Co., Philadelphia. **Colossus at Churchill Falls**, by Paul Friggens, *Reader's Digest*, December '69 (Churchill Falls—Billion-Dollar Dream Come True). **A Walk in the Wilds**, by Fred Bodsworth, *Reader's Digest*, April '68 (The Bruce Trail—A Walk in the Wilds), condensed from *Maclean's* (July 3, '65), ©1965 by Maclean-Hunter Pub. Co. Ltd., Toronto. **Escape to Canoe Country**, by Fred Bodsworth, *Reader's Digest*, May '68 (Paddle Your Own Canoe), condensed from *Maclean's* (April 16, '66), ©1966 by Maclean-Hunter Pub. Co. Ltd., Toronto. **The Fabulous Yukon**, by Ben Lucien Burman, *Reader's Digest*, February '69. **Incredible British Columbia**, by Bruce Hutchison, *Reader's Digest*, August '67 (The Incredible British Columbia). **Botanical Columbus**, by Robert O'Brien, *Reader's Digest*, January '71 (David Douglas: Explorer Extraordinary). **My Saskatchewan Boyhood**, by Robert Collins, *Reader's Digest*, September '70. **Seven Crows a Secret**, by Ernest Buckler, *Reader's Digest*, February '69, condensed from *Ox Bells and Fireflies*, ©1968 by Ernest Buckler, reprinted by permission of The Canadian Publishers, McClelland and Stewart Limited, Toronto. **A Son's Discovery**, by Ernest Buckler, *Reader's Digest*, November '69, condensed from *Ox Bells and Fireflies*, ©1968 by Ernest Buckler, reprinted by permission of The Canadian Publishers, McClelland and Stewart Limited, Toronto. **The Rooster Who Served The Lord**, by H. Gordon Green, *Reader's Digest*, November '63, condensed from *Christian Herald* (October '63), ©1963 by Christian Herald Assn., Inc., New York. **". . . And All His Wealth Was Wandering,"** by Harry J. Boyle, *Reader's Digest*, January '71, condensed from *The Beaver* (Winter 1967), ©1967 by Hudson's Bay Company, Winnipeg. **So Much to Live For**, by Ivan Cormier with Derm Dunwoody, *Reader's Digest*, January '61 (I Came Back From The Dead), condensed from *Maclean's* (October 8, '60), ©1960 by Maclean-Hunter Pub. Co. Ltd., Toronto. **The Vision of Eddie Baker**, by Frank G.J. McDonagh, as told to David MacDonald, *Reader's Digest*, February '70 (Canada's Unforgettable Eddie Baker). **Rehabilitation Is Good Business**, by Jeannine Locke, *Reader's Digest*, March '68 (Helping the Handicapped Help Themselves). **"Yessir, I Sure Would!,"** by David MacDonald, *Reader's Digest*, March '68 (Up The Cliff). **Without Fear or Favor**, by Paul Friggens, *Reader's Digest*, July '70 (The RCMP: World's Most Extraordinary Lawmen). **Her Majesty From Ontario**, by C.W. Harvison, *Reader's Digest*, October '68, condensed from *The Horsemen*, ©1967 by C.W. Harvison, reprinted by permission of The Canadian Publishers, McClelland and Stewart Limited, Toronto. **Whiskey Whiskey Papa**, by Lawrence Elliott, *Reader's Digest*, February '71 (Whiskey Whiskey Papa: Highest Flier in the High Arctic). **Somebody Buried *Something* Here**, by David MacDonald, *Reader's Digest*, January '65 (Nova Scotia's Mysterious "Money Pit"), condensed from *The Rotarian* (January '65), ©1964 by Rotary International, Evanston, Ill. **Canada's Wonderful "Wishing Book,"** by Robert Collins, *Reader's Digest*, March '70. **Stratford on Avon—Canada!**, by William French, *Reader's Digest*, September '69 (How Glory Came to Stratford). **CUSO: A Word for Partnership**, by Janice Tyrwhitt, *Reader's Digest*, January '69 (CUSO: Canada's Foreign Aid Extraordinary). **New School for Old Values**, by David MacDonald, *Reader's Digest*, September '70 (St. John's: New School for Old Values). **The Cats That Conquered Winter**, by Ronald Schiller, *Reader's Digest*, December '68 (Snowmobiles: The Cats That Conquered Winter), condensed from *Rod and Gun in Canada* (November '68), ©1968 by Rod and Gun Pub. Corp. Ltd., Montreal. **But . . .**, by Jack Olsen, *Reader's Digest*, December '70 (Time to Control Snowmobiles), condensed from *Sports Illustrated* (March 16, '70), ©1970 by Time Inc., New York. **Vive le Canada!**, by George Ronald, *Reader's Digest*, February '70 (The Understanding). **Two of the Greatest: The Big Guy . . .**, by David MacDonald, *Reader's Digest*, November '69 (Gordie Howe—Hockey's Marvelous Methuselah). **. . . and The Commando Raid**, by Bill Surface, *Reader's Digest*, February '71 (Hottest Man on Ice), condensed from *The Kiwanis Magazine* (February '71), ©1971 by Kiwanis International, Chicago. **City of the Future**, by J.D. Ratcliff, *Reader's Digest*, November '70 (Tomorrow's City—Here Today), condensed from *National Civic Review* (September '70), ©1970 by National Municipal League, New York. **The Triumph of Janis Babson**, by Lawrence Elliott, *Reader's Digest*, June '63, condensed from *A Little Girl's Gift*, ©1963 by Lawrence Elliott, published by Holt, Rinehart & Winston, Inc., New York. **"Look, Man! Look!,"** by Nelles Silverthorne, *Reader's Digest*, April '62 (My Most Unforgettable Character). **The Gift for Inspiring Hope**, by David MacDonald, *Reader's Digest*, October '70 (Canada's Doctor for the Disabled). **Little Man, Lonely Man**, by Keith Munro, *Reader's Digest*, August '51 (The Most Unforgettable Canadian I've Met). **Darby of Bella Bella**, by Hugh W. McKervill, *Reader's Digest*, January '66 (The Most Unforgettable Character I've Met). **Dr. Dave, GP**, by Percy Wray, *Reader's Digest*, October '69 (My Most Unforgettable Character). **Miracle of the Big Honkers**, by Manly Miner, *Reader's Digest*, May '69 (My Most Unforgettable Character). **The Good Life of Gleason Green**, by Mary Coburn, *Reader's Digest*, July '62 (My Most Unforgettable Character). **Mr. Commonwealth**, by George Ronald, *Reader's Digest*, January '71 (Meet the Commonwealth's Mr. Smith). **The Joyous Feast of Family**, by Isabel Stevenson, as told to David MacDonald, *Reader's Digest*, December '68 (Bachelor Mother), condensed from *The United Church Observer* (November 15, '68), published by the United Church of Canada, Toronto. **Maverick from the Miramichi**, by Irwin Ross, *Reader's Digest*, April '64 (Beaverbrook: Maverick From the Miramichi). **No Sense At All in Stopping**, by Irwin Ross, *Reader's Digest*, August '68 (Lord of the Newspaper World). **The Indomitable Nurse Bennett**, by H. Gordon Green, *Reader's Digest*, January '70 (Newfoundland's Indomitable Nurse Bennett). **Bound To Be Known as Joey**, by Jeannine Locke, *Reader's Digest*, October '68 (Joey Smallwood: Newfoundland's Supersalesman). **The "Unadoptables,"** by Janice Tyrwhitt, *Reader's Digest*, January '68 (She Finds Homes for the "Hopeless" Child). **The Stunning Birds of Fen Lansdowne**, by David MacDonald, *Reader's Digest*, August '69. **God's Greatest Nuisance**, by John R. Chafe, *Reader's Digest*, October '62 (The Most Unforgettable Character I've Met).

Picture credits

Credits are from left to right and from top to bottom, with additional information as needed. A single credit indicates that all illustrations on that page or pages are from the same source. Extensive effort was made to determine the ownership of photographs; the publishers welcome any additional information. These abbreviations are used:

AP: Associated Press. **CGTB**: Canadian Government Travel Bureau. **Churchill**: Churchill Falls (Labrador) Corporation Limited. **COI**: Central Office of Information, London. **CW**: Canada Wide. **Eaton's**: Archives, Eaton's of Canada Limited. **Evans**: Mary Evans Picture Library. **Feheley**: M.F. Feheley Arts Company Limited. **MS**: Montreal Star. **NFB**: National Film Board. **PAC**: Public Archives of Canada. **RCMP**: Royal Canadian Mounted Police. **RIM**: Rehabilitation Institute of Montreal. **Stratford**: Stratford Shakespearean Festival. **UCC**: United Church of Canada.

Inside front cover: Bruce Weston. **Following page**: NFB/John Reeves. **1**: Richard A. Vroom. **2**: Michael Liu. **4-5**: Michael H. Reichmann (top 2); Mary Asselin-Daemen; Bob Brooks; Henry Kalen. **6-7**: Mary Asselin-Daemen. **8-9**: Don Newlands; Horst Ehricht. **11**: Freeman Patterson. **12-13**: Malak, Ottawa; Freeman Patterson. **14-15**: NFB/Egon Bork; NFB/Paul Baich; Henry Kalen. **16**: James Quong; Don Newlands; Horst Ehricht; Chris Bruun. **17**: Henry Kalen. **18-19**: NFB/Malak; René Delbuguet; Horst Ehricht; Mary Asselin-Daemen. **20-21**: John de Visser; Bob Brooks (3). **22-23**: Richard A. Vroom; Paul Baich; Edi Klopfenstein; James Hayes. **24-25**: Henry Kalen; Bob Brooks (center and top right); Don Newlands (bottom left); Michael Liu; Joan Powell (bottom right). **26-27**: Freeman Patterson; Michael Semak; Prism/Garth Scheuer (p. 27 top); NFB/Wilf Doucette; Henry Kalen. **28-29**: Edi Klopfenstein; Richard A. Vroom. **30**: Richard A. Vroom. **32-33**: John de Visser. **34-35**: Harry Rowed; Hans Fuhrer; John de Visser; Harry Rowed. **36-37**: Harry Rowed. **38-39**: Hans Fuhrer; Harry Rowed (2 top right). **40-41**: Alberta Government Photo; Hans Fuhrer. **42-43**: Fred Bruemmer (top); John de Visser (2). **44-45**: John de Visser (2 left); NFB/James Sproat; Fred Bruemmer. **46-47**: NFB/Ted Grant; James Quong; NFB/John Reeves (right). **48-49**: John Powell (left); Joan Powell; John de Visser. **50-51**: John de Visser; Joan Powell; George Hunter (right). **52-53**: John de Visser. **54-55**: Churchill; Malak, Ottawa. **56-57**: Malak, Ottawa; Churchill (2). **58-59**: Churchill. **60-61**: R.N. Lowes (left); Malcolm Kirk (2); Ontario Department of Tourism (lower right). **62-63**: Ontario Department of Tourism (topmost); Malcolm Kirk (3). **64-65**: Fred Bodsworth; John Powell. **66-67**: John de Visser (top); Fred Bodsworth (2). **68-69**: NFB/George Hunter; George Hunter (top); John de Visser. **70-71**: John de Visser. **72-73**: James Quong; John de Visser (2). **74-75**: Malak, Ottawa; NFB/Freeman Patterson; Greater Vancouver Visitors and Convention Bureau. **76-77**: Toby Rankin (top 2); John de Visser; Malak, Ottawa. **78-79**: Hans Fuhrer; Chuck Diven; Toby Rankin (bottom left); Don Newlands (2 right). **80-81**: NFB/Egon Bork; Hans Fuhrer; CGTB. **82-83**: John de Visser. **84**: Royal Horticultural Society, London; John de Visser. **85-91**: Bruce Johnson. **92-99**: Michel Doyon. **100-104**: Bruce Johnson. **105-108**: Michel Doyon. **109-110**: Michael H. Reichmann. **113**: Bob Brooks. **114-115, 117**: Courtesy Jessie Cormier. **118-123**: Canadian National Institute for the Blind. **124-125**: Ian Brown. **126-127**: Ian Brown (2); Rehabilitation Foundation for the Disabled (2). **129**: E.N. Wilcox (courtesy Ottawa Benson). **130-131**: Vernon Bagley; E.N. Wilcox (courtesy Vernon Bagley). **133-134**: Antoine Désilets. **136-137**: RCMP; Henry Kalen. **138-139**: PAC (left); RCMP (2). **140-141**: RCMP (2); PAC. **142-143**: PAC. **144-145**: A. Aufderheide; Lawrence Elliott; Barry Ranford. **146-147**: John de Visser (2); MS/CW. **149**: Triton (James Pickerell). **150-151**: Reader's Digest; Weekend/CW (2). **152-153**: Weekend/CW (2); Triton (James Pickerell). **154-155**: Triton (James Pickerell). **156-157**: Eaton's; John de Visser. **158-161**: Eaton's. **162-163**: Eaton's (bottom left); John de Visser (4). **164**: Stratford; Douglas Spillane. **165**: Evans; Stratford; Stratford (Peter Smith); Stratford. **166-167**: Stratford; Douglas Spillane; Stratford (Peter Smith); Stratford (3); Stratford (Robert C. Ragsdale). **168-169**: CGTB; Douglas Spillane. **170-173**: Courtesy CUSO Information. **175-179**: St. John's School. **180-181**: Mary Asselin-Daemen (2); John de Visser (top right). **182-185**: Courtesy Bombardier Ltd. **187**: James Hayes. **188-189**: Courtesy the Howe family; MS/CW. **190-191**: Courtesy the Howe family; except bottom left (NHL). **192-193**: AP/CW; Weekend/CW; Horst Ehricht (2). **194-195**: Horst Ehricht (2); James Hayes. **196**: Canadian National; Associated Commercial Photographers Ltd.; Paul Gélinas; Associated Commercial Photographers Ltd. **197**: Mary Asselin-Daemen; James Hayes (2 middle, bottom left, bottom center); Vincent Ponte (snow scene and bottom right). **198**: Louis Hamel and James Hayes. **199**: Bob Brooks; Vincent Ponte (bottom center); James Hayes (3). **200**: James Hayes. **201-224**: John Creel. **225-226**: Prism/Joan Latchford. **228-229**: Courtesy Dr. Nelles Silverthorne. **230-231**: Mead Johnson Canada; The Hospital for Sick Children (3). **232-233**: RIM. **234-235**: RIM; MS/CW (3). **236-237**: MS/CW; RIM (2). **238**: John de Visser. **242-243**: Acme/CW; Toronto Star Syndicate; courtesy UCC. **244-245**: British Columbia Provincial Archives; courtesy UCC. **246-247**: Courtesy UCC. **248-249**: George Hunter; Keith Giles (courtesy Dr. David Lander). **250-251**: Keith Giles (courtesy Dr. David Lander). **252-257**: Jack Miner Migratory Bird Foundation Inc. (courtesy Manly Miner). **259-261**: Courtesy Gleason Green. **263**: AP/CW. **264-265**: Press Information Bureau, Government of India (bottom left); Arnold Smith (4). **266-267**: Fox-Waterman Photography Ltd.; courtesy COI. **268**: Salihu A. International Photo; The Singapore Herald. **269**: Courtesy COI (3); Arnold Smith (bottom left). **270-271**: Dr. Isabel Stevenson; Islen Cole (3). **272-275**: Dr. Isabel Stevenson. **276-279**: London *Daily Express*/CW. **280-281**: Radio Times Hulton Picture Library (extreme left); Bob Brooks; CW. **282-283**: Thomson Newspapers Limited; *Timmins Daily Press*. **284**: *Timmins Daily Press*. **286**: London *Daily Express*/CW. **288-289**: Weekend/CW; Myra Bennett. **290-291**: Myra Bennett. **292-293**: Government of Newfoundland. **294-295**: Government of Newfoundland (2); Toronto Telegram Syndicate. **296-297**: Bill Croke (2); Bob Brooks. **298-299**: Ontario Department of Social and Family Services; Reader's Digest. **300-301**: Ontario Department of Social and Family Services. **303**: Dudley Whitney (courtesy Feheley); Feheley. **304-305**: Feheley. **306**: Dudley Whitney (courtesy Feheley). **307**: NFB/Nick Morant. **308-309**: Nova Scotia Information Service. **310-311**: Coady Institute (2); NFB/Nick Morant. **316**: Bob Brooks. **318-319**: Prism/Joan Latchford; NFB/Michael Semak. **320**: Freeman Patterson. **Following page**: Freeman Patterson. **Inside back cover**: British Columbia Government.

EDITOR: George Ronald

ASSISTANT EDITOR: Jeannette Gibbs

ART DIRECTOR: James Hayes

DESIGNER: Lucie Martineau

PHOTO RESEARCHER: Beverley Renahan